Edinburgh
Food Guide

Introduction

Welcome to the ninth edition of the Edinburgh Food Guide, the most established guide to eating out in Scotland's capital city, bringing you up-to-date reviews of the best places to eat.

Edinburgh offers a huge choice of restaurants, cafés, pubs and bistros, featuring cuisine from the continent. New places open all the time and the Guide will keep you informed of all the latest developments. There are separate sections for areas including Leith, the City Outskirts, Fife and the Borders. In addition, the delivery menus section, if you just want to stay in and the Caterers section – new for this year – is ideal if you have something bigger than a romantic meal for two in mind.

We have featured establishments by area so that wherever you are it's simple to find what you're looking for. At the back there is a category index that lists establishments by the type of cuisine they serve, alongside an alphabetical index with telephone numbers for quick reference. With our comprehensive colour maps to help you find your way about, all you have to do is eat and enjoy!

Contents

	page
Our Top Five New Places to Eat	4
Edinburgh Food Guide's New Places to Eat	6
Our Top Five New Places to Eat 1999/2000	8
Our Top Five New Places to Eat 2000/2001	9
Eating Out around Greyfriars	11
Eating Out in New Town &	35
Eating Out around the Market	69
Eating Out in ...	88
Eating Out in Bruntsfield, Morningside, Mayfield & Marchmont	101
Eating Out Vegetarian in Edinburgh	108
Eating Out in Leith with colour map	111
Eating Out in Café-Bars, Pubs, Cafés & Coffee Houses	121
Eating Out in the Outskirts	135
Eating Out in the Lothians, Borders & Fife with colour map	140
Delivery Menus	149
Category Index	166
Caterers	168
Alphabetical Index	182
Map of Edinburgh & Leith	189

Duck's at Le Marché Noir

Intimate, white linen, candles,
fresh Scottish fish, meat and game.
Excellent vegetarian dishes.
Superb wine + malt whisky selection
Professional friendly service.
Private rooms available.

2/4 Eyre Place, Edinburgh. Tel 0800 698 1411
e-mail: enquiries@ducks.co.uk   www.ducks.co.uk

TOP 5 NEW PLACES

Edinburgh
Food Guide

Edinburgh Food Guide's Top 5

Capital Cuisine

Not many people would refute the claim that Scotland is home to some of the best produce in the world. Top restaurants all over the globe feature Scottish ingredients and many home-grown chefs have earned world class reputations too. In our ceaseless search for delicious food and exceptional atmosphere we've picked out our own personal favourites from the wealth of eateries in Edinburgh.

We chose these five because we were particularly impressed with the quality of the cooking and we were won over by their style and service. But there'll be many more featured in these pages that you'll love just as much. So have a good browse, eat some really good food and have fun compiling your own hit list.

**30A CHAMBERS STREET,
Tel: 0800 698 1404**

Festival Inns have transformed the old dental school on Chambers Street into the city's newest, some would say most stylish bar-restaurant. Beluga has an unashamedly upmarket appeal. Mixing blond wood, glass tiling, shining steel and leather booths, the interior is a fusion of modern design ideas that succeeds by never overdoing its attempts to impress. There's even a waterfall tumbling down the staircase that leads to the basement bar. The restaurant menu is as colourful as the stained glass windows that light the dining area, mixing a world of culinary ideas with the freshest local ingredients to wonderful effect. Definitely for the style-conscious, a place to see and be seen but with wonderful food that would appeal to all appetites - if only all dentists were like this. See our review on page 22.

(fitz) Henry
A BRASSERIE

19 SHORE PLACE, LEITH, TEL: 0800 698 1460

While (fitz) Henry is not strictly new, the improvements made since its recent re-opening under new ownership are so distinct that it might as well be. Alan Morrison & Valerie Faichney were themselves regulars of (fitz) Henry mk.1 and, whilst striving to maintain the décor and ambience present before, have transformed the menu with the help of surviving chef Hubert Lamort. The dishes on the monthly-changing selection are consistently inventive and adventurous, while never being less than first-class in terms of taste and presentation. The brasserie itself is situated beside the Water of Leith and was a warehouse in previous times, allowing for high ceilings and spacious seating arrangements. Combine this with velvet drapes and subdued lighting for an intimate, elegant atmosphere with an almost medieval feel. All of these factors together ensure that dining at (fitz) Henry is a special experience, and certainly not one to be missed. See our review on p114.

The longest running guide to eating out in Edinburgh

Edinburgh Food Guide

www.edinburghfoodguide.co.uk

2001-2002

INCLUDING OUT OF TOWN, CAFÉS-BARS, DELIVERY & CATERING SECTIONS

ISBN 0-9528878-5-1

£3

Features 204 of the best places to eat in Edinburgh

BOROUGH

Distributing to the necessity of saints; given to hospitality (Romans 13:14)

Restaurant
- Lunch; 3 courses - £8.95, from 12 noon until 2.30pm
- Dinner; 6pm until 10pm, Sunday - Thursday - until 11pm Friday and Saturday

Bar
- Bar Food and coffee served throughout
- Fabulous cocktail menu
- Champagne Happy Hour daily from 5pm-8pm;
  House Champagne £15; Bollinger, Veuve Clicquot £25; Dom Perignon, Krug, Cristal £70

Hotel
- 9 en-suite bedrooms
- Satellite TV and DVD
- Private bar available for hotel clients and members

72-80 Causewayside, Edinburgh   EH9 1PY   0131 668 2255

TOP 5 NEW PLACES

New Places to Eat

THE STOCKBRIDGE RESTAURANT

54 ST. STEPHEN STREET, TEL: 0800 698 1451

Chef and proprietor Juliet Lawrence's recent move from the world of outside catering to that of the inside variety has provided the Edinburgh restaurant scene with a welcome portion of classic dining. Tucked away in a basement on St. Stephen Street, this delightful dining room is adorned with refined furnishings, the walls peppered with grand mirrors and the works of the Scottish Colourists. It makes an ideal setting for food that is a selection of the finest quality fresh Scottish ingredients, transformed into dishes as creative as the art that graces the walls. This is a venture aimed at the high end of the market and every aspect of the experience has been carefully considered, yet the prices remain within most budgets. With so much effort put in and such worthwhile results, Stockbridge looks set to be the place to eat in 2002. See our review on page 80.

COCONUT GROVE

3 Lochrin Terrace, Tel: 0800 698 1409

Mexican restaurants are often amongst the most popular in town: many make a name for good value, some for great atmosphere and others occasionally for great food. So when one came along that combined all three, it was guaranteed a place in this year's Top Five. This bright, welcoming cantina, recently transformed by new owner Perdip Singh, is cosy enough for romantic dinners and accommodating enough for group celebrations – and it proves popular with both. Authenticity is guaranteed as the chef trained and worked in, amongst other places, Mexico. His experience shines through in the quality cuisine, and everything is dished up in the usual Mexican hurry, but always worth ten times the wait. The bright décor and yellow and orange crockery make one feel like the summer sun is shining, no matter what the time of year. Combine this with friendly staff and excellent food and everyone ends up with a smile on their face. See our review on page 92.

PLAISIR DU CHOCOLAT
— EDINBURGH —
251-253 Canongate, Tel: 556 9524

In the heart of Edinburgh's most historic streets lies a slice of the finest in French indulgence. Plaisir is the labour of love of Parisian Bertrand Espouy and his team of dedicated French pastry chefs. Bernard is better known as founder of the Auld Alliance bakery chain but he's now focusing his attentions on this smaller, more luxurious concern. The name tells you a lot about what's on offer – the finest chocolate, cakes, pastries and desserts any chocoholic could dream for – but there's a lot more besides. Plaisir combines a pattiserie and chocolatier, with a salon du thé and a proper restaurant. Great pride is taken in using only the best ingredients, importing what Scotland can't provide and creating all dishes and chocolate in-house. So next time you're feeling in need of a pick-me-up, be it savoury or sweet, head for The Canongate and let the pleasure be all yours. See our review on page 121.

NEW PLACES

Edinburgh
Food Guide

Edinburgh
Food Guide's New

Alongside our Top Five we bring you a selection of recommended new restaurants. Sticking to the same search criteria of delicious food and exceptional atmosphere we've chosen some personal favourites. Why not try them out for yourself, see how they compare to your favourites and all those old established gems.

**50-54 Henderson Street, Leith,
Tel: 0800 698 1504**

This charming restaurant is but a stone's throw from Leith's Shore area and specialises in Indian and Bangladeshi Cuisine. Whatever tickles your taste buds, you are sure to find the perfect meal on the expansive menu.

The gargantuan selection includes traditional dishes, unique recipes, delicacies and an array of vegetarian choices. If you can't settle on one meal, a buffet is available, so you can pick and choose to your heart's (and your stomach's) content. Buffet-goers are invited to eat as much as they can, and for just £6.95, once the high quality of the food becomes apparent, they often do! This delicious, value-for-money food is coupled with friendly, courteous and helpful service, making the King's Spice a highlight amongst Edinburgh's selection of Indian restaurants. See our review on page 114.

BOROUGH

72-80 CAUSEWAYSIDE, TEL: 668 2255

This address used to be home to one of Edinburgh's toughest snooker halls. But green baize and red faces have been replaced by a restaurant, hotel and bar with an undisputedly stylish streak. Borough has a look you would more associate with the city centre than the south side, but it's combination of looks, charm and excellent food is set to divert much attention from the glass and chrome of the usual George Street hot spots.

The restaurant itself is intimate and refined, with many of the tables seated at gorgeously comfy leather booths. The menu fuses Scottish fayre with twists of International flavours and has enough variety and downright good taste to suit any palate. Okay so there are no snooker tables, but with food and drink this fine, who'd have the time to play, let alone the inclination? See our review on page 106.

**Carlton Highland Hotel,
19 North Bridge, Tel: 472 3022**

The Carlton Highland Hotel on North Bridge was recently revamped as part of a multi-million pound refurbishment scheme. The Hotel offers much to local residents and visitors to the area as well as to its guests. There's a leisure complex with a pool, squash court and a gym, but most importantly from our point of view is the restaurant. The transformation of the hotel to the height of style and luxury is reflected in the dark intimacy of The Bridge, situated on the first floor. This chic eaterie offers a delightfully refined modern Scottish menu which reflects the heritage if its old Edinburgh surroundings and the style of the Hotel's new look. The menu makes the utmost of fresh Scottish produce, the dishes all have an extra touch of culinary class and the decadent surroundings help make this add up to an extra special experience. See our review on page 21.

Edinburgh Food Guide — NEW PLACES

Places to Eat

NAMASTE
North Indian Frontier Cuisine
41-42 West Preston Street, Tel: 0800 689 1435

So new is this venture from Indi and Perdip, (owners of Top Five New Places entry Coconut Grove), that it was barely open by the time the Guide hit the streets. But what it loses through innocence is quickly regained, and more, with the knowledge that the menu is based on recipes many of which are over 300 years old. The dishes are mainly Mugahli and Punjabi in origin and are of the kind enjoyed by North Indian royalty for many centuries. It's not just the content of the recipes that impresses but also the adherence to time-honoured cooking methods. The selection of meat and vegetables are prepared with over fifty spices and slow-fired in a customary clay oven. The décor too is a million miles from the usual Indian offerings, with authentic styling and waitresses resplendent in traditional dress. Namaste well and truly takes Indian cuisine to a new frontier. See our review on page 106.

 alphabet
BAR RESTAURANT HOTEL
92 ST JOHNS ROAD, TEL: 316 4466

Recently opened by the Clark Pub Company, which runs Uisge Beatha and Alphabet Yard in Glasgow, this new Edinburgh offering combines a 28-room hotel with a stylish restaurant and bar. Situated close to Murrayfield Stadium and the Zoo, Alphabet is ideally placed for tourists visiting the city's attractions, as well as for locals seeking refreshment outwith the city centre. The bar serves a diverse selection of wines, beers, cocktails, juices and smoothies and the restaurant menu is varied and also includes a large delicatessen selection, offering a range of freshly prepared sandwiches, wraps and salad bowls. Despite the innovative design Alphabet maintains a friendly and relaxed atmosphere, there's even a purpose built children's' indoor play area and outdoor seating on heated timber decks. All in all there's enough variety to ensure that everyone leaves satisfied. So with this new offering, your search for somewhere to eat and drink will be as easy as A, B, C. See our review on page 136.

Inn over the Green
24 Milton Road East, Tel: 0800 698 1428

The Richard Corsie Conference Centre caters for seminars, celebrations and dances, amongst other grand occasions. Part of this wider facility, and in our view the highlight, is the Inn Over the Green restaurant. With wonderful views of the East Lothian countryside the restaurant makes an ideal venue for everything from a business lunch to a special, private celebration. Head chef Martin Butterick and his team prepare simple fresh food using the finest Scottish ingredients, all served in a wonderfully relaxed atmosphere by delightful staff. So whether it be business, a family get-together or just simple pleasure-seeking, you never need an excuse to enjoy the finest of food. See our review on page 138.

TOP 5 NEW PLACES 1999/2000

Edinburgh
Food Guide

Edinburgh Food Guide's Top 5 New Places to Eat 1999/2000

MUSSEL INN (See page 48), **POTTERS FINE DINING** (See page 106), **TAPAS OLE**, **THE TOWER** (See page 15), **SOUTHERN CROSS CAFÉ**.

Food fashions change with the seasons, trends come and go, but great food never gets forgotten. So just in case you missed them first time, here's a reminder of the highlights of the previous two editions' Top Five New Places to Eat.

MUSSEL INN

61-65 ROSE STREET, TEL: 225 5979

The success of this seafood restaurant has been such that they recently opened another branch in Glasgow's Hope Street. The product is always fresh as the owners farm much of it themselves in the sparkling lochs off the West of Scotland. It's a guarantee of quality that has made Mussel Inn such a success. What we said then: "The Mussel Inn is owned and run by shellfish farmers and it's proving a winning combination. The clean, modern interior, friendly staff and magnificently fresh seafood at remarkably reasonable prices, makes the Mussel Inn one of the best new places in town to eat." See our latest review on page 48.

POTTERS fine dining RESTAURANT

Kildonan Lodge Hotel, Tel: 662 9010

One of the highlights of the south side of the city, Potters has a reputation amongst restaurant reviewers that's second to none. What we said then: "Book a table here and it's yours for the night, so you'll never be rushed through your pudding and hustled out for the next booking, and the plethora of little extras intensifies the feeling of being pampered. But this is not a showy, over attentive kind of restaurant. The atmosphere is genuine and the food is really top quality. In fact, our reviewer has confidently stated that Chef Don Potter served up the best meal she's eaten in Edinburgh and she can't wait to go back."

See our latest review on page 106.

TOWER RESTAURANT

Museum of Scotland, Chambers St,
Tel: 0800 698 1485

Since its conception in 1999 The Tower has gone from strength to strength, developing a solid reputation for stunning surroundings and equally impressive modern Scottish cuisine. What we said then: "The Tower served up cutting edge Scottish cuisine that is truly impressive, although the view alone is enough to make a visit worthwhile. Add to this a beautifully styled interior, and you have a great advert for the best of contemporary Scottish architecture, design and, most importantly, cooking." See our latest review on page 15.

8

Edinburgh Food Guide — TOP 5 NEW PLACES 1999/2000

Edinburgh Food Guide's Top 5 New Places to Eat 2000/2001

THE APARTMENT, BRITANNIA SPICE (See page 116), THE CARRIAGE HOUSE (See page 92), THE MARQUE, RESTAURANT MARTIN WISHART.

BRITANNIA Spice — *Exclusive Exotic Cuisine* — 150 Commercial Street, Tel: 555 2255

Since arriving in Leith two years ago Britannia Spice has gained a name for taking diners on enchanting culinary voyages. The mix of stylish food and extravagant décor ensures Spice remains the favourite ship in port. What we said then: "The itinerary takes in a carefully chosen selection of dishes designed to allow you to sample a wide range of traditional cuisine from Bangladesh, Northern India, Nepal, Thailand, and Sri Lanka. Combine this all-encompassing list with the finest produce, fresh seasonal native vegetables and over twenty-five tears of restaurant experience and you're definitely cruising." See our latest review on page 116.

The Apartment
7-13 Barclay Place Tel: 0800 298 3462

This much talked about Bruntsfield eaterie gained a place in the Top Five for its stylish interior as well as for providing Edinburgh diners with an innovative menu that cut through all the hype. What we said then: "It may not bowl you over to learn that this restaurant has a buzz surrounding it that would drown out the work of a million busy bees. What may get you to sit up and take notice is to hear that the food actually does most of the talking. The menu dispenses with starters and gets straight on with a selection of dishes that combine Oriental, African and Mediterranean flavours into a selection of dishes that do their best to spoil you for choice."

RESTAURANT MARTIN WISHART
54 The Shore Tel: 553 3557

Now fully established on the Leith's Shore, Martin Wishart has developed a reputation that attracts discerning diners from across the country. What we said then: "…the highlight of the Shore experience, providing everything you'd expect from the setting. This is a cool, modern environment in which the young master creates classic dishes from the best Scottish seafood, game and steaks. So if you're looking for a taste of the finer side of life, Martin's got a name for it."

OFF THE WALL
RESTAURANT

Lunch 12.00-2.00pm   Dinner 5.30-10.00pm

Corporate/group menus from
£15.00 Lunch, £25.00 Dinner

'Chefs' table (6 people only)
from £65.00pp

Exclusive use of restaurant for groups of 20+

See us at www.off-the-wall.co.uk

105 High Street, Royal Mile, Edinburgh EH1 1SG
0131 558 1497

Edinburgh Food Guide — OLD TOWN & GREYFRIARS

Eating Out in the Old Town & Greyfriars

Edinburgh's Old Town is ever popular with visitors to the city. The area is steeped in history with architecture dating back to the 11th century. There's much to see here including the Castle, Holyrood Palace and the fledgling Scottish Parliament. The diversity of choice is further proof, if any were needed, that this old city isn't afraid to move with the times. Some of the very best Scottish restaurants are tucked away here. The Witchery is renowned for fabulous food in a romantic setting, the delightful Wee Windaes provides the best of Scottish produce, and the ultra-modern Tower has become an architectural and culinary landmark.

Neatly occupying the space that used to be a dental school on Chambers Street is Beluga, a new restaurant and bar that looks set to become one of the city's most frequented spots. Cockburn Street plays host to Viva Mexico, one of Edinburgh's most colourful restaurants. Further up the hill is the Grainstore, renowned for its elegant light lunches, and new arrival Maison Bleue, where French food becomes an innovative, sharing experience.

Ayutthaya E5

Its location opposite the Festival Theatre may make this an obvious choice for pre-theatre dining, but you don't need an excuse to enjoy Ayutthaya's sumptuous cuisine, relaxed atmosphere and helpful service. The menu fully explains each dish, an essential here, and the wine list not only boasts good house selections (£8.95 a bottle or £2.10 by the glass) but a featured wine of the month. We began our meal with the Ayutthaya mixed starter for two, showcasing a range of Thai appetisers including fish cakes, spring rolls, chicken satay and spare ribs with sweet chilli and peanut sauce dips. For the main course I chose gaeng phed ped yang (shredded roast duck cooked in a mild curry with coconut milk, tomatoes and pineapple, £7.50). Meanwhile, my partner tried goong ob mordin (king prawns, ginger and spring onions served with vermicelli and black bean sauce, £7.50) and we shared kao plao (steamed Thai fragrant rice, £1.50). There is a reason Thailand is called the Land of Smiles and, judging by Ayutthaya, the food may have a lot to do with it! Open 7 days, 12noon-3pm and 5.30pm-11pm. **DDR**

Off The Wall E4

Overlooking the historic Royal Mile, a culinary heaven exists serving the finest Scottish cuisine. The standard of food and service combined with the relaxed atmosphere makes for a most pleasurable evening. We began with an exquisite appetiser of seared oyster on a bed of buttered leeks. Suitably enticed we moved to starters of warm beef salad with confit of onion in red wine jus (£7.95), and escabache of sea bass with langoustine vinaigrette (£7.95). These were accompanied by a crisp Chilean sauvignon blanc (£13.95) from a good list. For main course we chose seared salmon with sweet pepper sauce (£16.95), and fillet of Scottish beef with celeriac, haricot blanc and tarragon jus (£18.95). The grand finale was the assiette platter of deserts (£15), a sample of all the deserts on the menu, the absolute in sheer indulgence! So indulge yourself! **CSR**

Golden Bengal D4

This traditional Indian restaurant opened in Leith in 1971, before moving to its more central location three years ago. Warmly decorated and keenly staffed, its menu has something to offer every curry lover with dishes from all over the subcontinent. After some papadum (£0.55), we started with vegetable samosa (£2.85) and chicken roll (chicken cooked with medium spices, garnished with spring onion and coriander leaves in deep-fried pastry, £3.25) both served with salad and a mild sauce. This was followed by Jaipuri chicken (pieces of chicken cooked in a curry sauce with fried

"...Oldest Indian Restaurant in Edinburgh"

THE GOLDEN BENGAL TANDOORI RESTAURANT EST 1971

Reservations
225 6633

5a Johnstone Terrace
EH1 2PW

OLD TOWN & GREYFRIARS

Edinburgh
Food Guide

mushrooms, onions, capsicums, and Punjabi massalam, £7.45; and tandoori chicken (spring chicken marinated in yoghurt and spices then barbecued on skewers and served with salad and sauce, £6.95) with fried rice (£2.05) and paswari naan (sweet stuffed bread, £2.35). The wine was a light, crisp white Rioja (£8.50). For dessert we tried pistachio kulfi (flavoured Indian style ice cream, £2.25) and orange bombe (vanilla ice cream and orange sauce on a wafer base and surrounded in chocolate, £2.65). **DDR**

Maharajah's D5
Glasgow was always known as the second city of the Empire but had Maharajah's been around a few years earlier I dare say Edinburgh would have stolen the honour. Step beyond its doors and you can delight in the opulence provided by pink drapery and painted vistas of Indian plains, not to mention the gentle accompaniment of a softly strummed sitar. The menu is customarily large, so after some debate I took the easy option of the all you can eat buffet (£7.95, Mon and Tues) which consists of two starters, two main courses (a korma and a bhuna) as well as rice, naan, salad and a vegetarian option. Meanwhile my friend opted for the king prawn puri (£4.25) followed by sag aloo delight (£5.50), a vegetarian dish of potatoes and spinach with coriander and mustard seeds. So, while I flitted back and forth sampling the treats offered by the well-stocked buffet (the tandoori chicken wings were particularly good) my friend enjoyed the subtly spiced prawns, and the outstanding sag aloo. Add a bottle of house red (£8.95) and you have empirical evidence of a good value, top quality meal. **JW**

Black Bo's E4
Black Bo's is a vegetarian restaurant with a difference. 'Not so much a way of life, more of a restaurant,' is their description and with accolades from Scotland the Best their billing as a gourmet restaurant is well deserved. My companion, the genuine article, and myself as a non-vegetarian were surprised and pleased on perusing the menu to find a wide variety of tempting and unusual dishes available. Vegetarian food has a bit of a reputation for being stodgy and over wholesome but at Black Bo's the menu reads more like an à la carte than your average wholefood deli. We began with garlic bread with basil and fresh tomatoes (£3.00) followed by haggis shish kebab flambéed with ginger and Drambuie (yes, it was vegetarian) and pasta with tomato, basil and capers topped with Parmesan shavings. (Both £4.95). Sweet potato and goats cheese baked in filo pastry with flavour rich red onion and garlic marmalade followed, along with peppers stuffed with blue cheese and almond soufflé with a Madeira and molasses sauce. A bottle of Carlos Serres Rioja (£10.50) washed everything down nicely before desserts of a light steamed lemon pudding with cream and rich dark and white chocolate Belgian ice cream. My companion spent most of the meal trying to convert me to vegetarianism. If you could convince me that the food would always be like this, I think I'd do it. **AB**

Ti Amo E5
Discreetly located opposite the Festival Theatre lies one of the city's finest Italian restaurants. Ti Amo has a spacious interior with high ceilings, polished wooden floors and ornate décor all providing an almost theatrical backdrop to quality Italian cuisine. The menu is extensive with enough pasta, pizza, meat, fish and vegetarian options to accommodate all tastes. We began with a generous portion of smoked salmon and fresh salad, and slices of mozzarella deep-fried in breadcrumbs, served with a spicy tomato dip (both £4.80). The main courses were equally well-portioned, the chicken risotto with rosemary, brandy, tomato and cream (£5.90) just out-performing the pepperoni-packed tagliatelle Ti Amo (£6.50). There is a large selection of desserts and coffees available but after generous servings we declined, soaked in the refined atmosphere and savoured the last of our bottle of house white wine (£8.90). Efficient, friendly service, the freshest ingredients and a superb setting makes Ti Amo one of Edinburgh's must-do dining experiences. **RRH**

Witchery D4
For an evening of romance, the finest food, first class service all set against a backdrop of Edinburgh's most historic scenery, look no further than The Witchery. The lavish care and attention that goes into each fine detail leaves nothing to be

BLACK BO'S
www.blackbos.com

Hailed as Scotland's best gourmet vegetarian restaurant

Amongst the very best in Scotland
SCOTLAND THE BEST

Not so much of a way of life, more of a restaurant.

Weekend Booking Recommended

57 - 61 Blackfriars Street,
off the Royal Mile
Edinburgh
Tel: 0800 298 2594

The Maharajahs

EGON RONAY RECOMMENDED

"Maharajahs more than fulfilled its eastern promise. 9 out of 10."
Gillian Glover, Scotsman

Magnificently designed, with hand painted murals, to resemble a tented pavillion set within a beautiful palace garden.

Opening Hours
Lunch 12 – 2pm
Dinner 5.30pm – midnight
7 Days

17-19 Forrest Road Tel 220 2273

Tower Restaurant

RESERVATIONS
0800 698 1487

mail@tower-restaurant.com
www.tower-restaurant.com

TOWER RESTAURANT
Museum of Scotland
Chambers Street
Edinburgh EH1 1JF

A TRUE DINING EXPERIENCE
Finest Quality Cuisine

Winner of TRINACRIA D'ORO
(Sicilian Golden Spoon Award)

Non-Smoking Area Available
Open 7 Days · 12pm till late

16 Nicolson St (opp Festival Theatre)
TEL 0800 698 1482
FAX 0131 622 7878

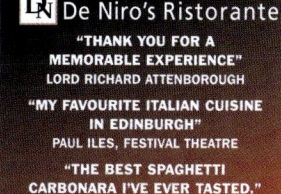

De Niro's Ristorante

"THANK YOU FOR A MEMORABLE EXPERIENCE"
LORD RICHARD ATTENBOROUGH

"MY FAVOURITE ITALIAN CUISINE IN EDINBURGH"
PAUL ILES, FESTIVAL THEATRE

"THE BEST SPAGHETTI CARBONARA I'VE EVER TASTED."
RORY FORD, EVENING NEWS

Open 7 days 12-11.30pm

140 Nicolson Street
Freephone: 0800 698 1481
Fax: 0131 622 7878

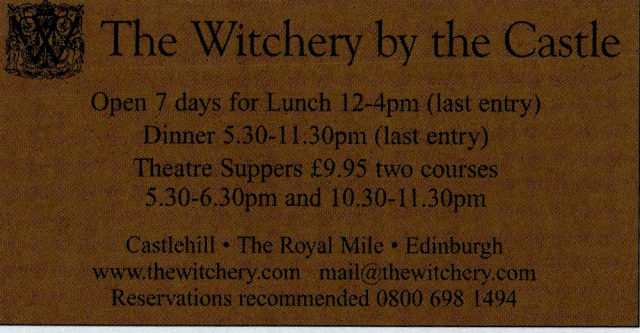

The Witchery by the Castle

Open 7 days for Lunch 12-4pm (last entry)
Dinner 5.30-11.30pm (last entry)
Theatre Suppers £9.95 two courses
5.30-6.30pm and 10.30-11.30pm

Castlehill • The Royal Mile • Edinburgh
www.thewitchery.com   mail@thewitchery.com
Reservations recommended 0800 698 1494

OLD TOWN & GREYFRIARS

Edinburgh **Food Guide**

desired. The menu is the finest selection of Scottish ingredients combined with creative flair. We began with the roast red pepper and chorizo soup, a spicy Spanish warmer (£4.95), and the Fife crab salad with lime mayonnaise, mango and basil (£8.95). After starters so sumptuous we could barely wait for mains of red onion and Roquefort tart with pesto crumble (£11.95), and honey roast Greshingham duck with Savoy cabbage, bacon and sweet potato rosti (£17.95). The desserts were amazing: a rumbaba with caramelised apple and praline mascarpone (£4.95) and a warm dark chocolate torte with white chocolate sorbet (£5.25). They also offer a light lunch and theatre supper with two courses at an incredible £9.95. The Witchery's reputation is as grand as the neighbouring Castle, and with food this good it's future appears equally rock solid. **RRH**

Bann UK D4

Bann UK has had a facelift and very gorgeous it's looking too. A myriad of subtle lighting effects, from rows of hidden up-lighters to a wafting blue gel, combine with candlelight and frosted glass to produce a sparklingly soft welcome. Solid wooden tables, fabric-covered benches and one brick red wall add warmth echoed in the friendly service and laid-back vibe. Enjoying an organic Italian Pinot Grigio (£10.90 a bottle), we chose crispy Thai potato fritters served with a trio of chutneys and relishes, and chicory baked in an emmental and Pernod fondue with herb lid (starters £3.90). Next came vegetarian haggis sausages on horseradish mash with red onion gravy, and crispy aromatic mock duck with stir-fried vegetables and dipping sauce (all main courses £9.80). We finished ourselves off with a vast Bailey's cheesecake gâteau and a chocolate and Cointreau mousse (desserts £3.90). This is gourmet vegetarian cuisine guaranteed to please avid meat eaters and vegans alike. You are invited to kick back and loaf at the urbannhangsuite on Friday and Saturday nights where a light menu and DJs promise to feed you up and chill you out from 11pm-3am. **EM**

Grain Store D4

Venture up stairs through an archway and you will find a series of intimate alcoves and open rooms in which to enjoy the very best Scottish fare. The choice of menus includes à la carte and tapas-style lunch options, an à la carte and a set dinner, which is well-priced at £15.50 for two courses and coffee. We chose from the à la carte lunch starters of toasted goats cheese with roasted pepper and watercress (£4.75) and soup of the day (£3), and main courses of venison with shallot

new
new
urbannhangsuite
Open 'til 3am
d.j. great food & drinks

'Innovative and adventurous vegetarian restaurant'
The Herald, 18.5.00

'Proof that style can accompany substance'
The Guardian, 16.6.00

Voted Best restaurant in Edinburgh 2000 by The List readers

modern vegetarian cuisine... with passion!

5 Hunter Square (Royal Mile) Edinburgh 0800 197 3515

OLD TOWN & GREYFRIARS

confit and port and rosemary jus (£11.75), and salmon steak with grapefruit and coriander butter (£9). The venison was tender and flavoursome, the salmon refreshed by the fruity tang of the butter. The homemade desserts – pear tart and crème anglaise and warm mango tart with pineapple sorbet (both £5) – were worth the temptation. The Grain Store provides a dining experience with many forward looking facets that never fails to refer back to the splendours of Scotland's natural larder. **RRH**

Tower D5

The recently opened Museum of Scotland celebrates Scottish culture, history and innovation so it is an appropriate setting for the Tower, a restaurant at the forefront of modern Scottish cuisine. The building is an architectural delight and the restaurant is both dramatically stylish and wonderfully light. I began with a trio of sushi (£5.95), served with a colourful display of pickled vegetables and fiery wasabi that tingled my senses. My partner chose smoked haddock risotto with poached egg, spinach and Parmesan (£5.95). Having had our taste buds tantalised we eagerly anticipated our main courses, a fillet of Aberdeen Angus served with fondant potato and sautéed shiitake mushrooms (£17.95) and scallops with a ragout of haricot beans and wild mushrooms with a butternut squash sauce (£15.95), accompanied by stir-fried spring vegetables (£1.95). The combination of flavours and textures was exquisite. Although replete, we indulged in a sharp and tangy lemon tart with a lime and ginger sorbet (£3.95) and a divine blueberry cheesecake (£3.95). An excellent range of international wines (from £9.95 to £680) and wonderful food served by charming staff in fabulous surroundings – what more could you ask for? **PC**

TOWER RESTAURANT

This stunning rooftop restaurant and terrace with views of Edinburgh's castle and skyline is open for lunch and dinner until late seven days.

RESERVATIONS
0800 698 1484

mail@tower-restaurant.com
www.tower-restaurant.com

TOWER RESTAURANT
Museum of Scotland
Chambers Street
Edinburgh EH1 1JF

OLD TOWN & GREYFRIARS

Edinburgh Food Guide

Gordon's Trattoria D4
On first arrival, Gordon's Trattoria appears to be a small café tucked into the Royal Mile, but surprisingly we were lead through the back to a cosy restaurant which was busy with Edinburgh folk and tourists alike. We settled in quickly and with an extensive menu to choose from ordered a bottle of house white, Lugana (£11.70) to sip while we selected. I started with bruschetta, garlic bread with chopped tomatoes (£3.40), simple but delicious, and my partner had the pâté della casa, chicken liver pâté with toasted bread (£4.90). For main courses we had bistecca al pepe, a sirloin steak with a brandy and green pepper sauce served with fries (£15.30), and a pizza fonteluna, spicy sausage pizza (£7.60). Even after such large portions I couldn't resist the profiteroles (£3), while my partner had a cappuccino (£1.85). Gordon's menu is very adaptable whether you want a cheap snack or a meal and they are open until 3am on Friday and Saturday, making it a great place to eat after a night on the town. **MJ**

Iggs E4
With the buzz of happy people and the summer breeze drifting in the open door, it could be Barcelona in late September - or Edinburgh early July. Iggs (above its sister Barioja, a city-chic tapas bar) has friendly staff who add a personable touch and a Spanish accent to proceedings. Ingredients are a mix of Spanish and Scottish in which neither is the foreigner. Lunch is value at £15.50 for three, £12.50 for two courses. We visited for dinner with starters £5.75, mains £15.75, and desserts £5.50. I began with a selection of air-dried meats with olives, sundried tomatoes and manchego cheese – a true taste of Spain. My partner had the gâteau of asparagus, aubergine, courgettes and red peppers topped with crispy shallots, pine kernels and an apricot dressing. Mains were breast of corn-fed chicken stuffed with manchego cheese, wrapped in jamon in a suprême and red pepper sauce, and baked fillet of Scottish beef on Anna potato with stuffed baby bell peppers and a sherry jus. Desserts were vanilla crème brulée with lemon sorbet and Spanish profiteroles with orange compote. For a taste of Spain in the heart of historic Scotland, head for Iggs. **RRH**

Barioja E4
Situated just off the Royal Mile above sister restaurant Iggs, this stylish tapas bar combines a contemporary interior with an excellent menu. We selected pinchos de pollo (grilled marinated chicken on a skewer, £3.50), patatas bravas (fried potato chunks with a spicy sauce, £2.00), gambas al ajillo (king prawns sautéed with garlic and chillies, £6.50), montadites de salmon (slices of bread topped with smoked salmon, £3.50), and

Gordon's Trattoria

ITALIAN RESTAURANT

Open 7 Days
Sun-Thurs, Midday-Midnight
Fri & Sat, Midday - 3.00am

"A taste of good food, good value, good atmosphere"
The Good Life.

231 High Street, Royal Mile, Edinburgh

Tel & Fax. 0131 225 7992

**THE AWARD WINNING
IGGS RESTAURANTE**

15 JEFFREY STREET   EDINBURGH   EH1 1DR
T: 0800 698 1501

**EDINBURGH'S
HOTTEST TAPAS BAR**

19 JEFFREY STREET   EDINBURGH   EH1 1DR
T: 0800 698 1499

OLD TOWN & GREYFRIARS

Edinburgh
Food Guide

pan con tomate (toasted bread with tomato, olive oil and garlic, £1.50). The excellent house white wine accompanied our meal (£10) and for dessert we had crême brûlée and the refreshing fruit soup (both £3.50). We found tapas a great way to experience different Spanish dishes and Barioja's reasonable prices enable you to enjoy a hearty selection. **MJ**

Viva Mexico   D4
Conveniently located on Cockburn Street, this popular restaurant has been delighting customers with its top quality Mexican cuisine since 1984. Viva Mexico offers a mouth-watering selection of dishes served in a bright and informal atmosphere by friendly staff. To begin, my partner and I opted to share plato national, a tasty selection of traditional Mexican starters (£6.50). My partner marvelled at the combination of ingredients in her mole poblano, a delicious Mexican speciality of chicken served in a chocolate, chile and herb sauce (£9.95). Meanwhile, I opted for flautas con salsa verde, a marvellous feast of crispy deep fried tortillas filled with chicken and covered with a tangy green salsa sauce (£9.95). To compliment our meal, we chose a bottle of house white La Ronciere (£10.85) from the extensive wine list. Following this, we indulged in a couple of delicious fruit sorbets (£3.25) – the perfect end to our Mexican feast. Viva Mexico is open for dinner (6.30-11pm Mon-Sat, 6.30-10pm Sun) and for lunch (12-2.30pm Mon-Sat), whilst a newly designed dining wing can cater for larger parties. **AD**

Bella   D4
Bella on North Bridge goes a long way to bring the Italian warmth and friendliness to Edinburgh. Serving traditional food with a modern twist, this is the place to come if you want some good, hearty fare. To start we went for cheese and garlic ciabatta bites (£2.10) and a lovely fresh insalata mozarella, a salad served with mozarella and dressed in nutty pesto and herbs (£3.50). For the main course I chose cellentani alpina, pasta spirals in a creamy cheese sauce with bacon and chicken (£6.99), while my friend opted for duck and caremelised onion pizza called papera (£6.40). We washed these down with the house red, £8.75, whilst deliberating over the desert menu which is full of tempting treats. We eventually chose torta di amaretto (£3.75), an amaretto cheesecake covered with cherry and kirsch sauce, and panacotta (£3.35), a dome of raspberry sorbet filled with ice cream and served with a berry sauce. Bella, also on Hanover Street, is open 10.30am-11pm (Mon-Sat) and noon-11pm (Sun). **AL**

Wee Windaes   D4
Situated in the heart of

New menus, new ideas, wonderful margaritas

Large groups welcome to our recently expanded dining room

41 Cockburn Street
Tel: 226 5145
www.viva-mexico.co.uk

OPEN
12-2.30pm MON-SAT
6.30-11pm MON-SAT
6.30-10pm SUN

18

Bella

Italian for beautiful food

Bella serve outstanding pastas and great pizzas as well as a wide choice of delicious starters, fresh salads and tempting desserts.

Your nearest Bella is located at:

54-56 North Bridge
0131 225 2044

9 Hanover Street
0131 225 4808

The Wee Windaes

SCOTTISH RESTAURANT & WEE DRAM BAR

If you want to enjoy high quality cuisine in a relaxed, friendly atmosphere, The Wee Windaes on Edinburgh's Royal Mile should be your first choice. Legend has it that the original windows on the building were stolen from a Kirk in the city's Cowgate. Nowadays you can gaze out onto the cobbled streets of the historic Old Town as you relish succulent Scottish fayre by candlelight.

From Scotch broth and haggis, to salmon and pheasant, to Angus beef, you'll find a menu cooked to perfection with a distinctive Highland taste - not to mention an excellent selection of wines, liqueurs and malt whiskies.

The Wee Windaes is an ideal spot for tourists and locals alike, providing the perfect venue for large parties, wedding celebrations and traditionally themed Scottish nights.

FREEPHONE: 0800 698 1455
FAX: 0131 226 1495
144 HIGH STREET, EDINBURGH

OLD TOWN & GREYFRIARS

Edinburgh Food Guide

Edinburgh's historic Old Town, Wee Windaes offers magnificent Scottish cuisine in a relaxed and welcoming atmosphere, and is enjoyed by locals and tourists alike. With a wide selection of dishes to choose from, we selected wild mushroom brioche (£4.95) and the more traditional cock-a-leekie soup (£3.95) to start. To follow, my partner opted for the fresh rainbow trout served in a tangy tomato essence and garnished with prawns (£11.95), whilst I chose the delightfully flavoured chicken breast stuffed with baby leeks and asparagus mousse (£11.95). Both dishes were washed down with a glass or two of house white Chateau de Lagarde 1998 (£11.95). Managing to squeeze in dessert after a short rest, my partner quickly polished off her chocolate éclair, whilst I thoroughly enjoyed the raspberry cranachan laced with Scotch whisky (both £4.25). Location, service and atmosphere are all excellent reasons to visit Wee Windaes. The sheer quality of the food on offer places this eaterie in the not-to-be-missed category. Wee Windaes is open for lunch daily noon-2.30pm (£2.95-£8.95) and also caters for tour parties and functions. Extended opening hours apply during the Festival. **AD**

Café Hub D4

The Hub is about much more than food. It's about drinking, concerts, art exhibitions, gourmet evenings and gathering with friends after work or before a night on the town. Many locals view Hub as a Festival-exclusive venue but with so much going on all year its more like a non-exclusive community whose sole aim is the nourishment and entertainment of all. We began our meal with seared halibut, vegetable and herb salad (£5.50), and basil and lemon risotto with Parma ham and prawns (£5.50). Mains were grilled corn-fed chicken with peas and mint (£11.50), and sweet pepper frittata, with spinach, ricotta and celeriac rosti (£9.50). Desserts were a dreamy cherry claflouti with choclate sorbet and sesame florentines with praline cream (both £3.75). Hub serves a large selection of teas coffees, malts, beers champagnes, so there's a tipple for every taste. The set menu offers two courses for £8 and three for £10 (Mon-Fri). With so much going on, why not put yourself at the centre of things, this summer, autumn, winter... **RRH**

Cafe Concerts, Culinary Evenings, Visual and Applied Arts
Brunch   Lunch   Dinner

cafe Hub

EDINBURGH'S FESTIVAL CENTRE
Main sponsor BANK OF SCOTLAND

Cafe Hub, Royal Mile, EH1 2NE
0131 473 2067   Open Daily

OLD TOWN & GREYFRIARS

Bridge D4

The Carlton Highland's recent refurbishment has transformed the hotel to the height of style and luxury, which is reflected in the dark intimacy of The Bridge, situated on the first floor. This chic eaterie, open from 6pm until 10pm, offers an exquisite three course menu priced at £18.95. We started with shallot and thyme soup with a wild mushroom and thyme chantilly, and ripe galia melon served with exotic fruit sorbet - both were delicious tasters priming us for the main course. I opted for a twice baked cheddar soufflé which was beautifully presented with an avocado and pine nut salad, while my partner chose pithivier of duck confit with apples and prunes in Armagnac with braised haricot beans and a Toulouse sausage. We sipped the lovely house red, Pierre Javert (£12.95) in anticipation of the desserts: a white and dark chocolate torte served with crème Anglais and a ginger brûlée, which made quite an entrance, covered in spun sugar. In our decadent surroundings, we finished off with a couple of liqueurs that completed the evening perfectly. **AL**

Maison Bleue D4

Nestled in the hub of Edinburgh's old town, Maison Bleue encourages a dining experience whereby customers order and share a number of dishes, thus rejecting the traditional three course path normally followed. The menu is eclectic and colour-coded to highlight different types of dish. Our chosen starters were the Vietnamese nems (£6.90), crispy rice pancakes with fresh crab,

The Bridge at the Carlton Hotel

0131 472 3022

19 North Bridge

Edinburgh EH1 1SD

21

OLD TOWN & GREYFRIARS

shrimp, garlic, mint and Chinese greens, and crunchy bruschetta topped with tomatoes, olives, basil and artichoke hearts (£4.90). For mains, we settled on the succulent coriander-crusted salmon served with braised baby leek on a garlic mash (£8.50), and a deliciously rich wild mushroom ragout in arborio rice with garden peas and fine herbs risotto style (£6.90), with a mouth-watering side order of creamed spinach (£2.90). A beautifully presented pineapple sorbet (£4.25) and royal nougat (£4.25) comprising nuts, almonds and chocolate followed for dessert, topping off a highly enjoyable meal. The service is both friendly and efficient, the atmosphere refined, while the décor is a stylish mix of both old and new. Not to be missed! **GB**

Suruchi   E5

On a boiling hot day, the last kind of meal you'd be hankering after is Indian. If you think this is true, you obviously haven't visited Suruchi's and tasted the coolest curries in town. And I'm not talking cool-as-a-korma either. In fact, in Suruchi's own words, they serve up some "beezers o' a curry"! The food at Suruchi is so out of this world that it's only the menu written in pure Scots, to remind you where you are. The refreshing atmosphere, flowers, beautiful tiles and subdued live jazz (Wed/Fri) lull you into submission to absolute pleasure - and the food is delicious! For starters try panir pakora; Indian cottage cheese fritters, and papdi chat; crunchy potatoes, yoghurt and mini popadoms (both £3.95). The main course, Nirvana, says it all; chicken cooked with lemongrass, mustard seeds, curry leaves and coconut (£8.25), matched only by the tandoori king prawn massalam (£12.95). A cool raita (£2.25) and an exotically Scottish upperi; crunchy cabbage with coconut (£3.95), completed our feast. So next time you're feeling the heat - you know exactly where to go. **PM**

Beluga   D5

Located in the old School of Dentistry on Chamber's Street, Beluga's interior is a modern fusion of blond wood and chrome. The menu is as colourful as the stained glass that lights the restaurant. I started my meal with a beautifully presented organic salad with spicy Mexican style sausage, mung beans, asparagus spears and balsamic dressing (£4.50). My companion finished off his roasted vine tomato and goat's cheese bruschetta with wild rocket and basil oil, while I ordered a bottle of Australian Chardonnay (£12.95). To follow, my partner tucked into collop of venison with mustard mash and baby vegetables drizzled with bacon and snowpea sauce (£15.95). I opted for seared fillet of sea bass, Thai style noodles and a black bean cream (£12.75). To round the evening off, I was treated to a rich chocolate tart and clotted

Maison Bleue
The new style of eating...
0131 226 1900
36-38 Victoria St
Map Ref: D4

SURUCHI RESTAURANT
Innovative Indian Cuisine
Large selection of vegetarian dishes
Live Jazz Wednesday & Friday evenings
Mon - Sat 12 -2
Mon - Sun 5 - 11.30pm
14a Nicolson Street,
Opposite The Festival Theatre
Telephone: 0800 298 3416

beluga

Bar & Canteen Restaurant

fine scottish produce with influences from around the pacific rim

open 9am-late
bar food also available

32a chambers street   edinburgh   tel 0131 624 4545

OLD TOWN & GREYFRIARS

iguana are offering a **2 for 1** offer on all drinks in the lists between 5-7 fridays & 9-11pm wednesdays-thursdays.

iguana provides **live entertainment** with selected quality djs, wednesday to sunday nights (7 nights a week during the festival). This is backed up regularly with special guest appearances.

eat at night food available 9am-10pm, 7 days (and nights) a week.

open@night

food & drink now served until

3am wednesday-saturday

iguana cafe & bar
41 lothian street, edinburgh
t. 0800 698 1425
www.iguanaedinburgh.co.uk

---

cream (£3.25) and my companion had a pretty papaya and raspberry panacotta (£3.50). A varied bar menu is available all day, and the restaurant menu changes regularly. **AMcC**

Iguana   D5
This trendy brasserie manages a heady mix: a bright, contemporary bar, imaginative food and a pre-club feel with live DJs at night. Quality service and an intelligent layout keep the focus, and our sights were firmly fixed on a meal a million miles from most people's idea of bar food! The menu is diverse, catering for small bites to three course meals, and portions are very generous. We had teriyaki chicken skewers with mixed leaves (£3.00) and steamed mussels with sweet chilli, coriander and tomato sauce (£3.00) for starters, either of which would have made a marvellous snack at any time of day. For a main course we chose wild mushroom risotto with Parmesan cheese and spinach (£5.60) and beef, mushroom and red wine casserole (£6.25). Apple & berry crumble with ice cream (£2.95) and ginger sponge pudding with golden syrup (£2.95) made for a perfect end, though I'm still wondering just how we managed to fit them in. A good selection of wines is available (£3.65/£2.65 by the glass and £10.95 by the bottle) as are all-day breakfasts (which are apparently excellent!). **DDR**

Vine Leaf   E5
When you put the amount of planning and care into a venture that Hala El-Berins has clearly invested in the new Vine Leaf, opposite the Festival Theatre, you can justifiably expect success. Having tested the menu on friends and family and built a welcoming atmosphere, she has produced a delightfully relaxing and intimate restaurant with an evocatively sunny Mediterranean menu. From the current selection of the seasonal variations, we enjoyed pan-fried polenta (£5.25) and a mezzeh platter, a mixture of various dishes (£5) to start. A fruity bottle of Tempranillo Merlot (£9.50) warmed us on the way to our coming banquet, consisting of sacchetini pasta with pesto sauce (£4.95), lamb and chicken brochettes with tahini sauce (£8.25), baby baked potatoes (£1.50) and an outstanding selection of Mediterranean roast vegetables (£1.50). We finished with a "small" piece of om ali - Middle Eastern bread and butter pudding (£3.50), a coffee and a herbal tea (£1.20 each). A two course lunch menu is also available for £5.95. If you don't leave here with a smile on your face, you haven't done it right! **JA**

Haw House   D5
The name might sound a little seedy but in reality the Haw House could not be a more tasteful establishment. Brightly lit with colourful decor and rhythmic modern music, this central venue has a fresh, exuberant, youthful feel about it, and its BYOB policy is ideal for large parties (£1.50 corkage). Mexican restaurant connoisseurs will know all about plentiful portions and this establishment is no exception to the rule. We began with a stacked plate of nachos de la casa (£3.65) and a crispy flauta (£3.75), before moving stealthily onto the beautifully cooked gambos al

The Vine Leaf

MEDITERRANEAN CUISINE

"...BRINGING A TOUCH OF SUN AND FLAVOUR OF THE MED TO EDINBURGH."

TEL: 0131 662 9191
22A NICHOLSON STREET

---

mexican cantina & grill

The Howl house

44 candlemaker row, eh1 2qe   tel: 0131 220 4420

OLD TOWN & GREYFRIARS

Edinburgh Food Guide

majo de ajo (£10.75) and a delicious beef enchillada (£7.95). Both main courses were served with rice and salad, and washed down with an excellent house red (£7.98). Two courses would have been more than sufficient but for the courageous there are also some mean cakes and desserts. We feasted on a portion of chocolate and chilli cheesecake and a more orthodox chocolate fudge cake (£2.95 each), and finished off with some extremely smooth filter coffee (£1). **JC**

Point C5

Walking along Bread Street, you can't help but stare in the large windows of The Point restaurant. It is part of the stylish Point Hotel, a very successful refurbishment of the old Co-op building. The restaurant is simple yet elegant with a warm atmosphere created with dim lighting and a candle at each table. We chose the Piesporter Michelsberg (£13.70) to drink and were pleasantly surprised to find that the food menu offers three courses for £12.90, offering you the choice of approximately four to six dishes per course. For starters we had bruschetta of charred vegetables and garlic with thyme olive oil and Cullen skink soup with Greenland prawns and basil chantilly. For my main course I had chicken and capsicum Thai style curry with fragrant rice, and my partner had hickory sirloin steak with scallion, potato mash and rosemary olive oil. Finally, for dessert we had warm apple pie, market fresh strawberries with vanilla custard and the dark chocolate torte with fruit purees and crème fraiche. The Point is the place to go if you want well-presented food in classy surroundings at great value. **MJ**

Lorenzo's D4

Lorenzo's has a rustic European charm, oil burners on the tables, a low ceiling with wooden beams and warm colours adding to the atmosphere generated by friendly staff. Champagne corks pop as romantic couples gaze lovingly and MSPs quietly debate alongside weekend pre-club revelry. There's also a summer terrace, which is extremely popular when the weather attempts to match the European feel of the décor. Many of the dishes on this Italian/Scottish menu can be ordered as starters or mains which cleverly opens the choice, making the menu seem incredibly varied. We chose roquette salad topped with crisp Parma ham and Parmesan

Lorenzo's RESTAURANT

Serving Excellent Italian Food 7 days a week

Lunch: 12-2pm

Dinner:
6-10pm Sun-Thurs 6-11pm Fri & Sat

Tel: 226 2426

shavings (£5.95) and sun-dried tomato and ricotta pizza as starters (£3.85), fresh, savoury and light enough not to weigh you down. Next up were gnocchi with chargrilled chicken, panchette and cream (£7.65) and pan roasted breast of duck with honey and orange jus (£12.95), both perfect as main courses. Desserts were lemon and blackcurrant sorbets (£3.25) and warm apple pie (£3.95). Lorenzo's is a fantastic little restaurant, a slice of Italian country charm in the heart of historic Edinburgh. **RRH**

Witchery   D4

For an evening of romance, the finest food, first class service all set against a backdrop of Edinburgh's most historic scenery, look no further than The Witchery. The lavish care and attention that goes into each fine detail leaves nothing to be desired. The menu is the finest selection of Scottish ingredients combined with creative flair. We began with the roast red pepper and chorizo soup, a spicy Spanish warmer (£4.95), and the Fife crab salad with lime mayonnaise, mango and basil (£8.95). After starters so sumptuous we could barely wait for mains of red onion and Roquefort tart with pesto crumble (£11.95), and honey roast Greshingham duck with Savoy cabbage, bacon and sweet potato rosti (£17.95). The desserts were amazing: a rumbaba with caramelised apple and praline mascarpone (£4.95) and a warm dark chocolate torte with white chocolate sorbet (£5.25). They also offer a light lunch and theatre supper with two courses at an incredible £9.95. The Witchery's reputation is as grand as the

The Witchery by the Castle

Edinburgh's most spectacular and atmospheric restaurants and luxurious suites located in an historic building at the gates of Edinburgh Castle.

Open 7 days for Lunch 12-4pm (last entry)
Dinner 5.30-11.30pm (last entry)
Theatre Suppers £9.95 two courses 5.30-6.30pm and 10.30-11.30pm

Castlehill • The Royal Mile • Edinburgh
www.thewitchery.com   mail@thewitchery.com
Reservations recommended 0800 698 1490

OLD TOWN & GREYFRIARS

neighbouring Castle, and with food this good it's future appears equally rock solid. **RRH**

Bay of Bengal   D4
The Bay of Bengal occupies a prime location in Edinburgh's Royal Mile with window tables that offer a great opportunity to watch the world go by while enjoying traditional Indian cuisine. This family-run restaurant offers a budget menu between 12-2pm and 5-6.30pm and also offers the option of late dining until 11.30pm. A lively mix of both visitors and locals ensured that two thirds of the tables were full throughout the evening and the attentive staff offered helpful advice on choosing from the range of dishes on offer. A tower of poppadums and chutneys kept us occupied while we made our selection. Starters of king prawn butterfly (£3.55) and lamb kebab (£2.95) were followed by a piquant platter of mixed tandoori (£9.50) with accompaniments of sag potato (£2.95) and bhindi bajee (£2.95). As an antidote to the rich spices we completed the meal with the cleansing qualities of orange sorbet and the more traditional mango kulfi (all £2.95). **KR**

Dial   D4
A bold hand is evident in this bright, contemporary restaurant with stunning décor. Everything is done with exceptional taste, from the printed fabric hangings and pale ice cream coloured walls to the Phillipe Stark chairs and even the choice of music. The à la carte menu is far from trendy, luxurious is more like it, and shows equal concentration and thought. For starters we began with cold omelette of cherry tomatoes, asparagus, red onion, artichoke and basil with a cauliflower cream (£4.50) and a delicious and unusual curried mussel and lychee broth topped with spring onion and crème fraîche (£4.95). A glass of the house white, Rocheburg Chenin Blanc (£10.95) prepared us for the main course: roasted rump of lamb with herb crusted mash and an apple and rosemary jus (£14.95) and fillet of Aberdeen Angus, fondant potato, baby tomato, mange tout and game jus (£14.95). For dessert, we sampled the richly fruity banana and blueberry cheesecake (£4.90) and decadent Belgian chocolate and Cointreau mousse (£4.50). Two café lattes (£1.55) helped us to digest our sumptuous meal before climbing the stairs back to George IV Bridge. In every way, Dial is restaurant with serious style. **AB**

Pancho Villas   E4
Found in historic Canongate, Pancho Villas provides revolutionary Tex Mex food at reasonable prices. The vibrant décor and lively salsa music coupled with an innovative Mexican menu has proved a winner for restaurant-goers over the past few years. As we relaxed with a bottle of the house Cabernet Sauvignon (£9.50 per bottle), we sampled the mixed nachos with refried beans (£3.95) and alitas de pollo, chicken wings cooked in garlic and butter and coated in honey (£3.25). Both provided the perfect entrees for the sizzling feast that lay ahead of us. For our main courses, I could not resist the generous portion of combination fajitas (£8.95) which comprised of chicken and steak served on a sizzler with onions, peppers and a selection of sauces. My partner tucked into the enchiladas suiza (£8.25), tortillas stuffed with chicken and cheese, topped with mild chilli cream and beans. We just managed to finish a large portion of the traditional ice cream (£2.95). Lunch is available all week and you can rest assured that the lively atmosphere and tasty menu at Panchos will add sizzle to any evening. **MM**

Il Castello   C5
Il Castello confirms every stereotype about Italian restaurants: the food is tasty and

Il Castello

Ristorante & Pizzeria

Dishing up Italian sun in the shadow of the castle

open 7 days
Lunch Hours 12-2.30, Dinner 5-11, Fri & Sat till 12 Midnight

36 Castle Terrace, Edinburgh Tel: 229 2730

Pancho Villas

MEXICAN RESTAURANT

For Something A Little Different

Now Open All Day
Friday and Saturday

26 Bell St, Merchant City, Glasgow
0141 552 7737

240 Canongate, Royal Mile, Edinburgh
0131 557 4416

OLD TOWN & GREYFRIARS

Edinburgh
Food Guide

the portions generous, the prices are reasonable and the wine a simple but pleasant accompaniment. The staff are friendly and even on a weeknight there was enough business to create a convivial atmosphere. Close to the Grassmarket and the Castle, it's ideal for almost any central location. While I enjoyed the ubiquitous insalate caprese, my partner tucked into a more elaborate insalata capriciosa (both representative at £3.60) before embarking on bistecca diana (£12.80) and veal 'al castello' (£9.80) respectively, somehow ignoring the enormous range of pizza, pasta and rizzotto at around the £6 mark. This was washed down with a generous litre of house wine, a steal at £9.20 a carafe for a very drinkable red, before topping off the meal with ice creams, a simple vanilla with chocolate sauce, and amaretto (£3.50 each). At this sort of price for this quality of food and service, Il Castello deserves to be amongst the busiest restaurants in the city. **CK**

City Restaurant   E5

The fact that the City Restaurant doubles up as a takeaway should not deter diners from trying out this popular, informal eatery. While traditional chip shop food is served up in the sit-in restaurant for those interested, the rest of the menu is impressively diverse and exceptionally good value for money. We ordered sizeable portions of onion rings (£2.00) and battered mushrooms (£2.20) for starters, before moving on to a delicious mushroom and sweetcorn pizza (£5.10) and a huge all-day veggie breakfast with toast and tea (£4.60). From the sweet menu, we then tried the knickerbocker glory (£2.95) and the tartufo (£2,95), and were far from disappointed with the size and flavour of both. The service is friendly and efficient while the décor is reminiscent of US diners, sporting booths, florescent signs and a counter running the length of the restaurant. The City is open 8am-1am, offers children's portions and is licensed, serving draught lager (£2.00) and wine (£8.20 per bottle), making it an ideal choice for all parties, whether for breakfast, lunch, dinner or supper. **GB**

Good old fashioned Scottish & Italian meals

OPEN ALL DAY
Haggis Suppers • Fish Suppers
All Day Breakfasts • Pizza + Pasta
Steaks & Burgers

**33 -35 Nicholson Street, next to Festival Theatre
0131 667 2819**

30

EDINBURGH'S TOP 20

YOUR GUIDE TO TWENTY OF THE BEST INDEPENDENT RESTAURANTS IN THE CITY

E.R.A.

EDINBURGH RESTAURATEURS' ASSOCIATION

WWW.EDINBURGHRESTAURANTS.CO.UK

EDINBURGH RESTAURATEURS ASSOCIATION

DANIEL'S BISTRO
See review on page 114
A much loved bistro specialising chiefly in Provincial French cooking but also in Scottish and pan European styles.
Reservations: 0800 542 4317
88 Commercial Street, Leith
MAP REF : 1

THE SHORE BAR & RESTAURANT
This historic eighteenth century hostelry specialises in Scottish fish and shellfish.
Reservations: 0800 542 4327
www.edinburgh-waterfront.com
3 Shore, Leith
MAP REF : 2

THE MAGNUM
This stylish, relaxed restaurant and bar, serves traditional Scottish dishes and is recognised for its welcoming atmosphere and outstanding value.
Reservations: 0800 542 4338
1 Albany Street,
MAP REF : 3

DUCK'S AT LE MARCHE NOIR
See review on page 48
Classic dishes cooked with imagination, using fresh Scottish produce, produced by homegrown, award-winning chefs.
Reservations: 0800 542 4293
www.ducks.co.uk
2/4/ Eyre Place **MAP REF : 4**

KWEILIN
See review on page 57
A unique selection of authentic Cantonese cuisine and an extensive wine list to suit many a palate and pocket.
19-21 Dundas Street.
Reservations: 0800 542 4296
MAP REF : 5

HALDANES
Award winning chef-proprietor, George Kelso creates classical and innovative dishes using the finest of Scottish produce.
Reservations: 0800 542 4302
www.haldanesrestaurant.com
39a Albany Street.
MAP REF : 6

LE CAFÉ SAINT-HONORE
Small, selective a la carte menu serving the best of Scottish fish, shellfish, vegetables, meat and game.
Reservations: 0800 542 4307
www.icscotland.co.uk/café-sthonore
34 NW Thistle Street Lane.
MAP REF : 7

MARTINS
An oasis of wild fresh fish, shellfish, game, lamb, organic vegetables, herbs, berries, summer fruits in clean, green and bright surroundings.
70 Rose Street North Lane
Reservations: 0800 542 4311
MAP REF : 8

SCALINI
Authentic Italian cuisine with the emphasis on antipasti, olive oils, balsamic vinegar served within an elegant dining room.
10 Melville Place
Reservations: 0800 542 4315
MAP REF : 9

WHIGHAMS WINE CELLARS
Varied and interesting selection of wines and champagne by the glass. Whigham is particularly renowned for their excellent value seafood platter.
Reservations: 0800 542 4325
13 Hope Street, Charlotte Square,
www.whighams.com **MAP REF : 10**

IGG'S
See review on page 16
The restaurant continues to offer its renowned quality of cuisine with the new extension of a tapas bar adding to the cosmopolitan atmosphere.
15 Jeffrey Street.
Reservations: 0800 542 4331
MAP REF : 11

DUBH PRAIS
A small cellar restauran offering the very best from the Scottish larder. Reservations are advisable and can be booked privately.
Reservations: 0800 542 4351
www.bencraighouse.co.uk
123b High Street. **MAP REF : 12**

CREELERS SEAFOOD BISTRO & REST.
The proprietors bring fresh fish, smoked products and game in their own boat from Arran to their restaurant in the heart of Edinburgh.
Reservations: 0800 542 4294
www.creelers.co.uk
3 Hunter Sq. Royal Mile **MAP REF : 13**

JACKSONS
A taste of Scotland Restaurant offers elegant, creative cuisine to satisfy discerning palates.
Reservations: 0800 542 4297
www.jacksons-restaurant.co.uk
209-213 High Street. Royal Mile
MAP REF : 14

THE WITCHERY BY THE CASTLE
See review on page 12
The Witchery's two historic dining rooms offer the finest Scottish cuisine and hospitality in unique surroundings.
Reservations: 0800 542 4305
www.thewitchery.com
Castlehill, The Royal Mile **MAP REF : 15**

MERCHANTS
Our regularly changing menus ensure good food in a relaxed and friendly atmosphere with personal service.
Reservations: 0800 542 4308
www.merchantsrestaurant.co.uk
17 Merchant Street. **MAP REF : 16**

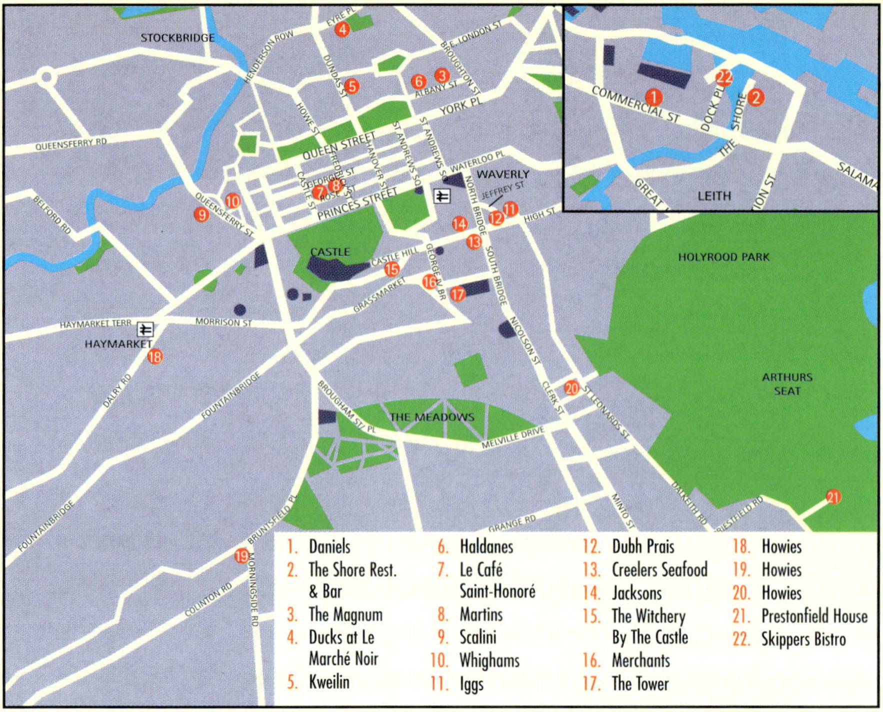

EDINBURGH RESTAURATEURS ASSOCIATION

1. Daniels
2. The Shore Rest. & Bar
3. The Magnum
4. Ducks at Le Marché Noir
5. Kweilin
6. Haldanes
7. Le Café Saint-Honoré
8. Martins
9. Scalini
10. Whighams
11. Iggs
12. Dubh Prais
13. Creelers Seafood
14. Jacksons
15. The Witchery By The Castle
16. Merchants
17. The Tower
18. Howies
19. Howies
20. Howies
21. Prestonfield House
22. Skippers Bistro

THE TOWER
See review on page 12
Tower is sleek, elegant and luxurious, serving the very best of Scottish produce, especially steaks and shellfish, with imagination and flair- totally unmissable.
Reservations: 0800 542 4312
www.tower-restaurant.com
Museum of Scotland, Chamber Street.
MAP REF : 17

HOWIES
See review on pages 76, 77, 92
A delightful trio of Scottish restaurants using the freshest of locally sourced food s to create inspiring fixed price menus.
208 Bruntsfield Place Reservations: 0800 542 4316
63 Dalry Road Reservations: 0800 542 5270
4/6 Glanville Place Reservations 0800 542 5268
www.howies.uk.com
MAP REF : 18,19, 20

PRESTONFIELD HOUSE
The Old Dining Room is open as an a la carte restaurant serving classic French and Scottish cuisine and there is extensive cellar of fine wines.
Reservations: 0800 542 4326
www.prestonfieldhouse.com
Prestonfield Road
MAP REF : 21

SKIPPERS BISTRO
See review on pages 114
Skippers is a cosy, atmospheric bistro waiting for your discovery. The seafood-orientated menu is selected daily and is subject to the day's catch of the Scottish fishing fleets.
Reservations: 0800 542 4332
www.skippers.co.uk
1a Dock Place, Leith **MAP REF : 22**

NEW TOWN, BROUGHTON AND LEITH WALK

Eating Out in New Town, Broughton and Leith Walk.

The New Town combines money, history and fashion in one of the city's most sought-after areas. The refined Georgian streets are a buzz of upmarket shopping, art galleries, bars and restaurants. Rick's on George Street was recently voted the world's most stylish bar and is a favoured hang-out for Edinburgh's in-crowd. Charlotte Square is home to the annual Book Festival so if after a day spent digesting diction you feel the need for sustenance, why not head for a meal at No.27?

Rose Street has shrugged off its reputation for smoky drinking dens and boozy pub crawls. Recent arrivals include the Easy Everything internet café, the famous Rhodes and Co, the delightful Thai Erawan Express, and the fabulous new Japanese restaurant YO! Sushi.

Your travels may well take you on to bohemian Broughton and its throng of cafés, bars and brassieres. Sip a cappuccino at the ever-popular Nexus Café, bounce to the beat with a buritto and a beer at The Basement, dine in style at the Smoke Stack or sample a slice of Spanish sunshine at the Tapas Tree.

Across from the Playhouse, Union Place is home to yet more international flavours. Amongst others, you'll find the French delights of La Gavotte, as well as Asian offerings at Modern India and Shezan.

No.3 Royal Terrace E2

With it's open fire, splashes of tartan and warm, muted lighting, No.3 Royal Terrace (sister restaurant to The Howgate) manages to be both plush and informal. Busiest at weekends, its broad, globetrotting restaurant and bistro menu (recently updated) feature both modish and traditional dishes, catering for adventurous eaters and those with less exotic tastes. From the myriad of dishes on offer, we opted for a generous portion of mussels in white wine, garlic and cream (both £4.95), and the sizeable Thai crab fish cakes with wilted spinach and Oriental sauce. Our mains consisted of a huge, tender Scotch lamb shank with roasted root vegetables and chive mash, and seared supreme of halibut with wilted spinach, asparagus and a red pepper butter sauce (both £8.95). These left no room for dessert and we just about managed to squeeze in coffee. Although it's a little off the beaten track, make an effort to search out No.3 because it boasts a comfy, congenial atmosphere, service is swift and courteous and prices are more than reasonable. What more could you ask for? **DK**

MP's Bistro E3

Tucked away behind Waterloo Place at the bottom of Calton Hill is the Parliament House Hotel, within which you may chance upon MP's. Fortunately, one may argue, not the political sort of MP but rather MP's Bistro, a far more appetising find! For dinner you can either choose two courses for £11 or three for £13. While contemplating the menu we sipped on a glass of Los Dominicos Chilean house white wine (£11.25 a bottle). My partner started with spicy chorizo and pepper stew served on a bed of noodles, while I opted for cherry tomatoes and feta cheese with an extremely tasty hazelnut dressing. For our main courses I chose slow-braised leg of duckling with a puy lentil and chilli ragout, which proved a delicious combination. My partner ordered sautéed lamb's liver, with bacon and a rosemary, red wine reduction - a fine dish that he is still raving about. We decided, hesitantly, to skip the delicious-sounding desserts on offer and finished our meal with some rich filter coffee (£1.50). MP's also offer a 'light bites' menu during the evening with prices starting at about £4. **LJT**

No. 3 ROYAL TERRACE
BISTRO AND RESTAURANT
No. 3 ROYAL TERRACE
0800 698 1438

NEW TOWN, BROUGHTON AND LEITH WALK

Edinburgh Food Guide

Lafayette B3

Whilst any building of this period has rarity value in Edinburgh, Tudor House is a black and white gem amidst the West End's grey grandeur. That it is now home to a stylish French restaurant is an added bonus. With true Gallic ceremony we were ushered up the timber staircase to the elegant dining room to peruse an impressive menu, assisted by an excellent Sauvignon Blanc (£12.50). My tartare of wild salmon with salad and a pickled pear coulis (£4.95) was a typically imaginative and successful combination, as was my companion's watercress salad with seared langoustines and lemon dressing (£4.50). The roasted halibut with fennel, stuffed tomato, fondant potatoes and mushroom sauce that followed (£15.95) was also delicious. Rather than ordering from the sweet trolley, we opted for coffee (£1.50) and shared a cheeseboard (£5.25). A table d'hôte menu of two (£18.50) or three courses (£22.50) is also available. And how did we cope with all this medieval splendour? Being middle-aged with creaky French we felt quite at home. **MB**

Number One D3

One Princes Street is a fitting address for Edinburgh's number one best kept secret, and Number One comes first in every detail. With the dimensions of a ballroom, and only 14 tables at a push, the ambience is surprisingly intimate. The service is just right: friendly but never overdone, and the décor is plush yet modern, with an elegant, jet set atmosphere. And here's the secret: you don't need a Concorde-sized budget to enjoy a five-star dinner. I chose from the market menu and for £37.50 cruised through three courses comprising: timbale of crab, artichoke and avocado; roast turbot topped with cheese and garlic potatoes, spinach soubise and lie de vin; and chocolate terrine with orange compôte and crème fraîche. My partner opted for à la carte: a rich assortment of foie gras (£16.50); succulent roast duckling (£19.50) with sautéed potatoes (£3.50); and a dark chocolate tart with hazelnut ice cream (£7.50). Each dish was lovingly prepared, lavishly presented and then lustily devoured – delicious! Lingering over coffee and petit fours, we kicked back and digested our taste of the good life. **PM**

Hadrian's D3

The Roman Emperor Hadrian considered north Britain so uncivilised that he built a wall separating it from the south. Why one of Edinburgh's top hotels

Traditional French Cuisine
Served in elegant surroundings

Extensive Wine List
Table d'Hote Lunch from £9.50
Table d'Hote Dinner from £18.50

Creative a la carte menu

Monday - Saturday 12-2pm, 6.30-10pm

All major credit cards accepted

Tudor House, 9 Randolph Place Edinburgh EH3 7TE
Tel: 0131 225 8678 Fax: 0131 225 6477

THE BALMORAL
EDINBURGH

RF
HOTELS

The Rocco Forte Collection

A member of
The Leading Hotels of the World

number one

Join us for lunch or dinner at this award winning restaurant.

Menus are created by our celebrated chef - Jeff Bland to suit any occasion.

☎ 0800 698 1439

HADRIAN'S

Breakfast, lunch or dinner ... enjoy a casual and relaxed dining experience at Hadrian's Brasserie.

Every Sunday brunch is served between 12.30pm and 2.30pm.

☎ 0800 698 1440

1 Princes Street
Edinburgh, EH2 2EQ

NEW TOWN, BROUGHTON AND LEITH WALK

chose his name for its stylish, contemporary brasserie is not immediately obvious, but it does underline just how cultivated Scots are today. This is reflected in both the restaurant's elegant décor and its new menu, which we were delighted to sample. My companion's terrine of osso bucco (£4.95) was a light, sophisticated interpretation of the Italian veal and tomato stew, whilst my smoked salmon and crab parcel was equally inventive with Scottish fare. Roast monkfish with ginger and garlic was imaginatively teamed with herb noodles (£10.95), whilst my confit of duck was beautifully complemented by puy lentils and pomme purée (£16.50). The house white was an extremely civilised 1998 Chardonnay (£13). Despite such exacting standards the atmosphere is lively and informal. Established favourites such as steak, fish and chips or haggis are still available, reminding us that there's nothing primitive about traditional food cooked to perfection and beautifully presented. But Hadrian might have found that hard to swallow. **MB**

Bella D4

Running in from the driving rain, Bella has a homely feel. The interior shying away from the usual Italian pastiche and instead aims for warm and welcoming. The menu was a welcome treat too. In order to maximise on the items on offer, we ordered the Assortimento Bella (£5.99) to start. This consisted of a tempting combination of chicken wings, pastella ravioli, cheese and garlic ciabatta bites and other Italian titbits. Suitably enticed, we waited for our main courses; pollo cacciatora with fettucine (£8.99) was deliciously fresh and tasty, and the pizza marinara (£6.99) looked perfection itself, and judging by the clean plate, looks didn't deceive. Although thoroughly sated, we completed our research, heading towards the dessert menu. I chose panacotto (£3.35), which was a raspberry sorbet with cranberry jelly; very refreshing and well presented. My partner opted for tiramisu (£3.45), every bit as good as Mama used to make. If you find yourself in the New Town and the shopping has given you a hunger for tasty Italian fare at reasonable prices, you could do a lot worse than head for Bella. Also open for lunches from £7.95. **DC**

Modern India E2

The top of Leith Walk is a very busy area these days and, with the impending arrival of the new cinema and leisure park, the area is sure to continue its increase in popularity. So if you're looking for pre-theatre/cinema/whatever cuisine, you have to try the delights of Modern India. Located opposite the Playhouse, this is the perfect venue for a warm-up to your evening. Fusing Indian cuisine with cultures from around the world in an elegant, minimalist setting, this unique venue is ideal for couples or groups. There's plenty to pique your curiosity on the menu and you wouldn't be disappointed by anything from our table: mushroom nihari (spiced mushrooms with onions and cheese) (£4.65), traditional onion bhajis (£2.95), goa fish curry (£8.45), and sarson ka saag with paneer (spinach, cheese and garlic) (£6.45). All accompanied by pilau rice (£1.95), nan bread (£1.95) and a pleasant house red (£10.00). Finish with a selection of kulfi (£2.95) and head off into the night to enjoy the rest of your evening. Whatever night you're planning, Modern India is guaranteed to be a good choice. **JA**

Est Est Est B3

The bustling, lively atmosphere within this Italian restaurant is particularly suited to celebratory meals or as a precursor to a big night out, with guests invited to doodle on tablecloths with crayons and balloons scattered throughout the modern interior. The friendly service only adds to this 'party' atmosphere, while the food more than matches these peripheral feelgood factors. We started with garlic pizza bread (£2.95), insalate Caesar (£4.50) and mozzarella e funghi fritti (£4.60), all of which were delicious and well presented. Pizza rustica (£6.20) and salmone griglia (£9.95) were later despatched from the busy open kitchen and were equally

---

Bella

Italian for beautiful food

Bella serve outstanding pastas and great pizzas as well as a wide choice of delicious starters, fresh salads and tempting desserts.

Your nearest Bella is located at:
54-56 North Bridge
0131 225 2044

9 Hanover Street
0131 225 4808

MODERN INDIA
restaurant Edinburgh

Sister Restaurants in Glasgow & Paisley

Pre-Theatre Available 7 Days
4.00pm - 7.00pm

•

A la Carte Available All Day, Every Day

•

Lunch Available Mon - Sat
12.00pm - 3.00pm

Modern India
20 Union Place
Edinburgh, EH1 3NQ
Tel: 0131 556 4547
www.modern-india.co.uk

PEPPERMINT RESTAURANTS

NEW TOWN, BROUGHTON AND LEITH WALK

impressive. As the music gradually gained volume we relaxed with a bottle of tangy, fruity Pino Grigio (£17.50) before ordering the luscious meringa con cigleggie e gelato (£3.45) and refreshing sorbetto di frutta (£3.40) from the expansive sweet menu. In case you wondered, the word 'est' means 'it is' and the tale of the restaurant's title is revealed on the menu itself. To find out, pop along for a feed yourself. Is it good? Est Est Est! **GB**

Rhodes & Co D3

Edinburgh is one of four in a chain that relies on more than a name for success. The truth behind the brand betrays fine British food with a modern twist, in stylish, understated surroundings, and all at very reasonable prices. We started with potted chicken liver parfait with refreshing Bramley apple jelly and toasted brioche slices (£4.10), and smoked salmon and peppered cream cheesecake with spring onions (£5). Main courses include crispy battered cod and chips (£7.90), roast breast of chicken (£10.90) and grilled rib eye steak (£12.95), traditionally British with enough flair yet never drowned in over-zealous and unnecessary attempts to impress. We chose the salt-and-peppered duck breast with spicy plums (£12) and the tender, slightly pink roast pork fillet with buttered cabbage and creamy wild mushrooms (£11.80). A little unnerved about ordering pink pork I was delighted with the end result, a cut of meat that melted in the mouth. Puddings (£4.35) follow the feel of the menu; we selected iced pear parfait with caramelised melba toast and crème brûlée, nothing overtly frilly but an undisputed thrill for the taste buds. With a formula like this, the Rhodes name will go a long way. **RRH**

A Room In The Town C2

Retreating from a bitter January evening, the need for warmth and a smile is always a comfort you are sure to be granted in A Room In The Town. Our anticipation grew as taste buds thawed with alcohol (BYOB, £1 corkage). My partner began with chorizo and avocado salsa wrapped in Parma ham with a lime sour cream (£4.75), whilst I chose a light spicy corncake, complemented by a parsley and red onion yoghurt (£3.45). For our main course we indulged in a roasted saddle of venison on grilled white pudding with juniper and thyme jus (£14.95) and fillet of monkfish wrapped in smoked bacon on grilled black pudding with red wine braised artichokes (£14.25). Both dishes were accompanied with a grand assortment of vegetables, which added to the fine selection of ingredients. Winter soaked brambles with beautiful honey and oatmeal ice cream (£3.45), and raspberry and almond torte with raspberry coulis (£3.65) gave us the courage to face the nippy extremes and we left glowing from the inside out. **JF**

Nargile Mezeriye D3

A second childhood is hard to come by, so when you find an experience that genuinely makes you want to dance with delight, you'd be well advised to hold on to it for as long as possible. Thankfully, as far as Nargile proprietor Seyhan Azak is concerned, your table is yours for the evening. So, while basking in this restaurant's light elegant splendour, try the meze (£5.95 per person) to begin – a selection of nine starters that will give you that "kid in a

---

RHODES & CO

All day eating available
from 11.30am - 9.45pm
Fixed price menu from
6.00pm - 9.45pm

Rhodes and Co
3-15 Rose Street
Edinburgh EH2 2YJ
Tel: 0800 698 1445
Fax: 0131 220 9199

---

a room in the town

SCOTTISH BISTRO

LICENSED & B.Y.O.B

OPEN 7 DAYS
Lunch from noon
Dinner from 5.30

18 Howe Street
0131 225 8204

EST EST EST
0800 698 1413
135A GEORGE ST

Turkish Cuisine
NARGILE
MEZERIYE RESTAURANT
73 Hanover St
Edinburgh
0131 225 5755

Business Lunch
£7.50
Lunchtime Meze
£6.50

see our menu at
www.nargile.co.uk

Bar Roma

The best Italian restaurant in Edinburgh Bar None. Salute!

For Bookings Freephone 0800 298 3471   Fax 0131 226 7172
Email reservations@bar-roma.co.uk
Website www.bar-roma.co.uk
39A Queensferry Street, Edinburgh EH2 4RA

Siam Erawan

Business lunch, a la carte and Banquet Menus

**Open for lunch
12-2.30pm
Open for Dinner
6-10.45pm**

T. 226 3675
48 Howe Street

NEW TOWN, BROUGHTON AND LEITH WALK

candy shop" feeling. You will have trouble choosing a main, and we can recommend the biber dolmasi (stuffed peppers) (£7.95) or kilich shish (chargrilled swordfish) (£8.95) and a bottle of Turkish wine, Dikmen (£8.95). To be fair, we suspected everything on the menu would have been just as good and rounded off a wonderful evening by sharing a traditional baklava (£3.95), a sweet, nutty pastry, washed down with two Turkish coffees (£1.50 each). If you really can't choose, set meals are available from £9.95 or two course business lunches for £7.50. Trust me, your inner child deserves a visit to Nargile. **JA**

Brown's C3

A perfect start to an evening in Edinburgh's cosmopolitan district can be found at Brown's, where the lively atmosphere complements the airy décor and subtle lighting. Although the restaurant is reassuringly crammed, the relaxed informality alludes to privacy. Catering for those who wish for either a quick fix or a leisurely meal, the service provided by the friendly staff is most impressive. From the menu, we selected grilled king prawns marinated in garlic, coriander, chilli and olive oil (£5.95) and smoked salmon with soda bread (£6.25). Having whetted our appetite we relaxed over an Australian Chardonnay (£14.50) and awaited with anticipation our main course. Scottish sirloin steak served with fresh vegetables (£12.95) put a gluttonous gleam in my partner's eyes whilst I was equally enamoured with the venison and rose haunch with potatoes and courgettes in juniper and thyme (£10.95). Anticipating the hard night ahead of us we almost declined desert, however, the offer of sticky toffee pudding in butterscotch sauce (£3.65) and hot fudge brownie with ice cream (£3.65) was too much to bear and our sensibilities left us whilst we indulged in pudding heaven. **CSR**

Bar Roma B3

Situated in Edinburgh's West End with a stylish modern façade, Bar Roma is an Italian restaurant with a personality. At only 7.30pm, the restaurant area is full and buzzing with everything from couples to families and birthday parties. The attentive waiters brought us a bottle of white Trebbiano D'Abruzzo (£10.25) before heading across the restaurant to sing happy birthday to an ecstatic eight year old boy. This atmosphere - combined with the open kitchen and bar (not to mention the tree in the middle of the restaurant!) - put us in the mood for pasta. We had the

---

BROWNS™
RESTAURANT & BAR

Great food, bustling atmosphere and no need to book

... THAT'S BROWNS

"Browns deserves its popularity"
EDINBURGH FOOD GUIDE

131-133 GEORGE ST, EDINBURGH EH2 4JS

MAIN MEALS SERVED ALL DAY

12 noon - 11.00pm
Monday to Saturday

12 noon - 10.30pm
Sundays & Bank Holidays

SEPARATE COCKTAIL BAR

OPEN 7 DAYS A WEEK

FULL MENU ALWAYS AVAILABLE

TRADITIONAL SUNDAY ROAST

For information call
0131 225 4442

BAR ROMA

The best Italian restaurant in Edinburgh. Bar none. Salute!

For Reservations Free Phone 0800 298 3471
Fax 0131 226 7172
Email reservations@bar-roma.co.uk
Web site www.bar-roma.co.uk
39A Queensferry Street Edinburgh EH2 4RA

rigatoni norcina, Italian sausage in brandy, cream and tomato sauce (£6.95), and the rack of lamb with the best fresh tagliatelle in butter and parmesan that I have ever had outside Italy (£13.95). These followed starters of New Zealand mussels grilled with garlic butter (£5.50) and chicken wings (£4.95). As full as we felt after our meal, we could not go Italian without an espresso to finish (£1.40) – ideal! **GG**

La P'tite Folie C3

La P'tite Folie on Frederick Street is unmistakably French with wooden bistro chairs, candles flickering in bottles, Catherine Deneuvre et al on the wall and wine served in glass tumblers. There's a welcome tang of Atlantic coast in the décor, mirrored by the freshest ingredients and the lightest of touches in the kitchen. Menu

La p'tite folie...

restaurant francais

LUNCH SERVED 12-3pm
(£6.90 – 3 Courses)

DINNER SERVED 6-11pm
(A La Carte)

VEGETARIAN OPTIONS

SET DINNER AVAILABLE FOR LARGER GROUPS

61 FREDERICK STREET
0131 225 7923
www.geocities.com/laptitefolie_uk/

---

boards change every day but we enjoyed starters of moules mariniere (£3.95) and grilled goats cheese, avocado and toasted walnut salad (£4.00), followed by roast breast of Barbary duck with ginger, orange and coriander (£9.75), and escalope of salmon in a wild mushroom and pink peppercorn sauce (£8.80). Special mention must go to the plethora of accompanying vegetables, which included a fantastic potato gratin. The house wine was flowing nicely (£8.10 a bottle) when we were presented with the piece de resistance: a truly sublime chocolate tart and a masterful tarte tatin (both £2.80), proving once and for all that there is nothing in the world to beat real French cuisine. La P'tite Folie is open for lunch from 1-3pm and for dinner from 6-11pm. **EM**

Hard Rock Café D3

The Hard Rock Café is everything you would expect; busy, buzzing and bursting with atmosphere. The bar near the entrance is popular in its own right, but add the great restaurant, serving all your American favourites, rock music and friendly staff, and you know you are in for a great ride. We settled into our booth, perused the cocktail menu and waited for our chicken wings in milder sauce (£5.25). With one order comprising 14 succulent and meaty wings, we decided to share and, as they say back in the ol' country, they were finger lickin' good. As a main course, my companion chose the steak sandwich (£9.95), while I devoured the ribs (£11.50). We were very impressed with our meal but decided to leave room for the tempting desserts. I chose cheesecake (£3.95), which was everything it should be -

baked, tall, rich, delicious and hard to finish. My companion became almost territorial about his outrageous hot fudge brownie (£4.25), even though it is usually a shared dessert. We finished up this great meal and moved on to the bar to let the party begin! **BO'R**

Gringo Bills C3

Gringo Bill's is in the city centre on Hanover Street, you enter through a brightly painted door and find there is an equally bright atmosphere upstairs. This lively, upbeat restaurant offers an extensive menu of Mexican style food. We ordered the House white wine, Villa Costa Bianco (£9.00) and then decided on very tasty barbecue spare ribs cooked in bone-suckin' sauce (£5.00) and wings of fire, tender chicken wings baked in Bill's special spicy sauce (£5.00) to start. I followed this with chicken fajitas, a sizzling skillet of chicken, peppers, onion with flour tortillas, cheese, sour cream and pico de gallo salsa (£11.50). Meanwhile, my partner enjoyed chargrilled shrimp tostadas, a jumbo toasted flour tortilla, topped with salad, black beans, salsa fresca, guacamole, sour cream and melted cheese (£11.50). Both meals offer a choice of filling including chicken, sirloin steak, duck, shrimp and chilli vegetables. Sweets are available from £2.50 to £3.50 but for those in the party mood there are cocktails and 80 different tequilas to chose from, which makes this a popular place for large groups. Opening hours are noon-2.30pm then 6pm-late (Mon-Fri), and noon-late (Sat). **MJ**

La Gavotte E2

This is one of a clutch of restaurants enlivening the newly-chic Union Street/Leith

Gringo Bill's
BAR-Y-GRILL

Opening Hours:
Lunch
Tue-Fri 12-2pm
Sat 12-4pm

Dinner
Tue-Sat 6-10.30pm

**110 Hanover Street
Edinburgh
Tel: 0131 220 1208**

Take your partner to...

La Gavotte
Cafe • Restaurant

For a Medley of French Food

Close to Edinburgh Playhouse

Pre-theatre menu
2 courses £7.90
3 courses £9.90

Sunday Lunch
2 courses & coffee
£6.90

Live entertainment every Thursday

8 UNION STREET, EDINBURGH · TEL/FAX: 557 8451

NEW TOWN, BROUGHTON AND LEITH WALK

Walk area. Open just three months, but formerly a Pierre Victoire, La Gavotte retains the best features of the now-defunct chain (flaming orange walls and simple wooden furniture, creating a French country atmosphere), while expanding and developing its own identity. The £4.90 lunch stays, but from 5-7pm Monday-Thursday, there's also a pre-theatre menu (£7.90 for two courses, £9.90 for three), which caters for audiences at The Playhouse opposite. There are plans too for an art gallery-bar in the cellar as well as live music. We whetted our appetites on deep-fried brie (£3.95) and chicken croquettes (£4.50) before moving on to lemon sole with smoked salmon in wine bourdelaise sauce (£9.90), and poellée de poisson, a selection of fresh fish and shellfish in white wine and tomato sauce (£10.95). Ingredients are mainly local with an emphasis on fish and game, simply but perfectly cooked and presented. The "Reserve La Gavotte" crisp house wine confirmed that this is a restaurant intent on making a name for itself. **MB**

Bellini D2

Bellini opened at the tail end of last Millennium and already has centuries of tradition behind it. Head chef Angelo trained with Italy's finest and his desire to mix the custom and style of his homeland is obvious; from the Renaissance art adorning the walls, to the exquisitely crafted, extravagantly portioned food. We started with the crespelle carlos, a light crêpe, with spinach, ricotta and a rich cream sauce (£5.50), and botoncini notturni, button mushrooms sautéed in olive oil and garlic with Dijon mustard (£3.90). We enjoyed the ornate surroundings and sipped on a glass of Refosco del Friuli (£11.95) before the main courses arrived. My filleto di sogliola Veronique, sole sautéed in a cream sauce, was enlivened with sherry and adorned with grapes (£9.90). My partner was equally delighted with her vitello Lafayette, veal in a dreamy gorgonzola sauce, crowned with Parma ham and wrapped in a light crêpe (£11.90). To finish we sampled chocolate cake made to the family recipe, a refreshing lemon gateau and coffee with petit fours (£1.90). One of Bellini's finest works, 'The Feast of Gods', hangs in Washington's National Gallery but fear not, Edinburgh has a Bellini masterpiece all of its own. **RRH**

YO! Sushi D3

YO! Sushi, Edinburgh's first conveyor belt sushi bar, surprised us with its huge range

BELLINI
RESTAURANT
Classically Italian
Specialising in regional cooking

8b Abercromby Place, Edinburgh   5 minutes from Princes Street
Reservations on 0131 476 2602

YO! SUSHI
THE WORLD'S MOST FAMOUS CONVEYOR BELT SUSHI RESTAURANT

YO! BELOW
THE WORLD'S MOST TECHNOLOGICALLY ADVANCED BAR

YO! to GO
DELIVERING SUSHI DIRECT TO YOUR DOOR OR DESK

www.yosushi.com/edinburgh

Hanover Buildings, Rose Street, Edinburgh EH2 2NN

(we're next door to easyEverything)

easyEverything
the world's largest internet cafés

NEW TOWN, BROUGHTON AND LEITH WALK

of dishes. More than just raw fish, we were tempted by over 150 dishes including sushi, salads, hot dishes and desserts. Keeping within our budget was easy with individually colour-coded plates priced £1.50-£3.50. Hot dishes include salmon & nori spring rolls (£3), vegetable yakisoba noodles (£2.50), seven pepper shrimp (£3.50) and chicken & soba noodle soup (£3). The sushi lover within us was spoilt for choice with a selection of nigiri, gunkan, maki, iso rolls and hand-rolled sushi, including cucumber maki (£1.50), hand-rolled lobster & avocado (£3.50), tuna maki (£2.50) and sweet shrimp nigiri (£3.50). Once we'd had our fill we headed downstairs to YO! Below which is gadget heaven. Each table features a self-serve beer tap so we could top up our glasses without moving and airline-style call button allowing us to order from a range of sakes, Japanese beers and cocktails. Had we have been hungry a selection of bento boxes, sushi, soups, noodles and Asian-inspired grills can be ordered in YO! Below. For more information, visit www.yosushi.com. **RRH**

Mussel Inn C3

Having heard only good things about the Mussel Inn, I went expecting it to be somewhat jaded. I was however, left eating my mussels as the Inn lived up to its given status and surpassed expectations. Its relaxed atmosphere is complemented by the kooky décor. The menu has the largest selection of fresh fish, including the famous kilo pot of mussels! With so much to choose from we mulled over the menu with a bottle of house red wine (£11.50), finally settling on a starter of escalopes Caesar salad style (£3.95), whilst my companion had deep-fried goats cheese served with a light salad (£3.95). To follow I had the catch of the day - sole served in garlic butter with a selection of vegetables (£13.95). Meanwhile the kilo pot of mussels in Mexican sauce (£8.95) did not stand a chance, the increasing pile of empty shells accompanied by a smug grin of delight! After taking a well-earned break we indulged our dessert passions and ordered banoffee pie (£2.95) and chocolate brownie (£2.95). The staff are friendly, helpful and up for a laugh, a feature often lost amongst the growing 'style' set **CSR**

The Dome D3

Stunning architecture and a fabulous glass dome roof with the circular bar directly beneath ensure you spend the initial part of a visit to The Dome looking

Enjoy mouthwatering Scottish seafood in a restaurant owned and run by shellfish farmers
Quality and freshness guaranteed

61-65 Rose Street
Edinburgh
Tel: 0131 225 5979
Fax: 0131 556 8303

157 Hope Street
Glasgow
Tel: 0141 572 1405
Fax: 0141 572 1492

View our menu @ www.mussel-inn.com

THE DOME

THE GRILL ROOM

Here you can dine from Noon until Late - everyday - choosing from our À la Carte menus with Starters from £3.50 and Main Courses from 8.00. Choose your wines from our award-winning Wine List. On Sundays, you can relax and enjoy our Brunch Menu whilst listening to Live music - 1pm - 5pm.

- Marble columns
- Mosaic Floors
- Fresh Flowers
- Stained Glass
- Crystal Chandeliers

Welcome to the relaxed and friendly atmosphere of The Dome.

14 George Street Edinburgh EH2 2PF

Incorporating The Grill Room • Frazers Cocktail Bar • Conference, Banqueting & Private Dining Suites • The Garden Café

Tel: 0131 624 8624   Fax: 0131 624 8649

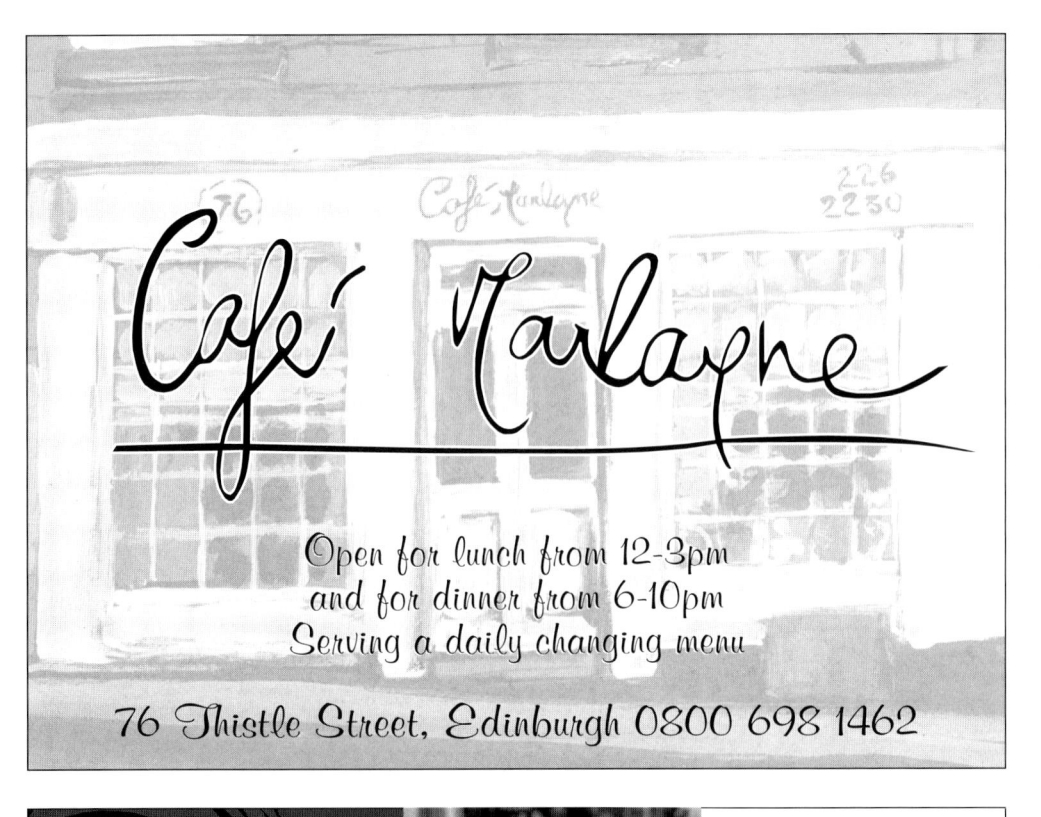

Café Marlayne

Open for lunch from 12-3pm
and for dinner from 6-10pm
Serving a daily changing menu

76 Thistle Street, Edinburgh 0800 698 1462

Great places to visit........
Great places to eat

The National Trust for Scotland

CELEBRATING 70 YEARS

Looking for some ideas for places to visit? Look no further than The National Trust for Scotland. With over 100 attractions in its care, you'll be spoilt for choice with castles, gardens, battle sites, museums and industrial heritage sites on offer – plus much more. Many have cafes and restaurants so you can have good food in some of the most spectacular surroundings. Tempted? Contact the Public Affairs Department for a free information pack or visit the Trust web site for all the essential information you'll need.

w w w . n t s . o r g . u k

The National Trust for Scotland (EFG), Wemyss House, 28 Charlotte Square, Edinburgh, EH2 4ET.
Telephone 0131 243 9300. Email information@nts.org.uk
Call in to No 28 Charlotte Square to find out more........and enjoy the Coffee House!

up. Once you've peeled your eyes off the ceiling, the immediate surroundings are just as impressive. Diners sit in a secluded raised area in the evenings, although more informal food is served in the bar during popular Sunday brunches and weekday lunches. We sipped Pinot Grigio del Veneto (£14.50 a bottle) and surveyed an equally impressive menu. We began with wild mushroom pâté with a tomato and tarragon chutney (£6.50), and crisp duck and rocket salad with a sweet Oriental-style dressing (£7.50). For mains, we followed up with confit of duck leg on garlic stove potatoes with an orange and ginger sauce (£13.50) and rack of lamb on sautéed potatoes with fresh spinach (£15.50). Lemon tart with citrus compôte and vanilla ice cream (£4.50), and a trio of miniature deserts with fresh fruit and a selection of coulis (£5.00) finished off a meal to remember. The service was excellent, the food fabulous and the setting prestigious. What more could you ask for? **AB**

Café Marlayne C3

On a cold and wintry night, Café Marlayne's warm and friendly atmosphere was just what we needed. Settling in, we ordered a bottle of the house white (£9), and contemplated the menu. For starters, my partner chose the mussels marinières (£3.70), which were delicious, while I had the exquisitely tender roast quail (£3.90). Knowing we were in for a treat, we awaited our main courses with bated breath. I had the mouth-watering Scotch beef fillet with creamed spinach and madeira jus (£12.90), while my partner enjoyed the salmon fillet with mango and avocado salsa (£8.20), which was beautifully presented and tasted as good as it looked. Both our meals were

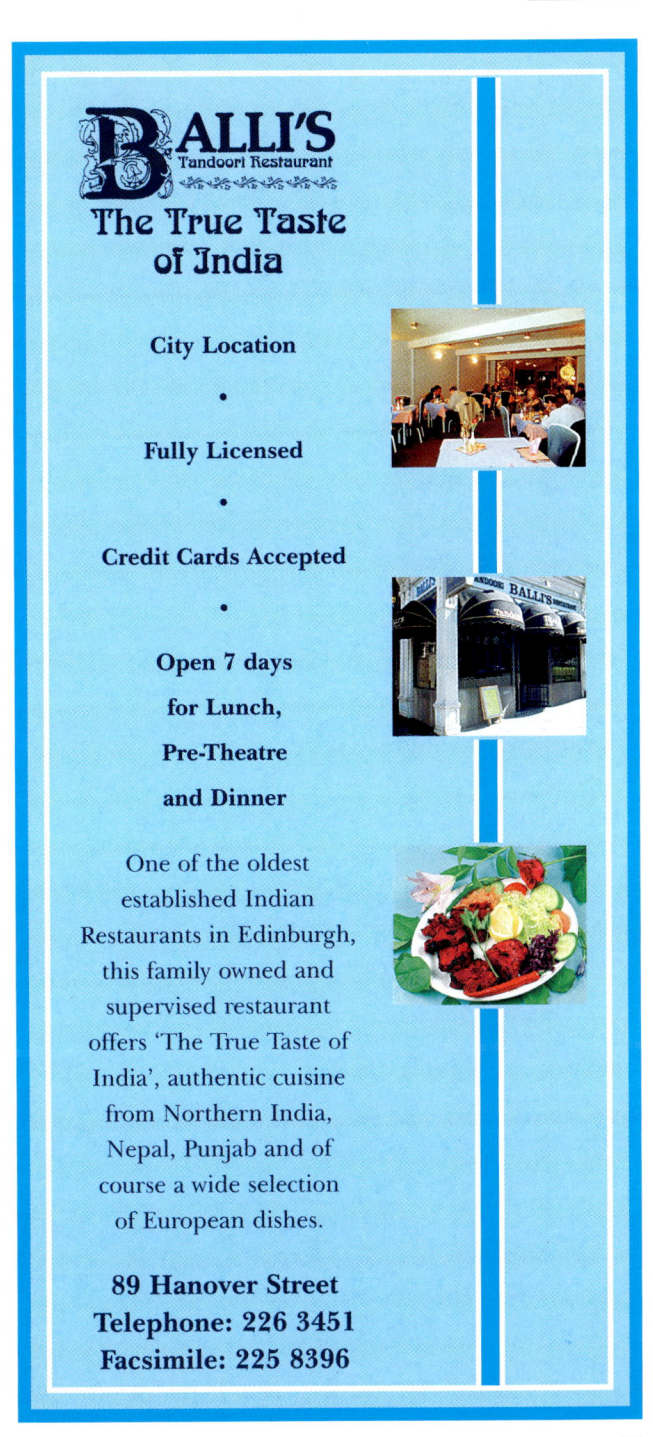

BALLI'S
Tandoori Restaurant

The True Taste of India

City Location

•

Fully Licensed

•

Credit Cards Accepted

•

Open 7 days for Lunch, Pre-Theatre and Dinner

One of the oldest established Indian Restaurants in Edinburgh, this family owned and supervised restaurant offers 'The True Taste of India', authentic cuisine from Northern India, Nepal, Punjab and of course a wide selection of European dishes.

**89 Hanover Street
Telephone: 226 3451
Facsimile: 225 8396**

NEW TOWN, BROUGHTON AND LEITH WALK

served with Champ potatoes and green beans. It is always a good sign when you finish two courses and are satisfied without being stuffed. With room left for dessert, my partner chose the pear and almond tart (£2.50), while I elected to go for the lemon tart (£2.50). Both were excellent: light and not too sweet in the first instance, and not too sharp in the second. Perhaps I was just in a positive mood, but even the coffee (£1.00) seemed to taste better than elsewhere!   **CP**

Balli's   D3

Balli's Tandoori Restaurant on Hanover Street is a welcome Indian oasis among a sea of Italian restaurants. This family-run business serves up high quality Indian cuisine, and their large and varied menu is bound to satisfy all customers. Our friendly waiter suggested we try their set menu, which gave my companion a good introduction to Tandoori cuisine. At £22.95 for two people, it is also great value. We began with the mixed starter, of birnjal bhaji, mushroom pakora and chott patt. All whetted our appetites and we looked forward to the meal ahead. For main course we had methi chicken with fenugreek, lamb bhuna and bindi sabzi, accompanied by pilau rice. These dishes were all complex in flavour and thoroughly delicious. Our meal was complemented by the house white wine (£10) which I would recommend. For dessert we had to try the kulfi in pistashio and mango flavours. Both were a perfect way to finish our meal, although the pistachio was my personal favourite. If you are after excellent Indian cuisine, with great service in a central location, then Balli's is a great place to go.   **BO'R**

The Tapas Tree   D2

A Spanish theme was just what we needed when we set out for dinner at the Tapas Tree. Welcomed by our host, we snuggled into the warm orange-hued interior and sipped the vino de casa tinto (£12.00 a bottle) while we perused the menu. The selection was so prodigious that we asked our host to choose for us and we were rewarded with an array of tasty dishes. These included pork and lamb meatballs (£3.85), green-lipped mussels (£4.70), breast of chicken cooked in paprika (£4.70), chargrilled chorizo cooked in cider (£4.60), a selection of Spanish Serrano ham, salami and cheese (£4.60), and deep fried prawn tails in their jackets (£5.80). There was barely room on the table for the feast but we eagerly polished off the majority. The warm sunny Mediterranean atmosphere and the relaxed informality of the surroundings greatly aided us in

> This restaurant is unusual in that it just keeps getting better and better.
> *(Scotland the Best)*
>
> Senior Luis Letelier and his energetic Spanish staff have been running this restaurant for over four years now and they certainly know what they're doing.
> *(Edinburgh Festival Eating Out Guide)*
>
> The Tapas Tree offers a great selection of Spanish fare. The atmosphere, décor and service is excellent.
> *(Daily Record Saturday Magazine)*
>
> Tucked away off happening Broughton Street, The Tapas Tree is the best of the city's Spanish restaurants.
> *(Pete Irvine – The Independent)*
>
> The Tapas Tree has been getting rave reviews since it opened five years ago. For good reason. The owner Luis Letelier, is interested in providing good food and even better service.
> *(The List)*

Authentic Spanish dishes, a superb selection of fine wines, a cosmopolitan atmosphere and a welcome as warm as the Mediterranean sun.

The Tapas Tree
RESTAURANTE ESPAÑOL

Open 7 days 11am - 11pm
0131 556 7118 • 1 Forth Street
www.tapastree.co.uk

NEW TOWN, BROUGHTON AND LEITH WALK

washing away the strains of the day and relaxing into the Spanish way. Crême caramel (£4.00) and white coffee (£1.55) ensured we were fully able to say "manana" before we rolled off into the night. Definitely one of the best tapas bars in town. **AB**

Erawan Oriental D3
Whether you are an aficionado or if this is your first taste of Thai cuisine, you are sure to love Erawan Oriental. With its broad slate floor and tall, elegant palms dotted amongst the blond wood tables, this restaurant manages to be both elegant and informal. We gladly let our waiter guide us through the menu, a good idea if you're not sure how hot you can take it. We started with mixed seafood tom yum (£4.75), a silky but fiery soup of fragrant herbs and spices, creamy tom kah (£4.75) and succulent fish cakes with dipping sauce (£4.75). The fresh flavours sung out, a perfect balance of spicy and subtle. A couple of bottles of Singha Thai beer (£2.70) cooled us down as we anticipated the delights of our main courses. Vibrant dishes of pad kraprao (£9.95), stir-fried mixed seafood with Thai basil and fresh chilli, and gaeng keow warn pak (£7.95), traditional green curry with aubergines, accompanied by steamed white noodles (£2.20) and steamed rice (£1.35) had us happily loosening our belts. Always the sign of a great meal! **EM**

Erawan Express C3
The name might suggest a quick takeaway but Erawan Express is a stylish Thai restaurant in bustling Rose Street. Lulled by gentle Oriental music and cosy terracotta décor we lingered over a menu for keaw poe kung; steamed flour skins with prawn and crabmeat stuffing (£4.50), and see krong moe tord; pork ribs marinated in garlic and black pepper (£4). We

ERAWAN
THAI RESTAURANT

Business lunch, a la carte and Banquet Menus

Erawan Oriental
14 South St
Edinburgh
EH2 2AZ
0131 556 4242

Erawan Express
176 Rose St
Edinburgh
EH2 4BA
0131 220 0059

Aiming to bring you the best Thai dining experience in Edinburgh

followed with pad king (£8.50); a stir-fry with ginger, yellow beans and vegetables, and gaeng pah (£8.50), a hot curry with red chilli and – the menu informed us – a root herb known as 'grachi'. We both selected chicken and were delighted, but dishes can be cooked with a variety of meats, fish or vegetables. Accompaniments were pad mee; noodles (£2.50), and kao man krati; jasmine rice cooked with coconut milk (£2.20). Those daunted by the menu's linguistic demands can order by number – as we did. A simpler lunch menu is available too with main dishes only £5.50. Service is unobtrusive but briskly efficient – hence the name perhaps? **MB**

Rick's C3

It takes more than design to render a place truly cool, and this combination of concept, décor and menu, is not only cool, but popular too. A modern twist on 'ye olde tavern', Rick's provides food, drink and accommodation together, and at last, somewhere in the New Town that actually feels 'new'! While avid readers of 'Wallpaper' will undoubtedly have checked out the striking minimalist interior, clean lines, rich wood veneers and oriental calm, Rick's is not a place for style snobs, and its staff exude a welcome that belies its trendy credentials. The day menu spans from 7am until 9pm offering everything from oysters (£9 for six) to egg's Benedict (£4.95). We chose the evening menu and began with tender king prawns (with sweet chilli dip), and a potato cake buried under a tower of herb smoked chicken (£4.75 each). My pan-fried sea bass with oriental sauce (£9.25) was beautifully created and mercifully low in salt, while my companion's chicken breast with ginger and lemon (£8.95) achieved a fine balance of flavours. I finished with a red berry pavlova (£3.25) which I unhesitatingly recommend. Selections of wines, cocktails and coffees are all well considered, and yes, quite cool. **NG**

Le Chambertin D3

Reassuringly grand décor surrounds you in Le Chambertin's dining area and the superior service is both knowledgeable and attentive. Although a special Taste of Scotland menu is available, offering such Celtic delights as Cullen skink and collops in the Pan, we opted for the main à la carte. The evening began with warm pigeon breast on continental salad leaves in a raspberry vinaigrette and toasted pine kernels (£8), and buffalo mozzarella and summer capsicum pin-wheels on sun-blushed tomato oil (£6.50). For my main course, I delighted in the pan-fried tranche of turbot with a herb and crab meat crust

rick's

rick's restaurant
Global inspiration from our chef offers innovative food from morning to night. Open for breakfast, coffee, lunch, dinner and supper.

rick's bar
Choice and quality are the underlying principles. Cocktails are our speciality. From Manhattans to Mohitos, we advise treating them with respect.

rick's bedrooms
10 superb rooms, providing uniquely designed city centre accommodation with entertainment and computers available. Ideal for work and play.

"top 21 hottest international hotels"
condé nast traveller magazine

"style bar of the year"

"cocktail bar tender of the year"
theme magazine awards march 2001

open from 7am–1am every day reservations 0800 698 1446
55a frederick street, edinburgh eh2 1lh   www.ricksedinburgh.co.uk

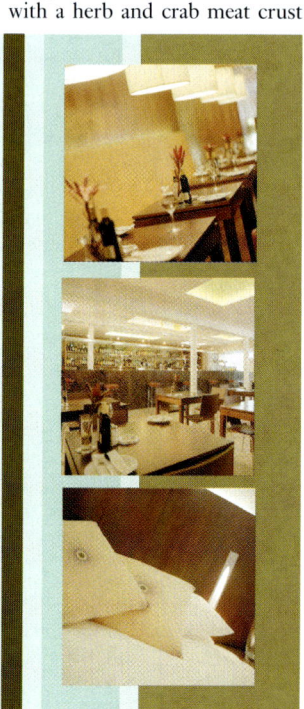

Innovative Scottish Cuisine

Affordable

Informal Ambience

Lunch: Monday to Friday
Dinner: Monday to Saturday

21 George Street, Edinburgh EH2 2PB
0131 240 7178

Le Chambertin

CARVERS

Spectacular Carvers Restaurant with marbled pillars and domed glass ceiling

Renowned for sumptuous buffets of local specialities and healthy dishes

Breakfast, Lunch and Dinner available Monday to Sunday

**GEORGE
INTER·CONTINENTAL
EDINBURGH**

19-21 George Street, Edinburgh, EH2 2PB
Tel: 0131 225 1251
e-mail: edinburgh@interconti.com
internet: www.edinburgh.interconti.com

on pecan and lime salsa (£18). My partner feasted on the prime Scottish fillet steak, topped with a hot duck liver parfait, accompanied by a cherry tomato and red onion salad with balsamic fresh horseradish dressing (£19.85). To accompany our meal, we enjoyed a bottle of the house white - a lovely Grenache Blanc (£13). We finished with mille feuille of blood orange sorbet on oven-dried orange wafers with pistachio crème fraiche (£4.25), and warm Grand Mariner marinated strawberries with green peppercorns over vanilla ice cream. This was a fanciful ending to an absolute dream of a dining experience. **AMcC**

Carvers at the George Hotel D3
To step back in time and experience some good old-fashioned British service, an evening at the George Hotel is the place. Charmed immediately upon arrival by the reserved warmth extended to every individual that dines here we were shown to an intimate table and attended to grandly for the rest of the evening. The selection of food from the largely traditional Scottish menu is, as the restaurant, sumptuous. I opted for the smoked salmon and warm potato pancake complemented by a dollop of sour cream (£8.75) whilst my partner speared an asparagus and wild mushroom strudel (£6.75). Approaching the carvery our mouths began to water and we piled our plates high of lamb, couscous, tuna loin upon a brown lentil tabbouleh and a choice selection of vegetables (£16.00 for two courses, £19.00 for three courses). Although we opted for rich foods there is an equally tantalising selection of healthy options to balance the menu accommodating the wishes of all. The romance of Carvers was completed with a generous serving of chocolate gâteau (£4.50) and a varied selection of traditional cheese and biscuits (£5.75). **CSR**

Stac Polly D2
Stac Polly takes more than its name from the grand Scottish mountain. It takes a measure of robustness, a degree of natural beauty and always leaves a desire to return. We visited for the à la carte dinner, (a two course lunch costs £12.95, or £15.95 for three courses, both with coffee) and began with haggis in filo pastry with a sweet plum sauce and warm salad of smoked haddock, new potatoes, cherry tomatoes and rocket leaves (both £5.95). We moved satisfied but still hungry onto baked supreme of halibut and chorizo sausage served with citrus mash and a drizzle of balsamic, chilli and vanilla reduction (£13.95), and roasted rump of Border lamb with buttered spinach and minted red wine gravy (£14.95). The pudding menu called across the heather and we duly followed to a sweet destination of lemon bavarois with ginger syrup and sticky toffee pudding with a butterscotch sauce (both £4.85). Our meal was washed gently down by a bottle of Merlot Domain Mont Auriol £12.50. All in all this is a Scottish experience that mixes fine natural ingredients into both traditional and modern recipes and, despite grand portions, always leaves an appetite for more. **RRH**

Est Est Est B3
The bustling, lively atmosphere within this Italian restaurant is particularly suited to celebratory meals or as a precursor to a big night out, with guests invited to doodle on tablecloths with crayons and balloons scattered throughout the modern interior. The friendly service only adds to this 'party' atmosphere, while the food more than matches these peripheral feelgood factors. We started with garlic pizza bread (£2.95), insalate Caesar (£4.50) and mozzarella e funghi fritti (£4.60), all of which were delicious and well presented. Pizza rustica (£6.20) and salmone griglia (£9.95) were later despatched from the busy open kitchen and were equally impressive. As the music gradually gained volume we relaxed with a bottle of tangy, fruity Pino Grigio (£17.50) before ordering the luscious meringa con cigleggie e gelato (£3.45) and refreshing sorbetto di frutta (£3.40) from the expansive sweet menu. In case you wondered, the word 'est' means 'it is' and the tale of the restaurant's title is revealed on the menu itself. To find out, pop along for a feed yourself. Is it good? Est Est Est! **GB**

PING ON
CHINESE RESTAURANT
EST. 1969

Superb cuisine from Canton, Peking & Szechuen

Vegetarian & seafood dishes a speciality

**32 Deanhaugh Street
0131 332 3621/8789**

EST EST EST

0800 698 1413
135A GEORGE ST

stac polly
THE SCOTTISH RESTAURANTS

Voted as one of the "Top 600 best restaurants in Britain"
GQ Magazine

"Food so perfectly prepared & so beautifully presented it was a shame to eat it"
Greg Russell - Evening News

"Brilliant, braw, scintillating, choose your own adjective"
Bill Clapperton - Evening News

"A sight of Stac Polly's menu is enough to set the heather alight"
Scotland on Sunday

Open 7 days a week

Member of
Taste of Scotland 2000/2001
Private dining facilities available

29-33 Dublin St, Edinburgh
FREEPHONE 0800 298 3427

8-10 Grindlay St, Edinburgh
FREEPHONE 0800 298 3428

If our line is busy your call will be diverted

NEW TOWN, BROUGHTON AND LEITH WALK

Kweilin C2

Dining at Kweilin served to remind this reviewer that quality Cantonese cuisine is a pleasure to be savoured. Sea bass, lobster and traditional Cantonese hot-pot on the menu signalled culinary treats in store and our appetisers of ha-kow, deliciously sticky prawn dumplings (£3.00) and perfectly steamed fresh scallops with black bean sauce (£5.00) happily confirmed our hopes. Spiced and salted half-shelled jumbo prawns (£14.00), soft noodles (£3.50) and rice (£2.20) were accompanied by aromatic lamb casserole, a dish that was recommended by our impeccably charming waitress. Refreshed by Chinese tea and hot towels we polished off ma-tai ko, hot water chestnut pudding with ice cream (£3.00) and stem ginger in cream (£2.75), their flavours beautifully enhanced by Campbell's Rutherglen liqueur (£3.75 a glass). The wine list merits a special mention and proprietor Derek Tang can be justly proud of it. Carefully selected, ready to drink wines from around the world rub shoulders with vintage malts, giving the visitor to Kweilin a consummate dining experience. Kweilin is closed on Mondays.   **EM**

Mountains of India C1

It is official, Asian food is the most popular in Britain and some restaurants, like Mountains of India, seem to have been around forever. With its friendly atmosphere, low-key eastern music and murals of ladies wearing far too little for the Scottish climate, I'm reminded of the unpretentious establishments of my youth. Situated at the bottom of Dundas Street the restaurant is popular with locals and tourists alike and business, sit-in and takeaway, is brisk. We opted for standard fare of poppadom (60p each), vegetable samosa (£2.30) and chicken kebab (£3.05) for starters. Main courses were chicken jalifrezi, bursting with chilli and coriander (£7.25) and the delicious tomato-flavoured king prawn rogan josh (£9.25). Accompaniments were perfectly cooked boiled rice (£1.60) and an aromatic garlic nan (£1.80). There was an ice cream dessert (£2-£2.60) but following tradition we had eaten too much by that point in proceedings. The restaurant is licensed but we drank water and finished off with coffees (£1.10 each). Alas, gone are the traditional five pints of lager, along with my youthful waistline. Still, maybe with the greenhouse effect we'll finally get an Indian summer. **MB**

Podricious C3

With Podricious former Rock chef David McCormack and his fiancée bring a brand new beacon of style, charm and quality dining to Rose Street. The look is a

KWEILIN

CANTONESE RESTAURANT

Authentic Cantonese Cuisine • Excellent Wine List

19-21 Dundas Street New Town
Tel. 0800 698 1430 Fax: 0131-557 3663

MOUNTAINS OF INDIA

Tandoori Restaurant
OPEN 7 DAYS

Mon-Sat: 12noon 'til 2pm & 5pm 'til midnight
Sunday: 5-11.30pm

3 course Business Lunches
£5.95-£6.95

Free Home Delivery
Min. Order £10

Fully Licensed • Parties Welcome • Carry out Available

146 Dundas Street, Edinburgh • 0131 556 9862

PODRICIOUS

Scottish Bistro & Grill

Contemporary Scottish cooking using the finest Scottish ingredients & specialising in Aberdeen Angus Steaks

"The duck was bold, deep-fleshed and tender as an opera singer's bosom"
Gillian Glover - The Scotsman

"The gateaux of wild mushrooms was a revelation - 'This is lovely!' "
Susan Dalgety - Evening News

"It was absolutely delicious"
Tam Cowan - Daily Record

192 Rose Street, Edinburgh, EH2 4AZ
FREEPHONE 0800 698 1442
www.podricious.co.uk   info@podricious.co.uk

smooth mix of violet and blue with pine floors and just enough candlelight. The wall space doubles as a gallery for up-and-coming artists and this further adds to the refined feel. The menu is a concise blend of quality Scottish ingredients: grass-fed beef, Crombies speciality sausages and fish, with just enough flair to feel fresh but never overdone. We began with Parmesan tartlet with roast cherry tomatoes and green pesto (£3.75) and salad of asparagus and Parma ham with light lemon dressing (£3.75). Main courses of Aberdeen Angus fillet steak with mushroom sauce, (cooked to perfection for £15) and loin of tuna with couscous and Niçoise garnish (£12) met expectations and then kept on going. Desserts of crème caramel with warmed strawberries and blueberries (£3.50) and chocolate marquis with orange confit (£3.75) were headed heaven's way along with the main courses. We sat back, supped the silky Chilean Santa Carolina red (£11) and pondered how we'd lived pre-Podricious. **RRH**

Nexus D2
Tucked away at the bottom of Broughton Street you will find three year old Nexus, a cosy café-bar which is definitely worth a look in. Open from 11am to 11pm for snacks, meals, coffees, drinks, and renowned for their Sunday breakfast, which is served all day. We arrived on a freezing evening to be welcomed by a blazing open fire, a friendly atmosphere and an offer of a bottle of wine which we, of course, accepted. The cabernet sauvignon (£9.00) warmed us up as we took ages to choose from a great snack menu that includes everything from soups to burgers and salads. After much deliberation I chose the chicken nachos which came in a giant portion smothered in melted cheese, guacamole, sour cream and salsa with a generous portion of chillies (£4.45). My friend went for the delicious vegetable satay served on noodles (£4.50). We finished off our meal with a couple of coffees and sat back for a chat very reluctant to get back out into the cold from this cosy home from home. **AL**

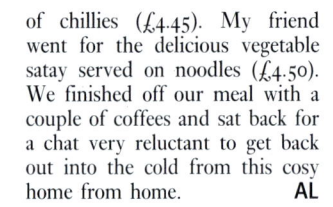

La Lanterna D3
As if the friendly glow emanating up to street level on Hanover Street - Edinburgh's Little Italy - wasn't enough, the welcome in La Lanterna is even warmer. The sense of tradition in this family run restaurant extends from the décor of wood and wine to the menu. There are two things you won't find here: a microwave (sacrilege) or a pizza (American). We started with a variation on garlic mushrooms, funghi trifolati (£3.95), and tre colore (£4.95), an excellent blend of tastes and textures. Mains were fresh and creamy rigatoni alla genovese (£6.75) and a fillet steak fiorentino (£15.45), whose brandy and cream sauce was subtly rich and smooth. All were accompanied by a half-carafe of silky medium dry Merlot (£5.55). Staying in a traditional mode, we finished with zuppa inglese, better than any trifle I've ever had, and of course, tiramisu (both £2.95) – "possibly the best ever" decreed my partner, and she would know. Cappuccinos (£1.20) and a homemade orange liqueur left us with one way to summarise our evening – mmm! **JA**

Howie's D3
The spacious, bright character of this restaurant provides the ideal setting for such an impressive menu. This Waterloo Place restaurant is the newest of four Howie's in Edinburgh and it maintains its individuality well. For starters I had Parma ham, marinated plum tomato, rocket

NEW TOWN, BROUGHTON AND LEITH WALK

and toasted pine nut salad with balsamic syrup whilst my partner chose a salad of feta cheese, cucumber and coriander with a red pepper dressing and fine herbs both of which were as good as their names were long. This was followed by our main course choices: the delectable chargrilled duck and orange sausages with celeriac & potato puree and balsamic roast dates, and a wonderfully textured risotto of fresh herbs and peas. We chose a medium dry white Moulin D'arvie from an excellent selection of house wines (£6.10-£9.55 a bottle). Dessert was sticky toffee pudding and roast pear with caramel sauce and mascarpone. Prices were surprisingly low for the quality of the fare: £13 for three courses, £11 for two and £9 for one (Sun-Wed) and £16.95 for three courses and £14.95 for two (Thu-Sat). Altogether, a treat that begs to be repeated. **DDR**

Smoke Stack D2
Situated on Broughton Street, the Smoke Stack has warm yet stylish décor and an eclectic menu featuring an impressive range of meat, fish and vegetarian dishes. With choices ranging from shrimp tails and crêpes to burgers and steaks, there really is something for everyone. Sipping a deliciously dry Cotes de Rouissollon (£9.50), we enjoyed succulent mussels in a white wine, tarragon and cream sauce (£3.95) and a crunchy corn on the cob with butter (£2.50). To follow, my partner's fillet steak (£14.95) with Drambuie and mushroom sauce (£1.00 extra) was cooked with skill and flair. I chose a chargrilled tuna steak (£11.95) with a superb texture that filled the mouth with flavour and was perfectly complemented by the crisp, fresh vegetables that

EAT DRINK ENJOY... Howies Restaurants

MODERN SCOTTISH COOKING WITH WORLD INFLUENCE ACCOMPANIED BY EAGERLY PRICED WINES.

208 BRUNTSFIELD PLACE
BRUNTSFIELD – 0800 698 1421

63 DALRY ROAD
DALRY – 0800 698 1422

29 WATERLOO PLACE
EAST PRINCES ST – 0800 698 1424

4/6 GLANVILLE PLACE
STOCKBRIDGE – 0800 698 1423

HOWIE'S OFFICE
(MARKETING, EVENTS, FUNCTIONS)
5 MARISCHAL PLACE – 332 1700

7 DAYS LUNCH, DINNER
& BY ARRANGEMENT
FINE FOOD WITHOUT THE FAFF

WWW.HOWIES.UK.COM

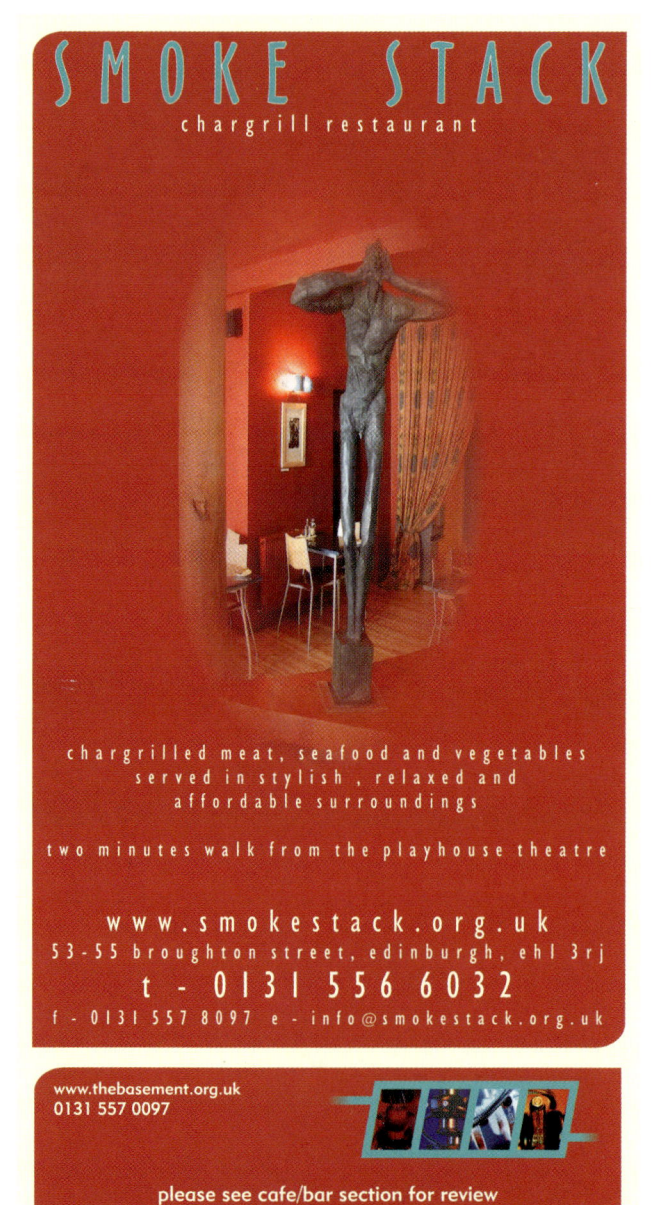

SMOKE STACK
chargrill restaurant

chargrilled meat, seafood and vegetables served in stylish, relaxed and affordable surroundings

two minutes walk from the playhouse theatre

www.smokestack.org.uk
53-55 broughton street, edinburgh, eh1 3rj
t - 0131 556 6032
f - 0131 557 8097 e - info@smokestack.org.uk

www.thebasement.org.uk
0131 557 0197

please see cafe/bar section for review of our sister bar - the basement again voted one of the top 3 restaurants in edinburgh by readers of the list magazine

the basement
10a-12a broughton street, edinburgh, eh1 3rh

---

accompanied it. We sat back and enjoyed the relaxed atmosphere before indulging in a dreamy bowl full of honey and Drambuie ice cream (£2.50) and a selection of fresh cheese and biscuits (£2.95). The great food is served by friendly and attentive staff who heighten the pleasure of dining here. **PC**

La Commedia E2
It's all too easy to miss this eatery as it is tucked away in a basement beneath London Road's Richmond House Hotel. Formerly an Italian restaurant, it's now run by Greg Fernandez, and its amended moniker reflects a globetrotting menu which features both European and Asian cuisine. Decorated in warm pastel shades, its walls are adorned with ornate Venetian masks and its loyal, contented clientele mainly consists of residents from the hotel. On our visit we chose from the à la carte menu (there's also a 3 course set dinner £14.50 and lunch £9.50). We kicked off with cazza alla marinara £5.50, huge mussels served with tomato and garlic sauce and sweet, spicy prawn gambaz £6.50. This was followed by delicately flavoured chicken Vietnamese curry (£9.50), and pork adobo - a Filipino dish in which the soy flavoured meat is complemented by unadorned steamed vegetables and rice (£8.75). These sumptuous stomach pleasers were accompanied by a beautifully mellow 1998 Cabernet franc (£12.85). All in all a fantastic example of East meeting West. **DK**

Miro's Cantina Mexicana C3
On a cold January night, a trip to Miro's convinced us that summer will come again. Established ten years, Miro's achieves an authentic and friendly taste of Mexico. All

La Commedia International Restaurant

Pearl of the Orient
at Richmond House Hotel ✱✱✱

Here at La Commedia you can have fun, mystery and excitement. We are sure you will enjoy yourself, especially with our excellent food and presentation, the company of your friends and a few glasses of our wine.

At "La Commedia" we provide you with the opportunity to sample some of the best products of the World mostly Asian, Filipino and European dishes. Our varied experiences in every kind of people, races and cultures blend with the recipes and ingredients served according to their traditional taste. Dishes are prepared and cooked from fresh and are produced in house.

20 Leopold Place
London Road
Edinburgh
0131 556 6748
0131 556 3556

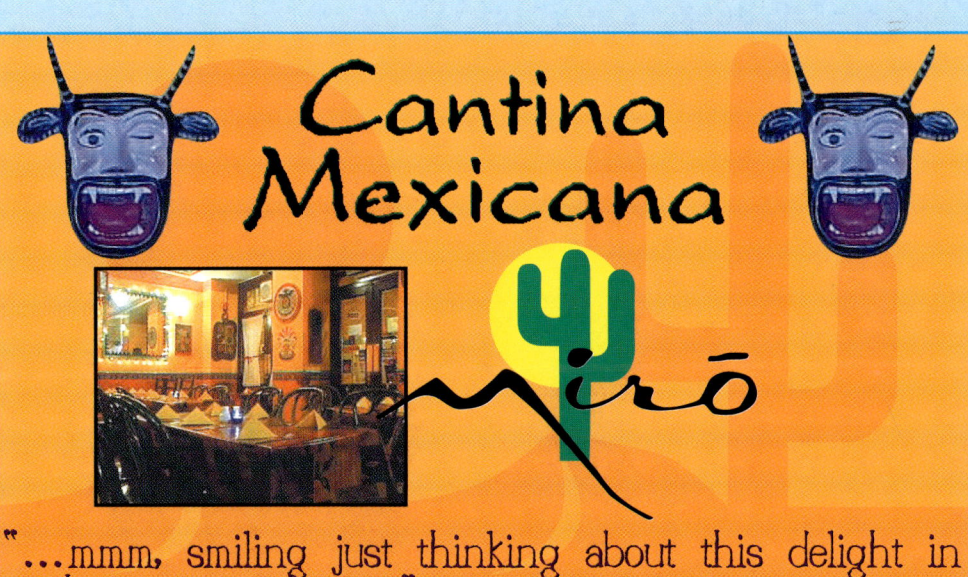

Cantina Mexicana

Miró

"...mmm, smiling just thinking about this delight in the centre of town" Liz & Freya's Guide to the Fringe

Freephone 0800 698 1433
184 Rose Street • Edinburgh

NEW TOWN, BROUGHTON AND LEITH WALK

dishes are freshly prepared, with a good vegetarian selection and lots of fish on the menu. Uncorking a bottle of house red (£9.95), we enjoyed starters of spicy wedges of grilled chorizo sausage (£3.75), and delicious goats cheese and pesto crostini (£3.85). Winter already just a memory, we followed with carne diablo (£10.25), strips of steak in a hot smoked chilli sauce, and a sizzling platter of huge, succulent king prawns served with flour tortillas, accompanied by rice, re-fried beans, salsa, guacamole and sour cream (£12.50). In a holiday mood, but with cold weather appetites, we greedily devoured a "best ever" Key lime cheesecake and a hot, sticky toffee pudding (both £2.95). Miro's creates an informal, cheerful and colourful environment, which made us feel like we were down Mexico way, but outside it was just Rose Street. Lunch is served Mon-Sat, noon-3pm, dinner Mon-Sun 6pm-10.30pm. **PM**

The Patio   C3

This family run restaurant stands out from the rest. The owner cooks his speciality of fresh seafood to order whilst customers are attended to by his wife and children in the restaurant. During the day there's a three course meal for only £5.75, whilst every night there are approximately fifteen speciality dishes. The head waiter announces these impressively from memory upon arrival at the table. After choosing a bottle of white Verduzzo (£9.45) to complement the vast seafood selection, we ordered princess scallops baked in butter, garlic and ground almonds (£6.25) and fresh crayfish (£6.50 including free lessons for beginners!) My partner continued on seafood for main course with a very generous portion of baked monkfish (£12.95), whilst I ventured on to a rack of lamb cooked perfectly pink without a trace of fat on it (£14.45): absolutely delicious. Both meals were served with potatoes and fresh vegetables included and we also tried some tagliatelle - cooked the way pasta should be. We finished the meal with espressos (£1.50) and a vintage port feeling very satisfied after a great meal with great homegrown Italian service. **GG**

Shezan Tandoori   E2

It might seem a daft idea, choosing a curry on the warmest evening of the year, but it works in countries with more experience of the sun than we'll ever have. Shezan is long established at the top of Leith

PATIO
ristorante ITALIANO

FRESH SEAFOOD SPECIALISTS

Family run, serving authentic Italian dishes.

Open Monday to Saturday for lunch and dinner.

Three Course Business Lunch
£5.75

87 Hanover Street, Edinburgh   0131 226 3653

NEW TOWN, BROUGHTON AND LEITH WALK

Walk, a once shabby area now reborn as the eastern edge of the ultra stylish New Town. The restaurant's interior, a jewel-coloured extravaganza, is defiantly opulent, but we found the atmosphere airy and soothing after the blistering heat outside. The menu is extensive with most dishes available to takeaway and, unusually, it includes a separate menu for children. We salivated at length before ordering starters of beautifully moist aubergine pakora (£2.85) and succulent king prawn tandoori (£5.50). Main courses of mushroom biryani (£9.50) and Punjabi garlic chicken masala (£8.65) were subtly spiced without being uncomfortably hot. We chilled further with a reviving carafe of house white (£10.95), along with the more traditional accompaniments of basmati rice (£2.20) and a massive masala nan (£2.95). Finally, deliciously tart lemon sorbets (£2.75) ensured we emerged as cool as the cucumber raita we had just demolished (£1.10). **MB**

Duck's at le Marché Noir C1

Discreetly located near Canonmills, this small restaurant has a huge reputation. The green and earth tones of the interior suggest a low-key sophistication which doesn't have to try hard to impress. The menu is minimal, with only a handful of choices per course, but the quality impeccable. We started with chargrilled vegetable salad, goat's cheese and pesto (£5.55), and haggis on leek and potato mash with whisky jus (£5.90). These were perfectly complemented by the intense flavours of sea bream on smoked salmon with lime, cucumber and caper dressing (£18.70), and scallops with carrot,

SHEZAN
TANDOORI
INDIAN CUISINE

OPEN
Monday - Thursday : 12 noon - 2pm & 5pm - midnight
Friday - Saturday : 12noon - 12.30am Sunday : 5pm - midnight

25 Union Place (Opposite the Playhouse) Edinburgh
Telephone 0131 557 5098

T.G.I. FRIDAY'S

The American Restaurant & Bar

JUST OFF PRINCES STREET (OPPOSITE THE CASTLE)

EXCELLENT LUNCH/EARLY DINERS MENU FROM £4.95

CHILDRENS MEAL DEALS (ALL INCLUSIVE)

FUNCTION/CONFERENCE ROOM AVAILABLE

26 CASTLE STREET, EDINBURGH

0800 197 3527

---

ginger and sesame salad and sweet chilli sauce (£18.90). An aromatic selection of Ian Mellis cheeses (£6.50) completed our meal. An impressive display of corks reflects another of this restaurant's glories – its wine list. We perused page after palate watering page before settling around the thousand pound mark. A mere jest unfortunately, but our £16.50 house white was delivered, served and consumed with all the care of a much more expensive vintage. If you're on a limited budget, the lunch menu offers two courses for £13.50 and three for £15.50.   **IB**

The Basement   D2

Broughton Street has a reputation as a place to see, and be seen, housing a number of stylish watering holes, The Basement being no exception. Here, you find a marriage of modern chic and murky charm laced with an industrial edge, most noticeable in the caterpillar track tables and gothic candlesticks. The smoky orange and blue walls are delicately lit, and the overall air is one of vibrancy, a fact reflected in a menu juggling Mexican, Scottish and international dishes with apparent ease. The bruschetta (£2.25), and smoked salmon with oatcakes (£2.50) were tasty precursors to our main courses of roast duck breast with a red peppercorn sauce (£4.95), and chicken burritos with rice and salad (£4.75), accompanied by a bottle of house red (£8.50). The size of the portions was matched only by the quality of the cooking and the produce used, and we finished off with sticky toffee pudding (£2.25), and Mr Boni's ice cream (£2.25). The menu changes daily, there is a special Thai menu on Wednesdays, and a Mexican menu at the weekend. Open all

NEW TOWN, BROUGHTON AND LEITH WALK

day and night (£5.95 for a two course lunch), you can enjoy this remarkably reasonable retreat at any time. **JW**

TGI Friday's   C3
TGI Friday's is located in the heart of Edinburgh's city centre and is a popular favourite for a quality meal within a fun environment. This popularity can be attributed to the varied menu, which has something to suit all tastes. An exciting new menu was launched April 2001, incorporating old favourites such as steaks and burgers, and adding new dishes along with a more varied lunchtime menu. We started with Aztec chicken soup (£3.50), which was spicy and packed with chicken. We also enjoyed wall to wall chicken (£9.95), which included different chicken pieces with a variety of dips. We followed with steak fajitas (£10.75), and a Friday's classic burger (£9.25). A wide selection of additional toppings are available, including the adventurous pineapple and avocado. Our meal was accompanied by Jack Daniels glazed ribs (£12.45). We finished with 'cookies gone bananas', a dessert of bananas and crunchy biscuit covered with chocolate and caramel fudge. To drink we chose from an impressive list of non-alcoholic and alcoholic cocktails and smoothies (from £2.15). TGI's also has a function room for hire for private celebrations or business meetings. **VI**

Vittoria   E1
After 30 years in business, Vittoria certainly has the welcoming atmosphere and great food down to a fine art. On the corner of Brunswick Street and Leith Walk, the caffé/restaurant has indoor and

---

Vittoria

ITALIAN RESTAURANT AND CAFFÉ BAR
Breakfast · Lunch · Dinner · All Day · 7 Days

LIGHT LUNCHES
Monday-Friday
A selection of dishes at
£3.40 per dish. Glass of wine £1.00
(11.30am to 2.30pm)

FULL A LA CARTE MENU
(2.30pm-11.30pm)
Homemade Pasta, Pizza, Grills,
Fish, Good Wine, Ice-Cream

· Coach Parties Welcome
· Large Menu for all tastes
· Seats up to 100
· Theatre groups phone for special menu and discounts

Outside seating area -
5 mins walk from
The Playhouse

Open 10am till late for breakfast, lunch and dinner or a genuine cup of Italian coffee.
Fully licensed, all major credit cards & switch welcome.

113 Brunswick Street, Leith Walk
FREEPHONE 0800 698 1454   Fax: 0131 478 7004
E-mail: vittoriaed@aol.com   www.vittoriarestaurant.com

NEW TOWN, BROUGHTON AND LEITH WALK

Continental outdoor pavement seating. We opted to sit inside due to the chilly winter weather and went about choosing from the menu. Not an easy task, there is a great selection of pizza, pasta and much more. I chose calamari fritti (£4.50) to start, which arrived with a lovely salad, and my partner chose polpetto, homemade meatballs in sweet and sour sauce (£4.50). Next we tucked in to a beautifully creamy spaghetti carbonara (£5.95) and vitello alla cinzia, veal served with three special sauces (£11.95). Then we sat back to finish off our bottle of Colle Secco (£10.95), Vittoria's house red, while we made room for pudding. I chose mint ice cream served with chocolate mints (£3.50) and my friend chose three ice cream flavours (£3.30) from the selection of twelve available. All in all, great value for money and perfect for all the family. **AL**

Baked Potato Shop D4

Situated on Cockburn Street, the Baked Potato Shop proves extremely popular with people working in the nearby shops and offices and passing tourists. Open from 9am 'til 9pm (later during the festival) this fully vegetarian/vegan delight is the perfect place to fortify yourself with a great value baked potato served with one of the delicious hot and cold fillings available. It isn't just wholesome spuds, there are also rolls, soup, pittas and salads. Most of the food is vegan and all of it is vegetarian. Even the mayonnaise is made from soya milk but the flavour and texture is not compromised even to a meat eater like me! This is primarily a takeaway but there is a small dining area where we sat and enjoyed a hot baked potato with egg and cheese filling (£2.85) and a salad tray (£2.45) which lets you choose any number of the fresh salads on offer. I made four delicious choices of curried rice and peppers, Greek salad, Waldorf Salad and mushrooms, chickpeas and tomatoes in a light oil. If this is all too healthy you may want to indulge in one of the gorgeous looking cakes (from 55p). **PC**

No. 27 B3

As yet relatively undiscovered, this elegant new the National Trust restaurant is situated in a Georgian house on picturesque Charlotte Square and occupies the former parlour/dining room. Absorbing our historic surroundings, including old family portrait paintings and original cornices, we turned to the menu. From a selection of Scottish dishes (the restaurant uses local produce) we chose roulade of two mousses, sole and salmon in watercress sauce (£3.95), and a tasty smoked haddock dish in cream sauce (£4.15) served casserole-style. Next, suprême of chicken with a spicy haggis filling and whisky cream (£10.45), and pan-fried venison, moist and tender, with shallots in a rich port wine and raspberry glaze (£14.50), both served with seasonal vegetables. Highland toffee cake (£3.65) and lemon fool with blue berries (£3.45) followed. A bottle of house red (£8.75) complemented our meal. All dishes were attractively presented and delicious, and the service was excellent. The pretty courtyard offers alfresco dining during summer. Do try this unique and reasonably priced restaurant, before the rush (open Tuesday to Saturday 6.00pm-11.00pm, last sitting 9.30pm). The Coffee House at No. 28 serves light snacks daily 10am-6pm. **MAB**

A Room in the West End B4

Situated in a quaint backstreet basement, A Room in the West End offers traditional Scottish cuisine with a contemporary edge, with all dishes prepared using fresh local produce. To begin our meal, we ordered the baked goats cheese and baby leek tart (£3.85) and salad of smoked salmon and smoked trout (£5.25), each uniquely-flavoured and impressively presented. To follow, the aubergine and red pepper hummus wrapped in rosemary pancake with heather honey dressing (£8.75)

THE STAND COMEDY CLUB

Live comedy every evening from 7.30pm and all day Sunday

Lots of laughs and delicious home cooked food, sumptuous coffees, well kept real ales and fine wines.

Private functions a speciality.

5 York Place   0131 558 7272

…

Eating Out in the West End, Haymarket & Stockbridge

Traditionally the financial hub, the bars and restaurants of the West End are immersed by the business thoroughfare all-day. Come the evening, however it transforms into an entertainment mecca, drawing an über-cool crowd through its doors. Stylish Indigo Yard is a popular venue for light snacks through to main meals or rub shoulders with the Rich and Famous at Caledonian Hotel's The Pompadour.

Continuing to serve up some of the best Indian cuisine in town is the Indian Cavalry Club, whilst the Caley Ale House at Haymarket has a fine range of cask ales, luscious food and soothing jazz.

Stockbridge is a little oasis of unassuming cool charm and style, reflected in the quality of its bars and eateries. With a 30 year history and pedigree in Chinese food the Ping On remains a favourite. In contrast new-comer, Stockbridge Restaurant is fast establishing itself as a high-quality dining experience. Another Stockbridge staple is Howie's, combining excellent dining at the right price.

maintained the high standard, as did the crispy polenta and tomato bangers on garlic and olive oil mash, with sweet red onion and chilli jam (£8.75). From the tasty choice of puddings, we plumped for the tangy bramble cranachan with shortie (£3.55) and the deliciously sweet banoffee pie (£3.85), washed down by the last of our smooth house white (£8.95 per bottle). The dinner menu, served from 5.30pm, is innovative and varied in price, so whether splashing out or on a budget, this brightly painted, candlelit restaurant fits the bill. A daily-changing lunch menu is also available from 12 noon, with two courses for £6.95 or three courses for £8.95.   **GB**

Pompadour   B4
Madame de Pompadour managed to entertain a bored Louis XV by organising suppers and festivities. The restaurant bearing her name has a large reputation transcending the centuries, bringing the diner ever closer to perfection. Unravelling into the welcoming glow emanating from the Caledonian Hotel, I chose from the set menu (£25 for 3 courses) whilst my partner became ensconced in a warm salad of Western Isle scallops and langoustine, served with a beetroot dressing (£13). The Toulouse sausage with couscous and a confit of red pepper exceeded my anticipation. To follow oven-baked chump of lamb on crushed potato, confit of vegetables and rosemary jus, merely confirmed my trust in fine cuisine, whilst my partner's grilled tranche of halibut with langoustine tortellini, served with a bouillabaisse sauce (£21) was met with similar approval. I braved on alone with a tangy passion fruit tart, mango sauce and vanilla ice cream – a combination of flavours that is to be treasured. Louis XV would have been delighted with the legacy his mistress has bestowed upon Edinburgh.   **JF**

Chisholm's   B4
The relaxed and informal brasserie of the five-star Caledonian Hotel is set in a huge conservatory-like room between the hotel's bar and foyer. With large windows looking onto the patio, and fresh retro-style décor, Chisholm's has a distinctly different atmosphere from the rest of the hotel. The menu is extensive and eclectic, with Thai fish cakes (£5.75) sitting alongside a salad of caramelised pear, stilton and spinach with a crème fraîche dressing (£6.00). Main courses range from the traditional to the modern, such as braised lamb shank with roast vegetables and rosemary mash (£13.50), and roast monkfish with ratatouille and saffron potatoes (£14.50). If you have any room left after all that, the impressive dessert menu may well tempt you. Pecan pie with butterscotch ice cream (£4.00) is deliciously indulgent, while orange sorbet in a brandy basket (£3.50) is wonderfully refreshing. A bottle of house Chardonnay (£14) provides the perfect

---

a room in the west end

SCOTTISH BISTRO

LICENSED & B.Y.O.B

OPEN 7 DAYS
Lunch from noon
Dinner from 5.30

26 William Street
0131 226 1036

WEST END, HAYMARKET AND STOCKBRIDGE

Songkran Thai

Authentic Thai Cuisine in the heart of the West End

Opening times:
Monday to Saturday
12.00 to 2.30 & 5.30 to 11pm
Sunday 6.00 to 10.30pm

Express Lunch
2 courses – £7.50
3 courses – £8.50

Takeaway available

Songkran Thai Restaurant
24a Stafford St
Edinburgh
EH3 7BD

FREEPHONE
0800 698 1449

*Songkran II
Opening June 2001
at 8 Gloucester St
Stockbridge*

accompaniment to a delicious meal in relaxed and comfortable surroundings. **CR**

Songkran   B4

Songkran is the traditional Thai new year, when people splash each other with water until everyone is drenched. Such behaviour would probably be unwelcome in this small West End basement, but if anywhere can whet your appetite for Thai cuisine this is it. The menu boasts a varied vegetarian selection and the background Thai pop music adds to a relaxed atmosphere. For starters we had kharom jeeb (steamed won ton cases stuffed with pork, prawn, crab, bamboo shoots and water chestnuts, £4.50) and tao hu tod (deep-fried tofu in breadcrumbs, Thai style, served with sweet peanut sauce, £3.50). My main course was ped pad kraprao (stir-fried sliced roast duck with chilli and Thai sweet basil, £8.50), whilst my partner chose gang ka ree pak (mild yellow curry with potato and carrot, £6.95) with which we shared kao pad khai (egg fried rice, £2.20). For dessert we tried the deliciously over-the-top Songkran bombe (deep-fried ice cream served with syrup and cream, £3.50) and freshly made banana fritters (£3.50). House wines are £2.20/glass, £9.95/bottle. **DDR**

Café Provençal   B4

There is a delightfully sunny feeling about Café Provençal due to the light and airy décor and the friendly disposition of the staff. The menu is traditional 'French peasant' fare and with a table d'hôte (two or three courses with coffee, £10.90 and £13.50) and a menu maison (two or three courses with coffee, £14.80 and £17.50), there is plenty to choose from. We opted for the menu du maison and chose a beautiful vegetable and pasta soup with crusty bread, and pâté du maison, which was delicious and obviously homemade. This was followed by braised lamb shank with flageolet beans and potato cake, which was a delight both to behold and to devour! My partner chose pasta with homemade pesto, which by all accounts was inspired. We finished off with the most incredible crème brûlée and surveyed the large selection of unique and interesting products, which the café also sells, such as rose petal preserve, imported directly from Provençe. So, whether for a welcoming morning coffee or a hearty evening meal, this reviewer will be heading to Café Provençal whenever he is in the West End. **DC**

Henry J. Beans   B4

See our review on page 129.

Café Provençal
CUISINE et PRODUITS
Coffee Shop ✢ Wine Bar ✢ Bistro ✢ Retail
34 Alva Street ✢ Edinburgh ✢ EH2 4PY
0131 220 6105

Caledonian Hilton

Princes Street, Edinburgh EH1 2AB

The Pompadour

At only £15.50 for a two course lunch you will experience the Award winning food and service enjoyed by the Rich and Famous

OPEN: Lunch: Tue-Fri 12.30pm-2.30pm,
Dinner: Tue-Sat 7pm- 10pm, Closed Sun/Mon

The Finest Fine Dining Restaurant in Edinburgh

Chisholms Bar and Brasserie

Mix old with new and dine where the old railway trains used to stop at the Caledonian

A wide selection of dishes from caesar salad to Haggis

OPEN:
Breakfast: Mon-Fri 7am-10am, Sat-Sun 7.30am-11.30am
Lunch: Sat-Mon 12.30pm-2.30pm, Dinner: Daily 6.30pm-10pm

For Reservations for the Pompadour and Chisholms Telephone 0131 222 8888

The focal point of Henry J Bean's is the bar where show bartenders mix a range of fun and coloured cocktails. The bar is crammed full of bottles of liquor displayed against a backdrop of mirrors and glass shelving encouraging guests to feel they can choose any drink imaginable. Henry J Bean's 35 cover restaurant serves daily from 12 noon until 10pm. With the best chicken wings in town and the best grilled chicken sandwich in the world, Henry J Bean's is a great place to enjoy new takes on classic American dishes.

The bar is open from:
12 noon - 1am Mon -Sat
12.30pm - 1am Sunday

The Rutland Street side of the Caledonian Hotel 0131 222 8844

HENRY J BEAN'S BAR AND GRILL

WEST END, HAYMARKET AND STOCKBRIDGE

indigo (yard)

"The space is a jigsaw of galleries and mezzanines with a contemporary mix of new and reclaimed materials; country oak tables with aluminium chairs designed for US prisons. Food is modern and international..."
Elle Magazine

indigo (yard)
7 Charlotte Lane Edinburgh
0800 298 3416
www.indigoyardedinburgh.co.uk

Indigo Yard B3
Indigo Yard is unusual for Edinburgh. Hidden in the west end of the city centre, you don't expect to find these uplifting, contemporary spaces to eat and drink. With such varied spaces Indigo Yard can be enjoyed for a meal, a drink or even a group function for up to 70 people, and has different menus to suit. We selected our meal from the evening menu and I began with duck spring rolls with sweet chilli dip (£4.85) and my vegetarian partner had black bean broth served with bread and butter (£2.85). From a wide selection of drinks we chose Sam's Island, a white Colombard Chardonnay (£12.95) to accompany the meal. For the main course we had chargrilled salmon with Asian greens and sweet ginger dressing on a bed of noodles (£8.85) and wild mushroom risotto with fresh Parmesan cheese (£7.95). To finish we both had banoffi cheesecake with toffee sauce (£3.25). Indigo Yard succeeds in combining excellent food and drink with stylish design and a buzzing atmosphere, an extremely popular mix. **MJ**

San Marco B2
A traditional family-run Italian restaurant, San Marco is as busy and popular today as it has ever been in its 16-year history. Situated on the main street of Stockbridge, it is clearly a favourite for locals, as many regular faces are greeted personally at the door. The restaurant itself takes up two large rooms, one of which is available to hire for private parties. The menu consists mainly of classic Italian dishes, such as calamari fritti (£4.30), a large plate of deep fried calamari served with lemon; and mozzarella carisma (£4.20), a huge portion of Italian cheese fried in breadcrumbs. The main courses include a risotto alla marinara (£6.35), with fresh shellfish complementing the tomato and herb rice, and tagliatelle al salmone (£6.25), a deliciously creamy pasta dish. A wide variety of ice-cream is available for dessert, from a refreshing lemon sorbet (£2.30), to vanilla ice cream with chocolate sauce and amaretto biscuits (£2.75). The house wine is also exceptional value at £8.75 for a litre carafe. The atmosphere is relaxed and welcoming, and the staff are friendly and attentive, assuring the restaurant's lasting popularity. **CR**

Skerries B4
Unseen rocks bring woe to sailors off Scotland's coasts but the hidden surprises of Skerries are delights to be uncovered. This

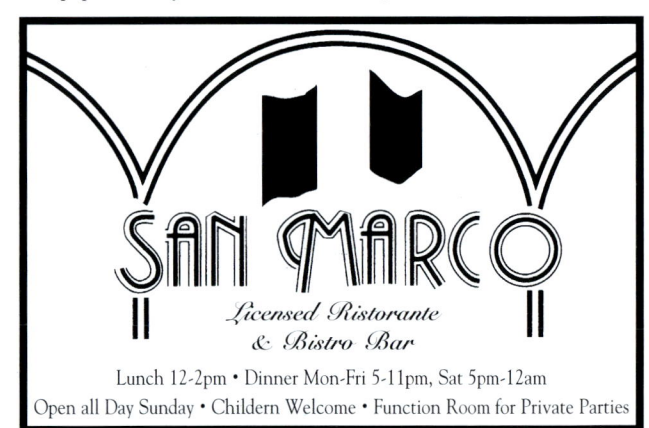

SAN MARCO
Licensed Ristorante & Bistro Bar

Lunch 12-2pm • Dinner Mon-Fri 5-11pm, Sat 5pm-12am
Open all Day Sunday • Childern Welcome • Function Room for Private Parties
10-11 Mary's Place, Raeburn Place, Stockbridge • 0131 332 1569

WEST END, HAYMARKET AND STOCKBRIDGE

family-run restaurant offers fine Northern Isles produce in an atmosphere of Orcadian tranquillity. Everything, including amazing mussel bread, is freshly prepared by Young Scottish Chef of the Year, Paul Temple, whose combinations, colourful presentations and myriad of flavours offer fresh waves of ingenuity. We started with tartare of monkfish with avocado mousse, a crême fraîche lemon dressing and rocket oil (£5.25) and the sublime chargrilled scallops salad with carrot, parmesan rosti and smoked garlic oil (£6.75). Our voyage continued with sea bass, saladaise potato and a balsamic and tomato reduction (£14.50). My red mullet and squid ink mussel fettucine with curry and coriander veloutte was as exciting as it sounded (£14.95). Our wine was Remy Pannier (£9.95). Banana and chocolate crême brûlée with Orkney shortbread (£4.95) and chocolate tort with coffee bean syrup and Grand Marnier ice cream (£4.95) concluded an invigorating evening. We ate in the intimate dining room but the friendly service is also offered in the private dining room and Stane Bar. Lunches, including business options, are available. JJF

Bell's Diner B2

Now in its 28th year Bell's Diner, a small, yet snug Stockbridge restaurant offers a simple choice: burger or steak? But, it's not that easy. Will it be the garlic burger or the pepper steak? The chicken burger or the homemade vegetarian nut burger? Mustard with that, or a big chunk of Roquefort cheese, or even an omelette or a tuna salad? The choice of starter added to the dilemma but eventually we opted for tomato, olive and basil salad, and mushrooms on toast (both £2.50). The steaks (around £11.00) were left for another day and it was with indulgent abandon that we tucked into a 4oz pepper burger (£6.45), and the meatier 6oz Roquefort burger

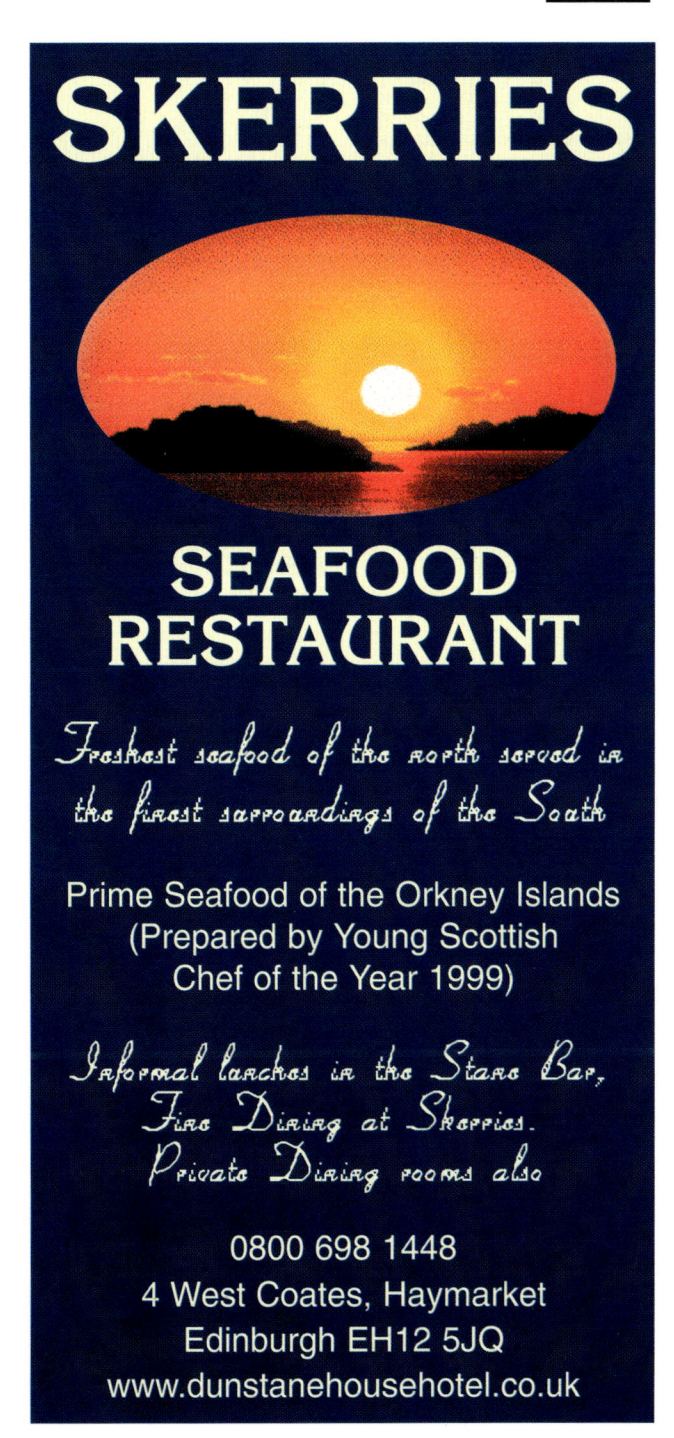

SKERRIES
SEAFOOD RESTAURANT

Freshest seafood of the north served in the finest surroundings of the South

Prime Seafood of the Orkney Islands
(Prepared by Young Scottish Chef of the Year 1999)

*Informal lunches in the Stane Bar,
Fine Dining at Skerries.
Private Dining rooms also*

0800 698 1448
4 West Coates, Haymarket
Edinburgh EH12 5JQ
www.dunstanehousehotel.co.uk

(£7.30), both complete with salad and French fries, and a bottle of house red (£7.45). For the health-conscious among us the burgers do come in a slim-line version which, minus the bun but with more salad, sounds like my kind of diet. We left with a belly full of peaches and cream pancake (£4.95), cherry Wednesday (£3.50) and a determination to come soon for that steak. **AM**

The Indian Cavalry Club A5
The epitome of style and elegance, the Indian Cavalry Club is an experience you will want to keep repeating. Conveniently situated in the heart of the city centre, the restaurant serves an extensive menu incorporating both meat and vegetarian options. There is a very wide selection of starters on offer including the colonel's pakoras which include chicken and fish pakora (£4.35) or king prawn butterfly pakora (£5.95). For our main course we tried madrasi sag chicken (£8.25) which was chicken with spinach, garlic, green chilli and spring onions. The menu also provides suggestions for the best side dish to accompany your choice, which in this case was Bombay potato bhaji (£3.50). We also tried lamb tikka massallam, which was lamb kebab in yoghurt, lime juice and spices in a creamy tandoori sauce (£8.45). We accompanied our meal with basmati pilau rice (£2.50) and a plain nan (£1.95). A wide range of temping desserts are also available. The Indian Cavalry was a treat from beginning to end. The food was excellent, staff attentive and the atmosphere intimate and friendly. **VI**

Dunedin Restaurant, Hilton Grosvenor A5
Sited amidst the architectural splendour of the West End, the Grosvenor Hotel combines nineteenth-century elegance with twenty-first century comfort. The restaurant too celebrates the City's past glories: Dunedin being the ancient name for Edinburgh. There is an abundance of traditional Scottish ingredients on offer, but dishes are varied and cosmopolitan. We were tempted by the excellent table d'hôte menu (starters £3.25, main courses £9.95), but finally decided to explore the extensive à la carte. On a freezing March evening my companion warmed himself with farmhouse broth from the daily stockpot (£3.25) and hot king prawns spiced with peppers and chillies (£10.75). Despite the weather I couldn't resist the cold smoked salmon platter (£6.75), but my chicken did come in an "overcoat" of skirlie with crowdie cheese and mushroom mousse (£10.95). We were soon thawed by the mellow atmosphere, attentive service and good food. The Kirkton Vale Chardonnay (£16.40) was redolent of warmer climes, and the shortcrust pastry basket, crammed with fruit and cream (£3.50), was a foretaste of summer. Finally, amply fortified with liqueur coffees (£3.45) we were again ready to brave those Edinburgh winds. **IB**

The Au Bar B4
The Au Bar is situated in the heart of the city's West End and is family run by husband and wife team Jim and Irene. The menu provides an impressive variety of choices, from traditional favourites to more adventurous options. We started by sampling the soup de jour, which was carrot and coriander and came served with a hot crusty roll (£1.75). We also had the classic Caesar (£3.75) from the varied salad menu. To follow we enjoyed chicken breast with a mild cream and mustard sauce (£5.25) and carbonnade of beef (£4.95), both came accompanied with seasonal vegetables and a choice of roast or mashed potatoes or chips. To drink we were impressed by the choice of wines, which could be purchased by the small (£2.35) or

---

Bell's DINER

CHARCOAL STEAKS, BURGERS, CHICKEN BURGERS & HOMEMADE NUT BURGERS

Licensed
Open Sundays
Booking Advisable

Sun-Fri, 6.00 -10.30
Sat, 12.00 - 10.30

We've been going 28 years and still going strong!

7 St Stephen Street
Edinburgh
0131 225 8116

THE INDIAN CAVALRY CLUB

The Best Indian Restaurant in Scotland.
Flavour of Edinburgh Award Winner.
Highly Recommended.

3 Atholl Place
0131 228 3282

Hilton Grosvenor

The Duncan Restaurant
0131 226 6001

Award winning food enjoyed by the rich & famous

OPEN 7 DAYS A WEEK
12PM - 10PM

5-21 Grosvenor Street
Haymarket, Edinburgh

Au Bar

Traditional Style Hospitality

Au Bar
201 Shandwick Place
Edinburgh
0131 228 2648

Au Bar 2
21 Lothian Road
Edinburgh
0131 228 3404

WEST END, HAYMARKET AND STOCKBRIDGE

large glass (£3.30) or by the bottle (£9.50). The Au Bar serves a selection of ice-cream desserts, cocktails, an excellent Sunday menu with an all-day breakfast (£3.95) and Sunday roast (£5.25). The Au Bar is the perfect choice for a high quality, excellent value meal within a comfortable and friendly environment. **VI**

Howie's B2
The various Howie's establishments in Edinburgh have developed a reputation for offering excellent dining at the right price. The Stockbridge restaurant holds this philosophy true whilst combining excellent design into the restaurant itself. My partner and I began with the soup for the evening, a beautifully rich and bolstering tomato & bean curd which set us up for the delights to come. The Katherine Hills Chardonnay would complement just about anything you choose to devour (£9.40).

Venison sausages with clapshot and roast onion gravy added to my satisfied glow whilst the grilled lamb cutlets with herb couscous and a cranberry jus could definitely become dangerously habit forming. The service is discreet yet attentive with none of the annoying pretentiousness you expect with cuisine of this quality. By now we were struggling to develop the merest hint of a sweet tooth but small effort is needed when presented with a juicy sticky toffee pudding. Set lunch and dinner menus of two or three courses are offered at a very worthwhile £5.50 – £ 9.50 respectively for lunch and £14.95 or £16.95 for dinner. For further news check out their website: www.howies.uk.com. **JF**

Tawan Thai A6
Mahogany tables placed around the large dining room give Tawan a very spacious feel. The emphasis is on enjoying your meal in a relaxed atmosphere. The waiting staff are very helpful and will talk any newcomers to Thai food through the menu. We ordered a bottle of the house white (£8.95) whilst we decided, eventually opting for Tawan spare ribs, marinated pork ribs, baked in honey and spices, and peek gai yud sai, deep-fried chicken wings stuffed with minced chicken and vegetables with a chilli plum sauce (both £3.95). For mains we had gai pad med manaung, stir-fried chicken and cashew nuts with dried chilli and onion (£6.95) and gratiam prig thai, king prawns fried in garlic and pepper (£7.95). We both had kao pad khai, egg fried rice to accompany our main dish (£2.00). Desserts range from £2.95 to £3.25 and we enjoyed the homemade coconut ice cream and lychees (£3.25). Tawan is one of the city's finest Thai experiences and comes highly recommended. **DH**

TAWAN
THAI RESTUARANT

Tawan Thai Restaurant is a great place to sample a taste of Authentic Thai cuisine with a warm & friendly service, prepared and freshly cooked with the finest ingredients by our highly experienced chefs.

We would like to introduce our menu which is selected from the popular dishes of Thai cooking found on every corner of Thailand.

0131 313 2797

Open: Tuesday – Saturday 12-2pm (Lunch)
Monday – Saturday 5.30-11pm Sunday 5.30-10.30pm

15 DALRY ROAD, HAYMARKET, EDINBURGH EH11 2BQ

Howies
A6

The Howie's menu takes Scottish produce and adds somewhat unusual twists to this year's fashionable choices. With dinner at two courses for £14.95 and three for £16.95 it's also great value. This is not concept food but food that's part of a concept which appears to try for little more than sheer customer satisfaction. We began with black pudding and egg terrine, wrapped in smoked bacon with paprika oil, and the feta salad with red onions, cherry tomatoes, roasted red peppers and basil oil. Mains were roast leg of Barbary duck with spring onion and Parmesan mash, and loin of pork with spiced red wild rice, caramelised apples and cider cream. Desserts of Dalry's banoffi pie, and iced orange and spiced honey parfait left us truly satisfied. All wines on the list are keenly-priced, (an excellent house red is £6.10/bottle) and with flavour descriptions on the menu you really can't go wrong. With the warmth of candlelight, happy eating and friendly chat, you could be in any of the four branches, proving that the unmistakable Howie's 'theme' translates to any location and is suited to any occasion. **RRH**

Bouzy Rouge
B4

The buzz about Bouzy is as warm as the welcome, worthwhile as the wine in your glass, (in this case a Chilean Merlot £12.95). Tables are separated into booths, some small and romantic, others big enough for groups. The rough stone walls are broken up by brightly coloured tiles and twisted Guadi-esque shapes, providing a Continental feel. The menu is split into Gourmet (starters £4.50, main courses £11.95 and desserts £4.50) and Casual (a selection of main courses from £5.95 to £16.95). From Gourmet we chose trio of Scottish puddings with Orkney cheese sabayon, and roast pigeon and beetroot salad with smoked bacon, toasted cashews and Dijon

---

EAT DRINK ENJOY...

Howies Restaurants

MODERN SCOTTISH COOKING WITH WORLD INFLUENCE ACCOMPANIED BY EAGERLY PRICED WINES.

208 BRUNTSFIELD PLACE
BRUNTSFIELD – 0800 698 1419

63 DALRY ROAD
DALRY – 0800 698 1420

29 WATERLOO PLACE
EAST PRINCES ST – 0800 698 1418

4/6 GLANVILLE PLACE
STOCKBRIDGE – 0800 698 1417

HOWIE'S OFFICE
(MARKETING, EVENTS, FUNCTIONS)
5 MARISCHAL PLACE – 332 1700

7 DAYS LUNCH, DINNER & BY ARRANGEMENT
FINE FOOD WITHOUT THE FAFF

WWW.HOWIES.UK.COM

WEST END, HAYMARKET AND STOCKBRIDGE

Bouzy Rouge

- Inspirational Atmosphere
- Stylish Decor
- Seriously Good Food
- Fresh Scottish Produce Embracing A World of Flavours
- Affordable Prices

Casual Gourmet Dining

11 Rochsolloch Road
Airdrie ML6 9BB
01236 763853

111 West Regent Street
Glasgow G2 2RU
0141 221 8804

1 Alva Street
Edinburgh EH2 4PH
0131 225 9594

At The Sheriffmuir Inn
By Dunblane
Perthshire, FK15 0LN
01786 823285

www.bouzy-rouge.com

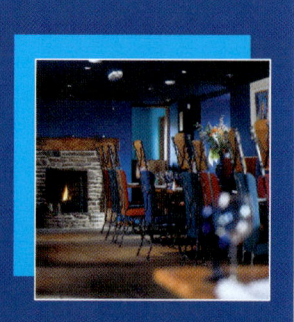

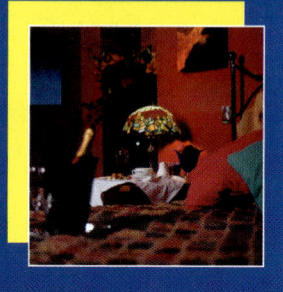

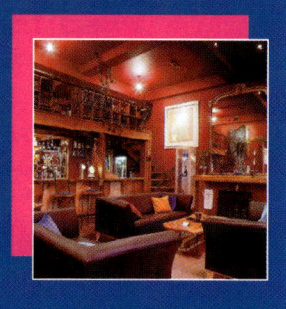

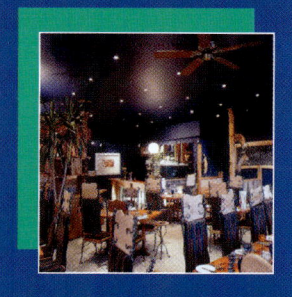

dressing. Main courses were saddle of Rannoch venison, lentil risotto with redcurrant and juniper reduction, and fillet of pork oatties with Bramley apple sauce, mushroom and peppercorn cream. The chefs here could teach some of the well-known 'Scottish' restaurants how to make the utmost of local produce. We relaxed after generous portions before desserts of sticky toffee pudding and banana crème brûlée. Loyal customers use the Rouge Rewards scheme but most require little more incentive than fine food in fine surroundings. **RRH**

The Bonham A3

I jumped at the chance to review the Restaurant at the Bonham as their mix of modern sophistication, Edinburgh elegance and truly excellent cuisine never fails to impress. Upon arrival we soon joined the leisurely chatter of Sunday afternoon brunchers. At this time two courses cost £12.50 and three £15, which is deservedly popular. We started with the cream of carrot and orange soup, and smoked haddock and chorizo risotto. Both were flawless. For main course I chose the seared tuna niçoise with an orange and grain mustard dressing while my companion raved about his baked salmon with new potatoes in mayonnaise and braised cabbage. Meanwhile, Cranswick Smith's Bin 12 Chardonnay (Australia 1999 £15.50) quenched our thirst nicely. To follow we chose rosemary crème brûlée and apple and banana crumble with vanilla custard were both divine. We finished off this excellent meal with cappuccinos served with brownies (£1.75). With regularly changing menus, modern décor and a team of talented chefs, the Restaurant at the Bonham is guaranteed to leave you satisfied and impressed. **BO'R**

Channings A2

Part of the Townhouse Hotel, this wine bar and conservatory

Channings

RESTAURANT
WINE BAR & CONSERVATORY

ROYAL MAIL
POSTAGE PAID
SCOTLAND
3495

Fancy joining me at Channings Restaurant for some distinctive and contemporary French cooking in homely surroundings? 8pm, Sat, table for 2. Meet me at 7.30pm, for drinks in the Wine Bar. £25 for 3 courses.

Reservations
0131 315 2225
restaurant@channings.co.uk

South Learmonth Gardens, Edinburgh EH4 1EZ
www.channings.co.uk

Lunch: Mon-Sat 12.30-2pm
Dinner: Sun-Thur 6.30-9.30pm Fri-Sat 6.30-10pm

RESTAURANT AT THE BONHAM

Good Mood Food: [Mood Food] Food to be consumed for specific emotional benefits; to calm down, be energised, gain a competitive edge. Faith Popcorn, Brainstorm, USA

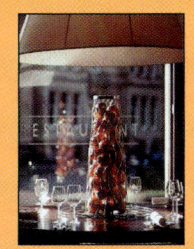

Reservations
0131 623 9319
E: restaurant@thebonham.com

Lunch: Mon-Sat 12-2.30pm Sun 12.30-3pm
Dinner: 6.30-10pm
35 Drumsheugh Gardens, Edinburgh EH3 7RN
www.thebonham.com

WEST END, HAYMARKET AND STOCKBRIDGE

THE KHUKURI
NEPALESE RESTAURANT

COME AND ENJOY A MEAL AT A FAMILY RUN RESTAURANT IN THE WEST END

OPEN SEVEN DAYS A WEEK

Mon-Thur 12.00-2.00pm
5.30-11.30pm

Fri-Sat 12.00-2.00pm
5.30-12.00pm

Sun Closed
5.00-11.00pm

TAKE AWAY/ DELIVERY SERVICE AVAILABLE

**8 WEST MAITLAND STREET
EDINBURGH EH12 5DS
0131 228 2085 / 2252**

---

restaurant, mixes a modern, elegant bar with the warmth of a converted townhouse dining room. We started with Chinese spiced duck confit, fondant potato, creamed spinach, puy lentils and a coriander jus, and the stack of marinated Mediterranean vegetables and buffalo mozarella with a slow-roasted ratatouille, pepper coulis and pesto. The latter looked much like an edible Picasso and tasted like a masterpiece. For mains we tried pan-fried sea bream with smoked fish cake, flavoured with lime and topped with a crispy battered oyster, and the sirloin steak with béarnaise sauce. Prices are very reasonable considering the quality, with two courses for £19.50, three for £24.50. Desserts were delicious pear bavarois with green apple sorbet and hot toffee apples, and the iced coconut parfait with a salsa of fruits, coconut praline and lime syrup. A painting of Lady Lonsdale hangs above the fireplace, keeping watch over a dining experience suitable for the landed gentry, but priced within less extravagant budgets. **RRH**

The Khukuri A5
The Khukuri, which faces a number of large, lavish-looking Indian restaurants, is something rather different. This welcoming restaurant has a unique charm and an extravagant menu constructed from Nepalese dishes which transcend their humble surroundings. We began with bara (£2.75), a traditional lentil pancake served with a delicious spicy dip, and trisuli poleko machha (£3.95), fish marinated in spices and cooked in a tandoori oven, which was bursting with flavour. We then moved on to gurkha bhenda, diced lamb in almonds, coconut cream and fresh herbs - similar to korma but with a lively spiciness - and solukhumbu bhenda, sliced lamb stuffed with mint and cooked with onions, ginger, garlic and tomato. These were consumed with the house wine, Chez Bouey from France (£9.95). On the side we had boiled rice (£1.65) and a garlic nan (£1.95). Having wiped our plates clean we were too full for desserts. The Khukuri is certainly giving its neighbours a run for their money. **JFW**

The Caley Ale House A5
Right next to Haymarket Station and atop the bustling Caley Ale House we were amazed to discover a cosy, candlelit restaurant with a mouth-watering menu based on the classic combination of Scottish and French ingredients. With three courses for a mere £16.95 (lunches available for around £5), my partner started with goats cheese, courgette, mushroom and roasted pepper mille feuille with a lime and coriander coulis, while I tucked into sumptuous pan-fried mussels in a tomato, garlic, basil and white wine sauce. To follow I sampled a generously portioned venison steak served on thyme roasted roots with a red wine and blueberry reduction, while my partner chose breast of pheasant stuffed with wild mushroom mousse on a leek and juniper cream sauce. A lovely bottle of Chilean Cabernet Sauvignon (£10.50) matched the bold flavours perfectly. To finish we enjoyed the chef's finest selection of cheeses accompanied, of course, by a glass of vintage port (£2.10). Such friendly and attentive service coupled with delicious food means my next trip to Glasgow will see me waylaid at the Caley before I can think about boarding a train. **SJM**

Stockbridge Restaurant B2
Juliet Wilson has exceeded her desire to create an upmarket eaterie. Stepping inside I was pleased to see that the stylish restaurant offered intimacy and character without pretence. An overview of the menu suggested we were in for a fulfilling evening. We started with the rich and flavoursome tomato and basil soup (£4.50) and a mussel tiger prawn bisque (£7.50) suitably

THE CALEY
ALE HOUSE & BISTRO

The Caledonian Ale House & Bistro is a traditional Scottish pub, furnished to provide that old world Edinburgh charm, in a relaxed, stylish atmosphere which also gives a distinctly European feel to Edinburgh's West End.

1/3 Haymarket Terrace
Edinburgh
0131 337 1006

THE STOCKBRIDGE RESTAURANT

FINE SEASONAL COOKING

"not for faint-hearts… as soon as you step into the Stockbridge Restaurant you know you are in for a sumptuous evening"

SUSAN DALGETY
EDINBURGH EVENING NEWS

0800 698 1451
54 ST STEPHEN STREET, EDINBURGH EH3 5AL

WEST END, HAYMARKET AND STOCKBRIDGE

Edinburgh Food Guide

Peter's Cellars Restaurant & Bar

Superb Scottish Cuisine

Corporate lunches catered for
Private dining room seats 18

Lunch: 2 courses £7.95, 3 courses £9.95
Dinner: 2 courses £17.00, 3 courses £19.00

BYOB £2.00 corkage
Wine list starts at £6.95

Unlimited tea/coffee £1.50

Open Mon-Sat 12-2.30pm, 6-10.30pm
Bar lunches served 12-5pm
Open Sundays 12.30-10pm

11a-13a William St,
West End, Edinburgh EH3 7NG
Tel: 0131 226 3161   Fax: 0131 538 7230
www.petercellars.co.uk (pre-book/order lunch)

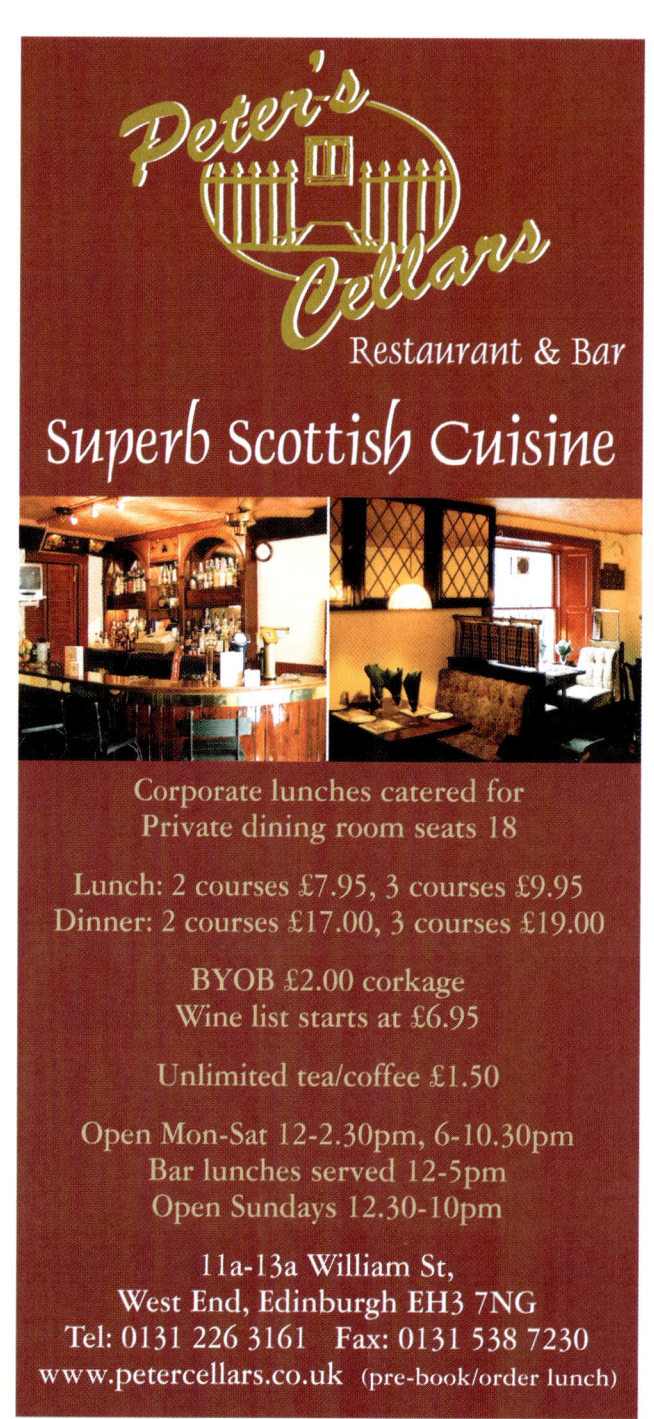

complemented by a bottle of house white chilled to perfection (£12.50). In between our courses we were given rumshoka, a crushed ice concoction of white rum, cola and lime which cleanses the palette and awakens senses. We had trouble selecting main courses from the wide and tempting menu but settled on fillet of beef with a cream and blue cheese sauce, served with sherry braised fennel (£22.50), whilst my partner braved the speciality, an enormous Arctic char served with a selection of vegetables (£19.50). After a necessary rest we dared a glance at the dessert menu. One of my all time favourite desserts, and I feel all quality restaurants should offer this, an assiette platter allowing one to indulge the desire to taste more than one sweet without feeling gluttonous. For a simple or special occasion Stockbridge provides all the elements. **CSR**

Peter's Cellars   B4

Tucked away in a quaint basement is a wee gem of a restaurant. Whether it's an intimate, softly lit romantic snug you desire, or a spacious setting for a lively gathering, (or indeed a private room for 18 diners), the cosy booths and various tables of Peter's Cellars afford whatever privacy you require. Newly decorated but with its renowned friendly staff still in place, this is an unassuming, friendly spot to enjoy some fine and imaginative Scottish fare. A fresh melon, mango and prawn starter set me delicately on my way, while my companion discovered what a 'quennel of haggis' was, and declared herself impressed with these little haggis castles in their moat of hot brandy cream. We didn't remember to 'BYOB' (corkage £2) and instead opted for the Rochberg Chenin Blanc (an extremely reasonable £7.95) to accompany medallions of pork with parmesan, served with a superb pepper/tomato concasse. The intriguing Cajun pepper

Ryan's

a la carte section	bar menu section
peppered mackerel	sandwiches
wild duck terrine	bagels
rack of lamb	croissants
roasted parsnip	baked potatoes
carrot and walnut ravioli	thai curry

Private functions for up to 150 people. No hire charges

Serving a menu inspired by variety, including a separate a la carte section in the evenings. We boast a relaxing and unique seating, including seven private alcoves. We create a perfect atmosphere for any occasion with quality service from friendly staff.

2-4 HOPE STREET, EDINBURGH   TEL: 0131 226 7005

WEST END, HAYMARKET AND STOCKBRIDGE

Edinburgh Food Guide

LA PIAZZA

FREEPHONE 0800 698 1432

Open: Mon-Thu 12noon-11pm,
Fri-Sat 12pm-12am, Sun 4pm-11pm

For a broad range of Italian dishes served in a warm relaxing atmosphere, choose La Piazza!

97/99 Shandwick Place, West End

crust enlivened my salmon fillet with its unusual flavour, and we finished with delightfully sinful confections from the ample dessert menu, and some fine coffees. All this for a mere £19 (two courses for £17). The lunch menu is similar (£9.95 and £7.95), while the bar and chargrill menus offer snacks, salads and steaks. **NG**

Ryan's Bar B4
Beneath Ryan's bar lies the Cellar restaurant, with private alcoves, and a flexible menu, making it perfect for romantic meals or a light bite during a heavy shopping expedition. We were shown to our alcove, which had plenty of room, and was beautifully painted with Grecian trompé l'oeil. We decided to go for the à la carte but there was also a main menu offering a huge selection of dishes from nibbles to haggis, neeps and tatties. I started with a rich cream of asparagus soup finished with crème fraîche and garlic croutons (£3.95), whilst my friend sampled the wild duck terrine, with fois gras medallions (£4.95). To follow, I chose marinated teriyaki fillet steak and crushed potatoes, served with pesto and Parmesan mushroom tartlet (£12.92), whilst my partner had herb crusted rack of lamb with rosemary and garlic mash. We drank a bottle of light and easy to drink Vin du Pays (£8.95 per bottle, or £2.30 per glass), and rounded things off with carrot cake and sticky toffee pudding (£2.95 each). Ryan's opening hours are as accommodating as their menu, doors open at 7.30 am, and close at 10 pm. **AmcC**

La Piazza B4
La Piazza is a busy, no-nonsense pizzeria on Shandwick Place down the West End - handy if you're passing. It's roomy enough inside to cope with a high volume of customers and was doing a brisk trade in couples, small parties and large groups the night that we dropped by. I was tempted by the fresh mussels in

Edinburgh's Finest Traditional Indian Cuisine

SHALIMAR
INDIAN RESTAURANT

Authenticity is everything at SHALIMAR whose traditional authentic curries are the order of the day. The QUALITY of the food in this fine restaurant is reflected by the fact that they have become a NEW ENTRANT in the 2001 Good Curry Guide to the best 1000 in Great Britain.

Extensive Menu
Highly Competitive Prices
Take away Menu Available
Free Delivery for orders over £10
(within a 2 mile radius)

Lunch Menu including a free bottle of beer for £5
5pm-8pm Special 2 for 1
Special prices for large party bookings
Fully Licensed

Open 7 Days a Week
29 West Maitland St Edinburgh
Tel: 0131 220 0603/0131 225 3199

WEST END, HAYMARKET AND STOCKBRIDGE

white wine as a starter (£5.45), while my partner picked out the homemade cannelloni half-portion (£4.75) - both of these dishes are available in larger sizes as main courses. And, it being a pizzeria, I opted for a great, steaming calzone ripieno for the main course, at the top end of the pizza menu for £8.50. From the carni menu (see? I'm almost a native) we also sampled the saltimbocca alla Roman (escalope with sage, Parma ham and white wine) at £12.95 and we washed the whole lot down with a bottle of the house white at £9.95. This is a cheery establishment that works hard to cater to a broad range of tastes. **JM**

Shalimar A5
The Shalimar brings an authentic touch of India to Haymarket with its unique, traditional Indian style décor and fine cuisine. We began our meal with the chicken pakoras (£3.35) and the king prawn puri, curried prawns sandwiched in a wafer thin puri (£3.95), and washed it down with a reasonably priced carafe of the house white wine (£10.95). The main course proved more difficult to choose due to the satisfyingly vast selection on the menu. I finally opted for the chicken tikka kebab, succulent boneless nuggets of chicken marinated in yoghurt, cumin, coriander and turmeric, served with pilau rice (£8.95) and my partner chose the chicken bhuna, a medium strength thick sauce of onions, tomatoes, fresh herbs and spices (£6.50). We also ordered garlic naan (£1.95) and chapatis (55p) to accompany our meal. We were very full and decided to skip dessert, but there was a good selection available ranging from £1.25 to £2.75. Shalimar is a very friendly place to eat with a standard of service close to perfection. A menu that tries to cater for everyone's taste and includes an excellent range of vegetarian dishes is bound to please. **DH**

Blue Parrot Cantina B2
This cosy Mexican restaurant is a great place to meet friends, the atmosphere intimate, without being over familiar. Their margaritas have quite a reputation so I was keen to try them (£2.50 per glass). We had the strawberry (freshly crushed strawberries, orange liqueur and tequila) and the traditional variety (tequila, orange liqueur and freshly squeezed lime juice). The feast began with nachos, smothered with melted cheese topped with jalapenos and capsicum pepper (£2.95) and songos as ajillo, mushrooms, garlic and chillies in a rich tomato salsa, served in a flour tortilla basket (£3.10). Our friendly waitress suggested the Mexican steak: Scotch sirloin covered in a smoked Chipotle salsa, served with cheese covered sweet potato and spicy garlic mushrooms (£10.95), succulent and well complemented by the sweet potatoes. My friend ordered the flavour-filled chicken and cashew burrito (£7.80). After such an impressive and filling meal, we just managed to squeeze in the mouth-watering banana chimi (Kahlua liqueur and banana wrapped in a tortilla, deep-fried, served with cream and ice-cream £3.30), my favourite way to eat Mexican. We waved good bye to the brightly coloured Parrot determined to return. **BO'R**

Loopy Lorna's B2
Opened in June 2001, this candlelit, mirrored haven can be found in a basement in the Stockbridge area - and what a find it is! A speciality teahouse by day, LL's transforms into a cosy, stylish bistro by night and is already proving to be a popular draw. The menu incorporates many different styles of food to provide a refreshingly original choice of dishes. One dish sure to become a legend is LL's own bloomin' onion (£4.20), served in a deep-fried batter with a choice of dips. Elsewhere, the lightly sautéed king prawns served with red chilli and ginger butter (£6.50) is a taste sensation. For mains, you cannot fail to be disappointed with the pan-fried woodland mushroom risotto with chive crème fraiche (£6.95), while the oak-smoked Highland salmon with lemon and basil cream (£8.20) will have you planning a return visit. The dessert menu is similarly eclectic, from which we sampled the chocolate and strawberry pudding (£4.00) and the summer fruits and mango crème brûlées (£4.00). As the owner plans to alter the menu regularly, the novelty of dining at Loopy Lorna's is unlikely to wear off. **GB**

Siam Erawan C2
As one of three great Erawan Thai restaurants in Edinburgh, I was looking forward to a meal at Siam. This basement restaurant has established a reputation for great Thai cuisine and friendly service. Once settled into our alcove table, we sipped the house white wine (£8.80) and perused the menu. Expect to find a mix that suits both conservative and adventurous diners. We opted for the set banquet for two (£18.50 per person), an opportunity to try a number of delicious Thai specialities, consisting of four starters, three main courses and filter coffee. The highlights of this delightful feast were starters of see krong moo tod, pork ribs marinated in garlic and black pepper, and kanom pang nakai, spiced minced chicken on bread, quick-fried with sesame seeds. The main courses were all worth a mention: panang chicken, a curry made with red chillies; mixed seafood and meat gratium prig Thai, a tantalising stir-fried dish with garlic and black pepper; and pad pak nammanhoi, mixed vegetables stir-fried with oyster sauce. Siam certainly plays its part in carving out the great Erawan reputation. **BO'R**

The Blue Parrot Cantina

Fine Mexican Food • Open 7 days
Booking advisable

49 St. Stephen Street, Stockbridge. **Tel: 0800 698 1405**

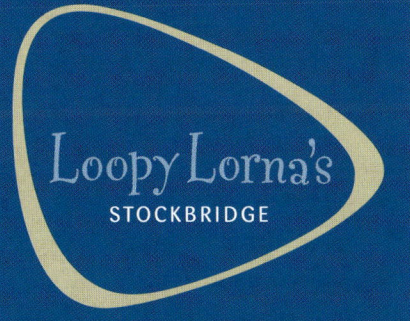

Loopy Lorna's
STOCKBRIDGE

email: info @loopylorna.com

24 Deanhaugh Street
Stockbridge
EH4 1LY

Tel: 0131 332 4476
Fax: 0131 332 4476

...Loopy Lorna's is a little different. Individual & personal, we believe that every part of your experience with us should be the best it can be - the service, the food, the drinks, the ambience.

By day - teas (over 30 to choose from!), coffee, light snacks, lunches & traditional afternoon teas.

By night - an illumination of flickering candles & mirrors combine with our superb bistro menu to create an evening to savour.

Eating out in Lothian Road, Tollcross, Bruntsfield & Morningside

Lothian Road is Edinburgh's new centre of business, entertainment and eating out. With new, impressive developments, cinema, theatre, pubs and nightclubs, the area caters for both the extravagant and the indulgent. If unadulterated luxury is what you desire then experience the Grill Room at the Sheraton Grand serving outstanding traditional Scottish cuisine or at the Terrace mixing top-quality ingredients and affordability.

Edinburgh's international feel is reflected by the diversity of cuisine on offer throughout the city. Tollcross and Lothian Road play host to a variety of restaurants: from Thai, French, Italian and African to Chinese, Cantonese and Indian. Whatever you choose, the quality of restaurants will guarantee your satisfaction. Let your tastebuds dictate.

As you reach the top of Tollcross, you amble into the Bruntsfield area, which begins with a grassy paradise where residents relax and while away the summer. A popular venue here is the stylish Montpeliers serving delicious and reasonably priced fare. Venture further down into Morningside's fashionable Carriage House, or spice it up at the Clay Oven.

Sukhothai C6

You really feel like you could be in the Far East when you dine at Sukhothai, with its traditionally dressed staff, authentic décor, exotic flowers and mouth-watering food. We began our meal by ordering a bottle of Ruitersvlei Chenin Blanc, a South African white wine (£10.45). For starters we had Sukothai prawns, marinated king prawns individually wrapped in a thin pastry leaf, quick fried and served with a spicy plum sauce (£4.75) and ka bueong talay, prawn and crab meat wrapped in flour skins with the same sauce (£4.70). For my main course I had pad nam man hoi, beef stir fried with oyster sauce and vegetables (£6.95) with egg fried rice (£2) and my partner had gaeng phed ped yang, roast duck in a mild red curry sauce (£7.25) with steamed fragrant rice (£1.50). For desserts we had coconut ice cream with jackfruit and lychee (£2.95) and orange sorbet (£2.65). Sukhothai offers the first Thai buffet in Scotland, giving you the chance to taste a wide range of Thai dishes at great value on a Sunday lunchtime for £9.95. Takeaway is also available. **DH**

Rainbow Arch B5

Centrally located off Edinburgh's busy Lothian Road, the popular Rainbow Arch offers a huge selection of authentic Chinese dishes served in a cosy and relaxing atmosphere. With two excellent value-for-money menus on offer - à la carte and dim sum - the only problem is deciding what to order. After due deliberation, we began with two deliciously light appetisers, Vietnamese spring rolls and deep-fried crispy wan-ton (both £2.30). To follow, we thoroughly enjoyed our generous portions of spicy kung po chicken (£7) and beef with green pepper and black bean sauce (£6.50). Both were served with a plentiful supply of egg fried rice (£2). After giving in to the temptations of the dessert menu, we concluded our feast with a couple of refreshing fruit sorbets (£2.50). The Rainbow Arch is open for lunch from 12-2pm (£5.50, 3 courses) with a menu that caters well for vegetarians and meat-eaters alike, whilst a pre-cinema set dinner is also available from 3-7pm (£8, 3 courses). **AD**

Stac Polly C5

Stac Polly welcomes you with far more comfort than the mountain it takes its name from. We wasted little effort in unwinding into intimate yet commodious decor. Stac Polly stakes its laurels upon fine Scottish ingredients with a turn and the menu confirms this fully. My partner indulged in one of the signature dishes, haggis wrapped in filo pastry with a plum sauce (£6.25). Whilst the tuna loin with soy and sesame dressing (6.25) brought a satisfying abundance of flavour with crispy garlic slivers adding a decent texture. A house Sauvignon (£12.95) gave a fine indication of the delights to come. As it was Spring I dare not pass by the baked lamb (£14.95). The parsley crust, thyme jus and calcannon potatoes only distinguished this classic. A sautéed sea bass, with chorizo and a chive oil (£14.95) was given a few "hmmms" - always a good sign. Fading appetites rambled onto dessert with a white chocolate mousse sprayed in Cointreau sauce (£4.95) and cheese (£5.95). If this restaurant were tucked under the shadow of a western peak rather than Edinburgh Castle it would remain a worthwhile destination. **JF**

RAINBOW ARCH
Chinese Restaurant

鵲橋居

Only Homemade Dim-Sum in
The City of Edinburgh

Patronised by
Clarissa Dickson
Wright

(of Two Fat
Ladies Fame)

Ho Ho Mei Noodle Shack

Informal Noodle Restaurant
Eat Cheap • Eat Plenty

8-16a Morrison Street • Edinburgh
Tel: 0800 698 1443   Fax: 538 7384

---

stac polly
THE SCOTTISH RESTAURANTS

Voted as one of the "Top 600 best restaurants in Britain"
GQ Magazine

"Food so perfectly prepared & so beautifully presented it was a shame to eat it"
Greg Russell - Evening News

"Brilliant, braw, scintillating, choose your own adjective"
Bill Clapperton - Evening News

"A sight of Stac Polly's menu is enough to set the heather alight"
Scotland on Sunday

Open 7 days a week

Member of
Taste of Scotland 2000/2001
Private dining facilities available

29-33 Dublin St, Edinburgh
FREEPHONE 0800 298 3429

8-10 Grindlay St, Edinburgh
FREEPHONE 0800 298 3430

If our line is busy your call will be diverted

LOTHIAN ROAD, TOLLCROSS, BRUNTSFIELD & MORNINGSIDE

Edinburgh Food Guide

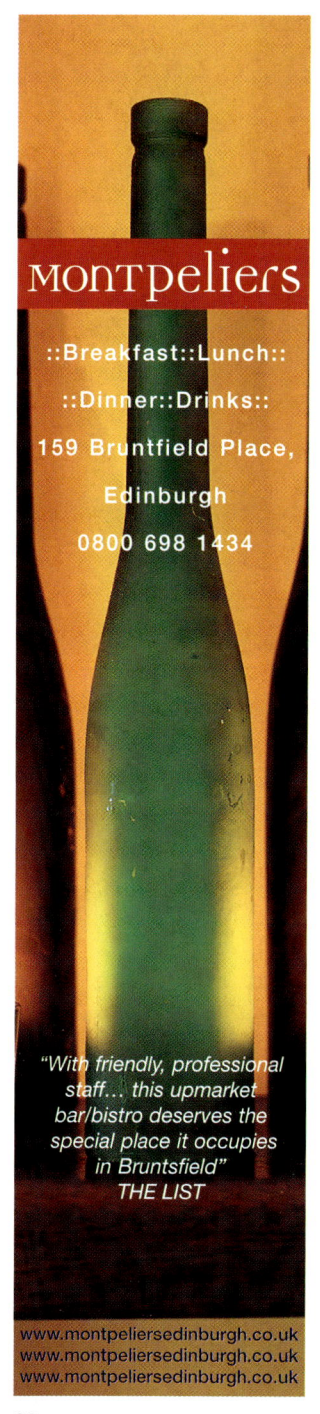

montpeliers

::Breakfast::Lunch::
::Dinner::Drinks::

159 Bruntfield Place,
Edinburgh
0800 698 1434

"With friendly, professional staff... this upmarket bar/bistro deserves the special place it occupies in Bruntsfield"
THE LIST

www.montpeliersedinburgh.co.uk
www.montpeliersedinburgh.co.uk
www.montpeliersedinburgh.co.uk

Montpeliers B7

Sunshine brings crowds to the pavements outside Montpeliers for a chat and a drink. On this occasion we ventured inside the stylish establishment to see what their menu had to offer. Serving breakfast from 9am and lunch from 12pm, we had come to sample the dinner menu. We ordered charred chicken skewers and peanut dip (£3.95) and crispy duck and watercress salad with plum sauce (£4.10), along with a bottle of the house red (£10.95). Next up I chose Caesar salad with charred chicken, pancetta and parmesan (£8.25), a huge portion, while my partner savoured the special, poached fillet of salmon on a bed of rice with water chestnuts, bamboo shoots and coriander (£8.65). Deserts couldn't be resisted especially since the banoffee pie (£3.25) had come with strong recommendations. It was as good as promised and polished off in seconds, as my partner relaxed with cheddar, stilton and brie with fruit, celery and biscuits (£3.35). Impressed by our meal we slipped over from the relaxed bistro to the lively bar to enjoy a few drinks. **AL**

Thai Orchid B5

What can you say about one of the most enjoyable meals you have had recently? That the food was superb, that the atmosphere was alive with happy diners, ourselves among them, or that when I think of that small Grindlay Street restaurant, I just want to go back. I recommend the banquet for two people (£19.50 per person) with house wine (£9.95), not only because each dish was just divine, but also because a table covered with excellent dishes is bound to induce feelings of decadence and celebration, on even the most ordinary of Scottish winter evenings. Although too many dishes to mention here were served to us, we particularly enjoyed the mixed starter, which incorporated flavoursome chicken, pork and prawn dishes. And as if all that food was not enough, we simply devoured the sticky coconut rice with mango (£3.50), which was even more flavoursome than it sounds. The Orchid banana fritters (£3.50), are the reason why banana fritters became so popular. I have been to many fine restaurants in Edinburgh, but there are not many that I have enjoyed more. **BO'R**

Potting Shed B6

Placed on the edge of Bruntsfield Links, The Potting Shed provides the ideal setting and cuisine for an elegant eating experience. The main dining area is extensive and light, with a conservatory looking onto the garden, perfect for the summer. You have the choice of one two or three courses on the set menu (£16.50, £19.50, £22.50 respectively), as well as casual and grill menus. I chose the set menu and began with tian of Galia melon and raspberry sorbet, drizzled with a light and tangy pineapple syrup, followed by grilled sea bass on couscous and a sweet pepper buerre noisette. My friend dabbled with the other menus and began with a salad of feta cheese, black olives and red onion with a herb oil (£2.95) from the casual menu, followed by fillet steak with tomatoes mushrooms and chips, from the grill menu (£18.50). We finished off our meal, and our wine (South African Chardonnay £13.00 per bottle) with a supreme selection of Scottish cheeses and the blackcurrant crême brulée served with melt in the mouth shortbread rounds (£4.95). **AmcC**

Made In France C6

This French café/takeaway, as its name suggests, brings an original and exciting array of fresh Gallic produce to the people of

Beautifully prepared, fresh, exciting food

DINNER MENU FROM AROUND £18.00. RESTAURANT OPEN 7 DAYS.

potting shed
Restaurant

AA Food Rosette

FOR RESERVATIONS TELEPHONE 0131 229 1393
69 BRUNTSFIELD PLACE, EDINBURGH EH10 4HH. www.thebruntsfield.co.uk

THAI ORCHID

Authentic Thai Cuisine in Elegant Surroundings

"The Thai Orchid dishes are positively addictive and positively the best Thai food we've ever tasted."

Bill Clapperton
Edinburgh Evening News

44 Grindlay Street, Edinburgh. Telephone: 0800 698 1452

Edinburgh. Its inspiration comes from Parisian owner Benoit who makes regular trips to his home city and returns with an exclusive range of French culinary treats, including an array of delights to aid and inspire your own home-cooking. The delicacies we savoured certainly made us feel as if we had managed to cross the Channel for an afternoon. Baguettes are freshly prepared and offer a range of delicious pâtés, hams and cheeses served with salads and cornichons (French pickles). We enjoyed a selection of fillings including conte, brie and roquefort cheeses, papion ham and the distinctive wild boar and goose pâtés (£1.80-£2.50). The wild mushroom quiche is also highly recommended (£1.40). Great value is offered in the combination of a baguette and coffee for £3 or coffee and a gâteau de jour (£2.20). We left with a jar of exquisite pesto and a determination to return and hire Benoit's raclette machine (£3 per day) to recreate a favourite French dish. **JJF**

Howie's   B7

Ushered into the softly lit small Bruntsfield restaurant, we sat down amongst a varied group of diners to examine an elaborate and imaginative menu. While I settled on pigeon breast with mushroom dressing followed by a salmon fillet with colourful vegetables on tagliatelle, my partner plumped for a tomato, goats cheese and olive tart with minty coulis and pheasant breast with a balsamic syrup. Despite a varied selection of puddings, neither of us could match those around us after the extremely delicious, satisfyingly enormous portions. There are three different house wines, fairly priced between £6 & £10, or you can bring your own at £2 corkage. Howie's also have an excellent list of non-house wines ranging in price from £10-£18 and, with four Howie's located throughout Edinburgh, you don't have to go too far for a great, reasonably priced meal. (The tiered pricing system offers: Sun-Wed £11 for 2 courses, £13 for three; Thurs-Sat £14.95/£16.95.) Also, check out their website: www.howies.uk.com. **CK**

Coconut Grove   B6

A saddle and sombrero hang in pride of place in this lively cantina, perhaps the chef had ridden into town and decided to stay? It transpires he trained in Mexico, making this experience one hundred percent auténtico. Smells and sounds spring forthwith, an effect upon the senses like sitting upon a cactus, minus the pain. We started with sopa de tortilla, Mexican soup with tortilla, freshly sliced avacado and cheese (£3.40) and caldo jalepeno, soup with garbanzo beans, chicken, avacado and cheese (£3.90), superbly spicy warmers on a cold January night. Upon a yellow plate that shone like the desert sun I enjoyed meat chimichanga (£8.95), where the meat was juicy strips of steak not the shredded corned beef you often receive, the tortilla crispy and light. My amigo feasted on tampiquena (£10.95), beef tenderloin with soft tortillas, refried beans, guacamole and Mexicana sauce, delicioso. Postre took the shape of jericalla, Mexican crème caramel with cinnamon, and coconut flan (both £3.25), sumptuous coolants to the heat. We drank Santa Helena, a Chilean Sauvignon blanc (£7.95) but there's five different kinds of tequila on offer. Let's just hope that saddle stays firmly fixed to the wall. **RRH**

Carriage House   B7

Although not quite an eighteenth century coaching inn, The Carriage House is an ideal place to refuel. A comparative newcomer to lively Morningside Road, this family run bistro has quickly established itself as a trendy place to eat. Traditional only in its use of fresh local ingredients, the menu is extensive and imaginative. The table d'hôte, offering two courses and a glass of wine for £11.50 (£9.95 between 5.30 and 7pm), is particularly good value. We opted for the à la carte, starting with grilled goats cheese, vine tomatoes and basil and arbequina oilve oil (£3.95), and smoked salmon with caper berries, shallots and lemon vinaigrette (£5.25). Main courses of salmon fillet with tomato, gin and juniper butter sauce (£9.50), and chicken topped with MacSweens haggis on brandy and lemon sauce (£9.95) came with vegetables and were very substantial. The dessert trolley beckoned (£3.95 each) but despite the delights on offer we resisted further indulgence with barely enough room for a glass of Chilean Chardonnay (£2.40). Still, there's always tomorrow; the Club lunch at £6.95 looks especially enticing. Now, where did we park the carriage? **MB**

Pasquale's   B6

Judging by the hundreds of photos adorning the walls of this traditional Italian restaurant, Pasquale's have built up a loyal and lively clientele over their 11 years in Gilmore Place. Having sampled the menu we discovered that this loyalty is not misguided. We started with pâté casalingo (£3.85) a rich pâté served with toast, and antipasto misto (£6.65) an impressive selection of Italian meats. Next I chose scampi fritti (£9.95), scampi with garlic dip, salad and chips while my partner went for cotoletta Milanese (£13.95) veal in breadcrumbs served with spaghetti bolognese which was declared 'wonderful!'. We washed our main course down with a lovely bottle of Montepulciano (£14.50). After deciding that we definitely didn't

Coconut Grove
Mexican Restaurant

A RED HOT FRESH SENSATION!!!

Relax, savour & enjoy our Mexican experience...
...and let your tongue dance, skip & sensualize...

0800 698 1409

3 Lochrin Terrace, Edinburgh

The Carriage House

The Carriage House's good food and polite service make for a truly Morningside experience.

*"A very civilised evening...
a great place for a relaxing night out"*

Susan Dalgety, Evening News

Try The Carriage House Bistro Now!

Serving lunch and dinner,
Table d'Hôte, Grill & A La Carte Menus.

**45 Morningside Road, Edinburgh
0131 466 7666**

Great Food at Great Value with Passion!

LOTHIAN ROAD, TOLLCROSS, BRUNTSFIELD & MORNINGSIDE

have room for desert we still couldn't resist gelato alla menta ice cream served with mint sauce and kiwi fruit (£3.85) and banana al gelato, banana split (£3.55). To finish we relaxed with espressos and liqueurs sure that we would be back soon to sample more of Pasquale's delicious menu. A three-course lunch menu is also available from 12pm until 2.30pm for £5.95. **AL**

Clay Oven C7

Tandoori isn't new to Scotland, but it's good to find authenticity that can still give a nod to more British Asian innovations. The atmosphere here is homely, the service attentive and the menu extensive. After being served the inevitable but welcome poppadoms with lime pickle and mango chutney, we tried king prawn on puri (£4.50) and fish kebab (£2.95). The first was presented in a sauce that was sweet, subtle and ineffably pleasing, whilst the latter came with two on the side: one mild, one spicy and both rich. We then had lamb pasanda (marinated and cooked in a mild, creamy almond sauce, £5.95) and tandoori murgh (half a spring chicken marinated in yoghurt with delicate herbs and spices then skewered and roasted in a clay oven, £5.95), all accompanied by sabzi pilau (basmati stir-fried with saffron and mixed vegetables, £2.25) and special rice (basmati with peas and vegetables, £2.25). Pistachio kulfi (flavoured frozen dessert, £2.25) and dahli mistin (sweet dumplings in yoghurt, £2.25) rounded the meal off perfectly. All in all, the Clay Oven is a truly satisfying and highly recommended dining experience. **DDR**

Great Wall B5

Edinburgh's Chinese restaurants cannot be mentioned without reference to The Great Wall, where excellent Chinese food is guaranteed, with service to match. After settling in to a nice corner table and perusing the extensive menu, we started with the aromatic crispy duck (half £12.95). The duck was meaty and succulent, and perfectly accompanied by the pancakes, spring onions and sauce. For main course my companion chose the chicken in satay sauce (£8.05) which she was very pleased with. I had the fried crispy shredded beef (£8.25), which had a perfect crispy texture to the tender meat. Both were served with fried rice (£1.90 each). We finished with pineapple fritter in syrup (£2.45) and toffee banana (£3.45), which was small balls of banana with a toffee crunch coating. This large, lively restaurant is perfect for both big parties and couples. With its guaranteed good food The Great Wall attracts a varied group of regulars. Their business lunches are great value and well worth a try, as are their evening

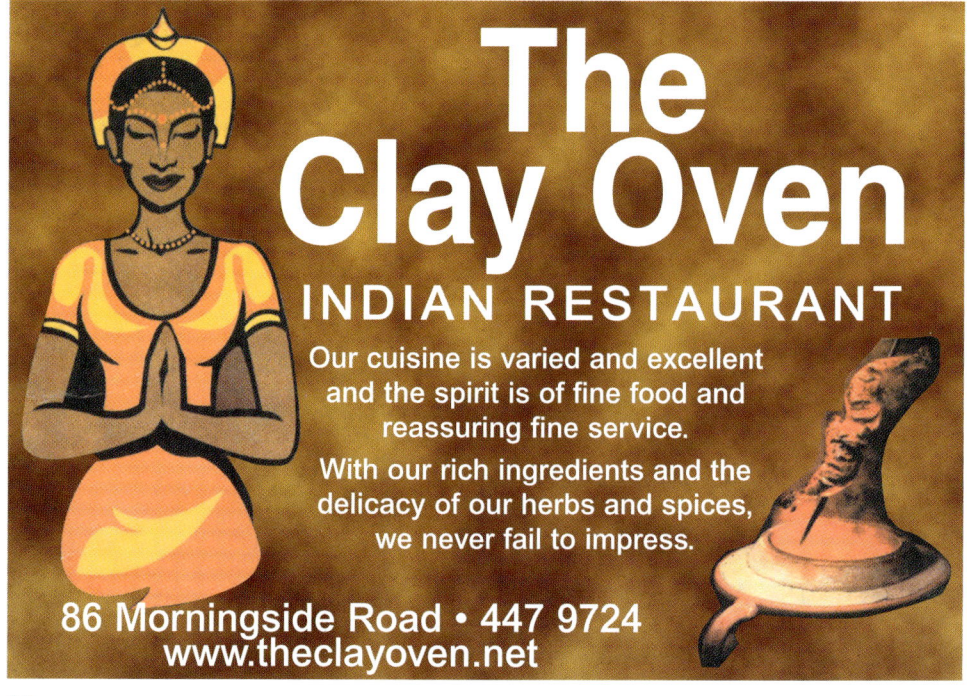

The Clay Oven
INDIAN RESTAURANT

Our cuisine is varied and excellent and the spirit is of fine food and reassuring fine service.

With our rich ingredients and the delicacy of our herbs and spices, we never fail to impress.

86 Morningside Road • 447 9724
www.theclayoven.net

GREAT WALL
CHINESE RESTAURANT
大富城大酒家

105-109 LOTHIAN ROAD EDINBURGH 0131 229 7747/7595

ENJOY CHINESE CUISINE AT ITS BEST IN OUR ORIENTAL SURROUNDINGS AND SOCIABLE ATMOSPHERE

Pizza & Pasta Italian-style Restaurant of the Year 1995. Joint winner with two others nationwide

L'Amore-D'Italia
Ristorante & Pizzeria
97-101 Fountainbridge
228 5069

Pasquales
Ristorante & Pizzeria

169 Gilmore Place
Tel: 0131 228 3115
5 mins from King's Theatre

LOTHIAN ROAD, TOLLCROSS, BRUNTSFIELD & MORNINGSIDE

Edinburgh
Food Guide

set menus starting a £14.90 a head. The Great Wall have got the mix of excellent food, good value, atmosphere and service just right. **BO'R**

L'Amore d'Italia B6
With so many Italian restaurants in Edinburgh, finding something a little bit different is a big achievement. That is definitely what we found here with a combination of excellent Italian food served within a friendly, dynamic and memorable environment. While we ate we were entertained by the owner, Guiseppe, who sang favourite karaoke classics, with many guests dancing and joining in. We began our meal with calamari fritti (£5.95), also available as a main course and snails in garlic sauce (£5.45). To follow we enjoyed pizza calzone (£7.45), which definitely earned its reputation as a speciality of the house, stuffed with salami, cheese, mushrooms and hot sausage. We also had spaghetti puttenesca, which was tomato sauce with capers, anchovies, olives and garlic (£6.45). We accompanied our meal with garlic bread (£2.30) and a bottle of house white (£9.95). To finish we had a very refreshing sorbetto del giorno (£2.95) and tiramisu (£3.45).

The restaurant also serves a special two-course lunch (£4.95) and a three course early evening meal, a bargain at (£7.50). A superbly varied menu, a real party atmosphere combined with high quality food and excellent service are enough to make anyone love this Italian. **VI**

La Bagatelle C6
A warm inviting glow and a classic French atmosphere welcome you to La Bagatelle, reminiscent of a peaceful restaurant in Provençe. We started with Kir Mousseaux at £2.85, refreshing and fruity. There is an extensive à la carte menu featuring a host of French classics and vegetarian dishes but we ate from the table d'hôte, excellent value at £19.95. All stocks and sauces are made on the premises and this shone out in the rich flavours. I started with salmon and prawn mousse served with tartare sauce, while my partner supped tasty cauliflower and blue cheese soup. We followed up with breast of pheasant with redcurrant and port sauce and chicken suprême filled with date forcemeat served on a sweet pepper coulis. A bottle of the house white: a crisp green Château Monereau Sauvignon Blanc at £10.95 washed it down admirably. To finish off some caramelised apple tart with Calvados and profiteroles filled with vanilla ice cream topped with warm chocolate sauce. Coffee with chocolates was well worth £1.50 extra. Lunch menus start at £8.50 for 2 courses and £10.50 or try a themed evening on the last Wednesday of every month. **AB**

Jacques C6
At Gillespie Place, convenient for the King's Theatre and Cameo cinema, Stephanie and Eric utilise their knowledge of the Mayenne region of France, to create attractive French cuisine in a comfortable setting. The cosy lamp-lit room is a haven for relaxed dining. Prices are given for main courses: the cost of your starters and desserts included. My partner started with the salade du chef of warm potatoes, smoked duck, salad leaves and shallot dressing, topped by a poached egg, while I settled for sumptuous smoked salmon with avocado mousse and lemon and basil butter. My partner progressed to an exquisite lemon sole with lardons, roast potato and lemon butter (£15.90) while I chose roast lamb shank with lentils, bacon, garlic and rosemary jus (£19.90) and we shared a vegetable platter. I luxuriated in the tasty tarte tatin, while partner thrilled to chef's extended deadline for his superb galette des roies. A nice, light Beaujoulais Villages (£13.25) rounded off the meal handsomely. We lingered over coffee, hesitating to leave. Jacques is open noon-2.30pm and 5.30pm-11pm. At lunch (£6.90) you can bring your own wine, pre-theatre including coffee is £8.20. **CT**

Lazio's B5
Lazio's is a welcoming and lively Italian restaurant and although it was mid-week in January when we dined, the place was exceedingly well patronized.

La Bagatelle
Restaurant Français

Fresh Scottish produce makes the French connection at La Bagatelle

Open: 12-2pm, 6pm-10.30pm

The auld alliance at its culinary best

Proprietors
Christophe Pelletier & Karen Perschke

www.leisurenet.co.uk

22a Brougham Place. Tel: 0800 698 1431

JACQUES

TRADITIONAL BISTRO FRANCAIS

Lunch Menu: £5.90 (2 crs) £6.90 (3 crs)
Pre & Post Dinner Menu: £8.90 (2 crs + coffee)
Dinner Menu: from £12.90 (3 crs)

Open 7 days a week • 50 yards from The Kings Theatre
Mon-Sat: Lunch and Dinner. Sun 5.30-10.30pm. BYOB (lunchtime only)

8 Gillespie Place Tollcross 0131 229 6080

Fri & Sat
12noon - 3am
Sun
12noon - 1.30am

Mon-Thurs
5pm - 1.30am

Ristorante
LAZIO

95 Lothian Rd • 0131 229 7788
www.lazio-restaurant.co.uk

LOTHIAN ROAD, TOLLCROSS, BRUNTSFIELD & MORNINGSIDE

Sipping the house red (£11.20 per litre carafe) we pondered over the comprehensive menu. My colleague started with cozze alla marinara, mussels in garlic and tomato (£5.50) while I had the insalata caprese, sliced tomatoes, mozzarella and basil (£4.80). The long-serving waiters are friendly yet the service is attentive, and the restaurant has a relaxed atmosphere. Our main courses were risotto Gloria, with mushrooms, ham and peppers, (£6.00) and tagliatelle crema, with cream, ham and mushrooms (£6.30), with a mixed salad to share (£2.20). All the dishes were nicely presented, tasty and the portions generous! And we somehow managed dessert. Homemade Sicilian cheesecake (£3.00) and cassata siciliana (£3.00), Italian ice cream, with a caffe latte (£1.20) to complement the meal. Lazio's is open Monday to Thursday 5.00pm-1.00am, Friday to Saturday Noon-3.00am and Sunday Noon-1.00am. An Italian restaurant worth a visit – and it now has its own gift vouchers, which are proving popular and rightly so! **MAB**

The Grill Room B5

A gold thistle motif shines proudly from the crockery, a mark of prestige that hints at the finest service and food Scotland has to offer. The menu explains, entices and enchants, whilst the set lunch menu is very popular with the neighbouring finance houses (two courses with a glass of wine/mineral water £24.50, three courses for £27.50), a slice of luxurious indulgence that fits neatly into any lunch hour. We began with appetisers of crêpe parmentiere with shallots and sage, roasted chestnuts, butternut and balsamic dressing (£9), and vigneronne salad with roasted quail breast and crisp truffle ravioli (£11.50). Entrées were tournedos of monkfish and Provençale crust, puy lentils and

lie de vin sauce with bacon adding a crisp kick to the melting fish (£21), and fillet of lightly smoked roe venison with caramelised endives, honey and thyme jus (£21.50). The venison is smoked on the premises, lightly flavoured and served medium ensuring a moist melt in the mouth experience. Desserts were gourmandise of chocolate with vanilla and chocolate sauce (£6.50) and coupe of homemade ice cream and sorbet with fruit coulis (£5.50), much like The Grill itself, a perfect mix of refreshment and enrichment. **RRH**

Terrace Restaurant at the Sheraton Grand B5

A terrace should always provide a great view and The Sheraton affords two - depending on which way you look. Outside, Festival Square has a brand new bubbling 'lunar rock' fountain, overlooked by The Castle. Inside are polished marble floors, new-colonial chairs and tables, much greenery and - ah - the buffet. Mouths watering at the prospect, we began at the salad table with our own selections of marinated herring, fresh and smoked salmon, rare roast beef, Greek salad, leafy greens and fresh olive bread. Cooked-to-order stir-fry followed, choosing shrimps, monkfish and salmon in a Thai green curry sauce, and minute steak and monkfish in a teriyaki sauce, both served with stir-fried vegetables. Refreshed, refuelled and ready we embarked on course two and a half – enjoying roast of the day, chicken and Greek cheese quiche with buttery potatoes and roast parsnip chips. Resisting nothing, dessert was a glistening pecan pie and mango cheesecake with ladles of homemade ice cream. At only £19.95 for three courses and £16.50 for two, a view of the bill is also a pleasure. **PM**

Samui Thai B6

This small but stylish Thai restaurant is slightly off the beaten track, but well worth the effort to find. With its elegant décor, friendly welcome and attentive staff, Samui offers the perfect venue for a quiet, intimate meal. The bilingual menu is extensive, with a great selection of vegetarian and fish dishes. To start, try the Thai fish cakes with Oriental salad (£4.95), or the prawn tempura with sweet chilli dipping sauce (£4.95). For main courses the choices are varied, including curries, stir-fries and noodle dishes. The duck stir-fry with ginger, mushroom and spring onion (£7.95) is delicate in flavour but delicious and filling, while the king prawn green curry (£7.95) is simply exquisite. A range of rice varieties to accompany the curry, and a bottle of house Chardonnay (£8.95) to wash it all down completes a truly special dining experience. Take away is also available at a 10% discount. Samui, a superb Thai treat. **CR**

New Bangalore C6

Named after the beautiful garden city in Southern India, the New Bangalore (by the Kings Theatre) is a cultivating, exciting and diverse tandoori eating experience. The emphasis is on providing delicious and plentiful dishes to meet all budgets and offering an extensive selection of Indian cuisine, including an impressive array of vegetarian options. After knowledgeable guidance from the cheery waiting staff I started with the intriguingly spiced murgh chat (£3.45), whilst my partner enjoyed her mildly spiced Eastern prawns with tamarind and coconut chutney (£4.15). We admired the spectacular, specially commissioned photographs of India adorning the walls as we

Samui Authentic Thai Restaurant

The Banquet is very good value for money, with 6 starters and 3 main courses at only £16.95 per head

"The food is excellent and service is charming"
Susan Dalgety, Evening News

BYOB Weekdays and Sunday
10% Discount on Takeaways
Home Delivery Service

95 Gilmore Place Edinburgh EH3 9NU, 0800 698 1447

Established since 1984
The Restaurant with a difference

BANGALORE
TANDOORI
RESTAURANT

Multi Award Winning
Authentic Indian cuisine
at very reasonable prices.
BYOB option available.

Mon-Fri Noon-2pm, 5.30pm-12.00am
Sat & Sun 5pm-1am

52 Home Street
(opp. Kings Theatre)
Tel: 0800 698 1408 Fax: 0131 221 9170

JASMINE

红茶馆

■Chinese Restaurant■

32 Grindlay Street

Edinburgh

Tel: 0800 698 1429

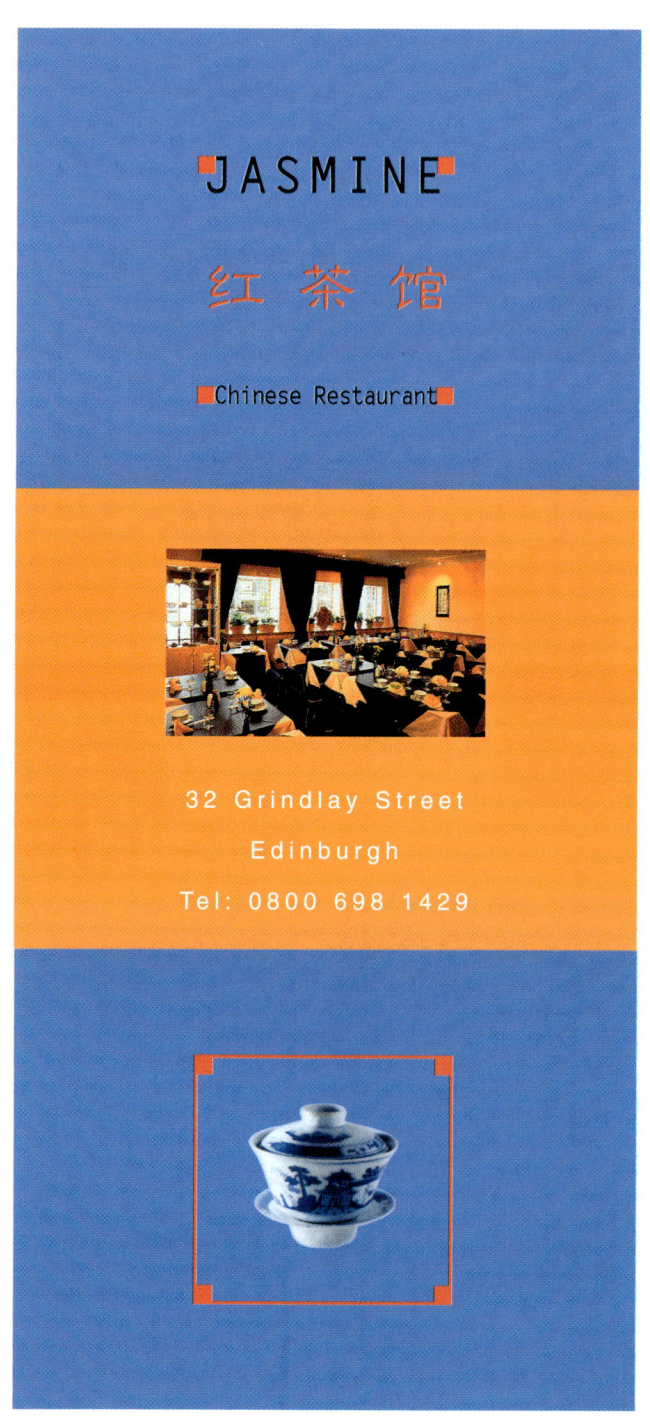

awaited main courses of nurjahan chicken pasanda (£6.95) and speciality jaipuri chicken (£6.95), which swiftly arrived in massive, colourfully presented proportions. Both were excellent. Somehow we managed to squeeze in peshwari nan (£2.20), pilau rice (£2.20) and the gorgeous and recommended bindi bhajee (crunchy vegetables, £2.70). As we polished off our Cobra beer (£2.20) we heard about the innovative plans for the artistic development of the restaurant. It will be well worth visiting to see how this intriguing venture continues to grow. **JJF**

Jasmine B5

It was a bitterly cold evening when we ventured into the exotic warmth that is the Jasmine Restaurant. An eaterie renowned for seafood specialities we were pleasantly surprised by the size and variety of the menu. Situated by bustling Lothian Road the restaurant was busy but unobtrusive, allowing for a hub-bub of noise but ensuring an atmosphere of privacy. We warmed up with a bottle of house white (£9) and the mixed starter for two, a platter containing a selection of crab, spring rolls, dim sum and many more (£12). The perfect way to whet your appetite. Both being unable to resist the temptation of seafood, my partner and I selected the spicy prawns Peking-style (£8.80) and mixed seafood in pineapple (£12.50) with fried rice (£2.50). They proved to be unashamedly delicious. Although we were deliriously sated, we felt we could not surpass the toffee banana (£4.50) and lychee (£5.20) desserts. Admittedly struggling with our coffee and mints (£1.60) we emerged from the Jasmine back into the frost without so much as a grumble. **CSR**

Eating out in Newington, Mayfield & Marchmont

Edinburgh's south side has seen a rapid rise in the number of bars and restaurants to throw open their doors and take advantage of the thriving hustle and bustle that characterises this area of town. Two of the most noticeable new comers are Borough, exhibiting an all-embracing quality and style that outstrips the rather overrated bars you will find on the main drag.

For really exceptional food, our year-in year-out favourite remains Potters Fine Dining, which offers culinary delight using the finest of Scottish ingredients. For an inviting atmosphere and contemporary cuisine, try the New Bell. If you fancy something from the orient, the Dragon Way had our reviewer in seventh heaven.

Serving African cuisine in an informal setting is Nile Valley, which comes highly recommended by anyone who's ventured in.

Nile Valley   E6

East African cuisine is largely an unfamiliar concept amongst the milieu of Edinburgh restaurants, but an evening sampling the aromatic array of food at Nile Valley and you will undoubtedly become a life-long convert. We started with chicken wings marinated in Sudanese spices, fried and served with shutta (£3.50), and a feta cheese salad complemented by flat bread (£3.50). The entrée left us positively salivating as we awaited our main course. Not to be disappointed, I was served up a truly delicious chicken breast garnished in sesame sauce with coriander and couscous (£8.75), whilst my partner devoured her fish in tomato and apricot sauce with vegetables, salad and couscous (£10.95). To complete our journey of East African delight, we shared coconut ice cream (£2.50) and baclava (£2.50). There are many more undiscovered delights on the menu and, as it is BYOB with free corkage, I will be back to sample some more. If you wish for a break from the norm then take a step inside the Nile Valley. CSR

Mothers Restaurant E6

This southside restaurant is bright, bold and sizzling and its helpful staff ensure that the atmosphere and décor as colourful as the food. You may think you've tasted the entirety of Mexican cuisine but Mothers' innovative menu opens up new worlds. For a starter I had mini quesadillas (three small flour tortillas filled and grilled with chorizo and cheese, £3.95) whilst my partner had deep-fried potato skins with melted cheese and spring onions, served with sour cream and chives (£3.95). My main course was an immensely satisfying Mexican paella (£12.25), strips of chicken and chargrilled beef, with chorizo, peppers, olives and chillies, bound in Mexican spiced rice and served with prawns and warm flour tortillas. Meanwhile, my partner chose the shrimp fajita-style salad (£8.95), served with salsa, guacamole, sour cream, and

---

Mother's Restaurant

Delicious authentic Mexican cooking in a relaxed, rustic environment

- Regular Promotions
- Student Discount
- Parties Welcome
  (disabled access)

Open Tuesday - Sunday
6pm til late

Fully Licensed

107-109 St Leonard's St,
Edinburgh
0800 698 1461

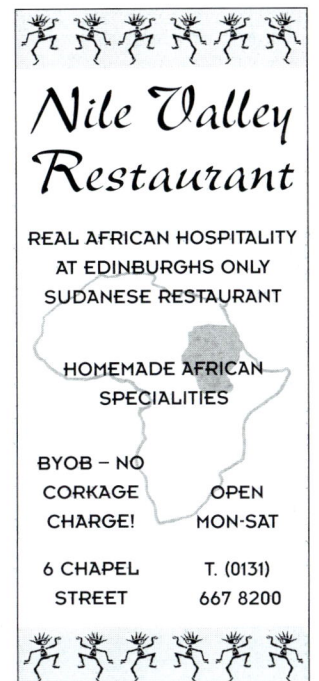

Nile Valley Restaurant

REAL AFRICAN HOSPITALITY AT EDINBURGHS ONLY SUDANESE RESTAURANT

HOMEMADE AFRICAN SPECIALITIES

BYOB – NO CORKAGE CHARGE!

OPEN MON-SAT

6 CHAPEL STREET

T. (0131) 667 8200

NEWINGTON, MAYFIELD AND MARCHMONT

THE NEW BELL restaurant

'a blend of traditional and contemporary cooking using the freshest scottish produce served in a casual and inviting atmosphere'

233 causewayside, eh9 1ph
two minutes from the meadows
0131 668 2868
www.newbell.com

warmed flour tortillas. Finally, we chose sticky toffee pudding (£3.75) and deep-fried tortillas (£4.25) from a selection of mouth-watering desserts. The drinks menu includes a selection of sociable cocktails (£2.95 glass, £7.00 half pitcher and £12.00 pitcher). **DDR**

The New Bell E7
Reached via the Old Bell Inn downstairs, the New Bell boasts low beams, crisp, white linen and gleaming wood panelling, whilst efficient and lively staff add relaxed warmth to the mix. Enjoying a crisp South African Chenin Blanc (£7.95 per bottle), we chose starters of tender steamed mussels in a white wine sauce studded with strands of saffron (£5.00), and seared scallops with basil and balsamic vinegar (£5.50). After a suitable pause we were served with equally excellent main courses. Wild boar sausages in a rich red wine and caramelised shallot gravy with creamy olive oil and garlic mash (£8.25) had my companion in raptures, whilst I savoured perfectly roasted monkfish served with an inspired tomato and red pepper butter (£11.00). We finished off with pistachio nut pavlova with seasonal fruits (£4.00), and traditional crêpes with lemon and orange sauce (£3.75). The best local ingredients are obtained to create an incredibly diverse, daily changing, modern Scottish menu, available from 5.30pm Tue-Sun **EM**

The Dragon Way E7
This Chinese restaurant makes you think you've stepped straight into the Far East. I took my Cantonese friend to judge its merits and she instantly felt at home in the colourful interior, full of curios from Hong Kong. Friendly staff helped us order and we were soon tucking into bean curd and mixed vegetable soup, and delicious hot and sour soup with bean curds, bamboo shoots, chicken and rice wine (both £3.50). A mixed platter of crispy

Dragon Way

where "Cooking is an art of living"

Newington 74 - 78 South Clerk St
Tel: 0800 298 3413
24 hour booking service: 07973 211228

Marchmont Takeaway
Tel: 0800 298 3470
Enjoy our delicious food
Takeaway or Delivered

Visit our new restaurant @ Port Seton
27c Links Road Tel: 01875 813 551

pastries followed, comprising wan ton, Cantonese spring rolls, prawn toasts, and crispy seaweed with a hot and sour dip (£9.00). A few glasses of the house Merlot (£8.90), set us up for main courses: one of the chef's specialities, lamb with ginger and spring onion, and Szechuan vegetables, hot, fiery, sweet and delicious. Both were accompanied by vegetable fried rice served inside a fresh pineapple. The dessert menu was tempting but we settled for coffee (£1.20) before returning to Edinburgh's grey streets. My friend's verdict? A taste of home! **AB**

Susie's Diner E6
This popular academic haunt works much like a standard canteen: look at the menu board on the wall, grab a tray then await service at the counter. I chose a large plate (£4.95), which entitled me to three hot choices and one salad portion. I plumped for spinach and ricotta flan, courgette and mushroom quiche and roasted tomato stuffed with red pepper and mushroom risotto. Opting for a medium plate (£3.95), my partner sampled two hot choices and one salad. The pincholada stuffed with mushroom, spinach and chickpeas was mildly spiced and came with an optional yoghurt sauce. This, together with rice and celery, apple and walnut salad, proved delightful. Bottles of organic wine (£9.95) are available, as are imported biers (£2.40) and 'smoothies' (£1.95). For dessert, the courgette and poppy seed cake (£1.75) and banoffi pie (£2.00) both highlights. Don't expect to be wined-and-dined at Susie's, but do expect rustic décor, an unpretentious atmosphere and, above all, quality vegetarian and vegan food. **GB**

Sambuca E7
A new addition to Edinburgh's southside, Sambuca deals in traditional Italian fare at refreshingly affordable prices. Relaxed, airily pleasant and awash with shades of lavender and baby blue, this diminutive, bustling eatery attracts a mixture of families and couples. Its menu is lengthy and as well as soups and starters it takes in pasta, pizza, salad, seafood, steak, veal and chicken. There are plenty of vegetarian options too. My partner started with cozze fresche (fresh mussels cooked in garlic, onions, breadcrumbs, wine cheese and cream at £4.50). I opted for a hefty portion of caprese (mozzarella, fresh tomato, olives and basil at £3.95). The main courses came in the shape of delicately flavoured scampi thermadore - scampi and rice, mushrooms, white wine, béchamel sauce and mozzarella (£7.80) and stecca pizzaiola – sirloin steak cooked in tomato, garlic, herbs and white wine served with Lionnaise potatoes (£10). Too full to even contemplate the list of desserts, we ambled out into the evening sunshine. **DK**

De Niro's E6
This fine Italian restaurant is a long-standing favourite amongst many due to its friendly, intimate atmosphere and, not least, the superiority of its food. The comprehensive menu contains a number of traditional dishes as well as several unique recipes that have to be experienced. We started with the flavoursome minestrone soup (£1.95) and a delicious plate of onion soup (£1.95), before moving on to the trustworthy penne quattro formaggi (£5.50) and tagliatelle caruso (£5.50), a traditional vegetarian dish comprising mushrooms, tomatoes, peppers, peas and cream. After washing down our main courses with a caraffe of smooth house white (£9.00), it was time to tackle the sweet menu. We plumped for the Caribbean sundae (£3.15), dairy chocolate & vanilla ice cream topped with cream, vermicelli, rum and raison, and coppa De Niro's (£3.25), strawberry and vanilla ice cream, fresh fruit salad,

PATAKA
"SIMPLY THE BEST"

Pataka is one of the Top Ten Indian restaurants in Scotland (Scotland on Sunday), also reviewed and highly recommended by many of the local papers, and food guides. We only use the freshest and finest ingredients to prepare authentic Indian cuisine. Our years of experience is your satisfaction guaranteed.

Home Delivery Available
(orders over £12.00 within 2 mile radius)

www.pataka.co.uk
190 Causewayside, Edinburgh. Tel: 668 1167 / 662 9434

Sambuca
RISTORANTE ITALIANO

It's like having your meal cooked by your Italian Grandmother.
Daily Record

IF YOU ENJOY ITALIAN TRADITIONAL FOOD AT REASONABLE PRICES SAMBUCA IS THE ONLY PLACE TO BE!

Starter & Maincourse £10

RESERVATIONS: 0131 667 3307

103 Causewayside, Edinburgh EH9 1QG

amarena cherries and Cointreau. A special lunchtime menu is also offered, which includes a good selection of dishes at very reasonable prices. **GB**

Bourough   E7
Callison Eaton's new venture is nothing short of impressive. Huge leather couches fused with a spacious interior simply invite you to unwind. The restaurant delights in sumptuous booths where couples dine intimately and larger groups revel in the comfort and space the designer has afforded them. The menu revealed a selection of Scottish fare with inspired international twists guaranteed to please the palate. I delved in to my vegetarian soup (£2.75), whilst my friend voraciously attacked her duck terrine (£4.25). We followed with sea bass in bouillabaisse sauce (£11.75) and roast duck breast in a chilli, lime and honey sauce, served with braised vegetables and side salad.

POTTERS
fine dining
RESTAURANT
A true taste of modern cuisine

"Potters affects a rather grand air, fortunately it matches it with food that ranks at the top of the evolutionary scale"
Neil MacLean
The Sunday Times

"We left convinced of the chef's talents"
Gillian Glover
Scotsman

T. 662 9010

Kildonan Lodge Hotel
27 Craigmillar Park
Newington
EH16 5PE

106

The hearty portions left us full to the brim and almost unable to face dessert, but the banana fritter with coconut ice cream (£4.25) and pana cotta with fruit compôte (£3.75) still found their way onto our table. Bourough offers delicious food, relaxed surroundings and professional, jovial staff - all of which ensure a great dining experience. **CSR**

Fenwicks   E7
This is the type of restaurant you walk by and wonder what's inside. Step in and find candlelight, casual music and warm colours; the kind of place you could take your lover, parents, or friends before a night on the tiles. From the dinner menu (£16.95 for 3 courses) we started with the platter of cured fish dressed with honey and mustard, and the saffron and pine kernel risotto. The risotto was supremely creamy, pine nuts adding interest and texture but fish was favourite, melting and drifting, an auspicious omen for that to follow. Main courses of lamb daube Provençale, and goat's cheese, pimento and asparagus tart with spinach and pepper coulis did not disappoint. Desserts of layered chocolate terrine with mango and raspberry coulis and plum and cognac crème brûlée formed an exclamation mark to the end of this culinary sentence. Fenwicks' lunch menu is a more manageable version of dinner, with the option of small plates (£1.75-£3.25) and large plates (£2.75-£5.50). **RRH**

Potters Fine Dining   E7
The chef and proprietor of Potters was once a member of the Canadian Junior Olympic culinary team, but has now graduated onto creating cuisine of gold medal standard at this captivating restaurant. The dining room exudes warmth and charm due to the combination of ornate surroundings and first class service. Dinner comes at a reasonable £23.95 for two courses or three for £26.95. We enjoyed starters of cream of spinach soup, and a roulade of corn-fed chicken stuffed with apricot and pine kernels, served with spiced pear chutney. Mains were Aberdeen Angus beef fillet on a bed of sautéed new potato, topped with a quenelle of pork liver pâté, and roast cannon of pork fillet rolled in a walnut and herb crust. Our wine was a new experience, a spicy Canadian Merlot (£16.95), from an unusual but well-chosen list. Potters' reputation for the finest fresh ingredients, combined with imagination and flair is safe and this gem of a restaurant remains one of the city's most worthwhile discoveries. **RRH**

Namaste North Indian Frontier   E7
Opened in August 2001, Namaste is a new sensation in Indian cuisine and serves dishes unlike any other restaurant in Edinburgh. Based on Mugahli and Punjabi food, the recipes used are over 300 years old and steeped in tradition. The method of cookery is another original feature of Namaste, with food being slow-cooked overnight in a clay oven, while the décor, service and atmosphere combine to offer an authentic northern Indian dining experience. Starters include crab shorba (£4.50), punjabi samosas (£3.50) and palak paneer (£3.75), homemade cottage cheese cooked in a spinach-based gravy. The main course options are equally appealing and include murgh tikka masala (£6.25), rogan josh (£6.95) and tandoori murgh chicken (half £5.70, whole £9.50). Try and leave a little room for the delicious sweets on offer too, such as the kulfi (£4.50) and the phirni (£3.90), an Indian milk pudding with cardamon and saffron. Namaste is open for lunch every day 12noon-2pm, and for dinner 6pm-11pm (Sun-Thu) and 6pm-11.30pm (Fri-Sat). **GB**

NAMASTE

North Indian Frontier Cuisine

41/42 West Preston Street
Freephone 0800 698 1435

Eating Vegetarian in Edinburgh

If you are vegetarian and looking for something to eat in Edinburgh then do not despair. There are plenty of places to find good vegetarian food and even the most ardent carnivores will find it hard not to appreciate the quality of ingredients and cooking on offer. The ever-popular Bann UK on the Royal Mile offers an expansive range of vegetarian and vegan options, boasting a loyal legion of diners. Just off the Cowgate you'll find Black Bo's, a restaurant that has dismantled the notion that vegetarian food is stodgy and over wholesome and serves a variety of tempting and unusual dishes.

For a veritable smorgasbord of tasty vegetarian fare pop into Susie's Diner, where the food is good and the options are limitless. A quick stroll away is the award-winning Kalpna with it's Gujarati inspired menu combines fresh ingredients and attentive staff to produce an informal restaurant which is a pleasure to dine in.

Kalpna   E6

The name of this vegetarian Indian restaurant is translated to mean 'a combination of imagination and creation', and such a name could not be more suited to the maker of such delicious, innovative food. For starters, we chose the Samosa (£2.50) served with dates and tamarind sauce and Aloo Firdoshi (£3.00), potato barrels stuffed with pistachio, raisins, coriander and a combination of herbs and delicate spice. Moving on to the main course, we were served dam aloo kashmeri (£7.50), with pilau rice (£2.25), and matar paneer (£5.00), a delicious recipe containing peas, homemade cheese, spiced onions, tomatoes and garlic, with coconut milk rice (£4.50). An impressive selection of wines and champagnes are available from £9.50, including connoisseur's choices. All desserts are £2.50 and very appealing, and we tried the mango kulfi malai (Indian mango ice cream flavoured with sweet spices) and the gulab jaman (milk sponge balls in spiced syrup). Kalpna also operates a buffet every Wednesday (5.30pm-11pm) for only £9.95 per person.   **GB**

Susie's Diner   E6

This popular academic haunt works much like a standard canteen, where you look at the menu board on the wall, grab a tray then await service at the counter. I chose a large plate (£4.95), which entitled me to three hot choices and one salad portion. As all options are visible at the counter, it was difficult to decide, but I plumped for spinach and ricotta flan, courgette and mushroom quiche and roasted tomato stuffed with red pepper and mushroom risotto. Opting for a medium plate (£3.95), my partner sampled two hot choices and one salad. The pincholada stuffed with mushroom, spinach and chickpeas was mildly-spiced and came with an optional yoghurt sauce. This, together with rice and celery, apple and walnut salad, proved delightful. Bottles of organic wine (£9.95) are available, as are imported

---

SUSIE'S DINER Wholefoods

Serving a great selection of vegetarian & vegan hot dishes & salads

Mon: 9am - 8pm
Tues - Sat: 9am - 9pm
(open Sun during Festival)

No need to book
Licensed & BYOB

51 - 53 West Nicholson St
Tel: 667 8723

Kalpna Restaurant

vegetarian wholefood restaurant

Lunch Menu £5.00
Buffet night every Wednesday only £9.95

Good Food Guide
Egon Ronay Recommended

2-3 St Patrick Square
Tel: 0800 698 1457

bann uk

Cafe | restaurant | bar

Cafe | restaurant | bar

new
**new
urbannhangsuite
Open 'til 3am
d.j. great food & drinks**

'Innovative and adventurous vegetarian restaurant'
The Herald, 18.5.00

'Proof that style can accompany substance'
The Guardian, 16.6.00

Voted Best restaurant in Edinburgh 2000 by The List readers

modern vegetarian cuisine… with passion!

**5 Hunter Square (Royal Mile)
Edinburgh 0800 197 3515**

VEGETARIAN

biers (£2.40) and 'smoothies' (£1.95). For dessert, the unusual courgette and poppy seed cake (£1.75) was tastier than it may sound, while the banoffi pie (£2.00) was the highlight. Don't expect to be wined-and-dined at Susie's, but do expect rustic décor, an unpretentious atmosphere and, above all, quality vegetarian and vegan food. **GB**

Bann UK   D4
Bann UK has had a facelift and very gorgeous it's looking too. A myriad of subtle lighting effects, add a warmth echoed in the friendly service and laid-back vibe. Enjoying an organic Italian Pinot Grigio (£10.90 a bottle), we chose crispy Thai potato fritters served with a trio of chutneys and relishes, and chicory baked in an emmental and Pernod fondue with herb lid (starters £3.90). Next came vegetarian haggis sausages on horseradish mash with red onion gravy, and crispy aromatic mock duck with stir-fried vegetables and dipping sauce (all main courses £9.80). We finished ourselves off with a vast Baileys cheesecake gâteau and a chocolate and Cointreau mousse (desserts £3.90). This is gourmet vegetarian cuisine guaranteed to please avid meat eaters and vegans alike. You are invited to kick back and loaf at the urbannhangsuite on Friday and Saturday nights where a light menu and DJs promise to feed you up and chill you out from 11pm – 3am.   **EM**

Black Bo's   E4
Black Bo's is a vegetarian restaurant with a difference. My companion, the genuine article, and myself as a non-vegetarian were surprised and pleased to find a wide variety of tempting and unusual dishes available. Vegetarian food has a bit of a reputation for being stodgy and over wholesome but at Black Bo's the menu reads more like an à la carte than your average whole food deli. We began with garlic bread with basil and fresh tomatoes (£3.00) followed by haggis shish kebab flambéed with ginger and Drambuie (yes, it was vegetarian) and pasta with tomato, basil and capers topped with Parmesan shavings. (Both £4.95). Sweet potato and goats cheese baked in filo pastry with flavour rich red onion and garlic marmalade followed, along with peppers stuffed with blue cheese and almond soufflé with a Madeira and molasses sauce. A bottle of Carlos Serres Rioja (£10.50) washed everything down nicely before desserts of a light steamed lemon pudding with cream and rich dark and white chocolate Belgian ice cream. My companion spent most of the meal trying to convert me to vegetarianism. If you could convince me that the food would always be like this, I think I'd do it.   **AB**

BLACK BO'S
www.blackbos.com

Hailed as Scotland's best gourmet vegetarian restaurant

Amongst the very best in Scotland
SCOTLAND THE BEST

Not so much of a way of life, more of a restaurant.

Weekend Booking Recommended

57 - 61 Blackfriars Street,
off the Royal Mile Edinburgh
Tel: 0800 298 2994

Eating out in Leith

Leith is a community in its own right and has flourished under careful regeneration in recent years. Steeped in history, it boasts a plethora of fine bars and restaurants, particularly down on the Shore where the locals and tourists gather to enjoy Leith's vibrant atmosphere.

Malmaison Brasserie dark and sleek, serving high-class cuisine is luxury without the fuss. Holding a prime waterside location on the Shore, you can dine al fresco and watch the world go by. A stone's throw away, set in a building historically used by James 1st, is the Kings Wark, cosy atmosphere combined with great food it's fit for a King! If elegant dining is your desire then (fitz) Henry comes highly recommended or for something a little more casual Starbank Inn allows relaxing views over the Firth of Forth while you eat.

Award-winning cuisine can be enjoyed at Britannia Spice offering a truly memorable dining experience, a little French fancy at Daniel's bistro, hands on Mongolian at Khublai Khans or dolce vita at Kavio's. Leith has much, much more to offer so get down there and sample!

Malmaison G8

With a philosophy of 'great places to eat, great places to meet', Malmaison is more than the sum of its parts. Set in a prime spot on Leith's up and coming Shore the key elements are fantastic atmosphere, friendly service, moody décor, great wine and simple yet delightful food. From a menu of the freshest ingredients, we started with vichyssoise soup with smoked haddock (£4.50) and crispy prawn and avocado salad with paprika roll (£5.95). Mains of citrus chicken wrapped in banana leaf, served with a spicy satay sauce (£11.50), and chargrilled steak bernaise (£13.95) were artful simplicity. We were lucky enough to sample four desserts (all £4.95) recommended by the chef, Mal's signature dish crème brûlée, pannacotta, apple strudel and summer fruits. With their own vineyard, many of the wines offered are exclusive to Mal. We sampled the excellent So Blanc de blancs (£3.50/glass). The express lunch menu offers two courses at £9.95, dinner is two for £12.95, and Sunday lunch has three at £14.95. All in, Malmaison makes for a great time at great value. **CSR**

King's Wark G8

Lying alongside the Water of Leith, the King's Wark does not rely on neon extravagance to haul you in the door. This establishment woos you through the door with a welcoming aura. Once nestled amongst the cosy interior we immediately relaxed into Wark speed. The menu bombards with all manner of freshness and the spicy mushroom soup (£2.50) and foie gras with roasted apples and ginger (£4.95) set a fine tone for the evening. The wild game casserole with root vegetables (£9.95) had a perfect burliness which was only matched by the succulent poached halibut fillet with mussels and white wine sauce (£10.95). Both dishes were accompanied by a heaped selection of vegetables. A frisky Pinot Grois of Argentinian (£11.50) complemented our trust of the service. As punishment for the excessive delight of the main courses we could only share a citrus crème brûlée (£3.50), a crisp and tangy twist to the old favourite. If you lack guilt and feel the need to indulge further there is a fine bar in which to drown your conscience. I can think of no less favourable places to pass an evening in search of gratification. **JF**

Joanna's Cuisine E1

Over the past two years this restaurant off Leith Walk has become a valued addition to Edinburgh's range of Chinese eateries. Specialising in the more elegant flavours of Northern (Peking) cuisine, a low-key 'living room' atmosphere makes you feel more of a guest than a customer. Both décor and music

Malmaison Brasserie

GRAND MENU

MALMAISON BRASSERIES INSPIRED BY THE STYLISH PARISIAN BRASSERIES OF THE TURN OF THE CENTURY.

WHOLESOME FRENCH COOKING FROM A TRADITIONAL BRASSERIE MENU

£9.95 FOR A TWO COURSE LUNCH MENU COMPRIS. MALMAISON GRAND FORMAT MENU, GRAND STYLE, GRAND FOOD, GRAND VALUE. AND NOT A WHIPPET IN SIGHT.

CALL IN OR CALL TO BOOK
EDINBURGH 468 5003

ONE TOWER PLACE LEITH
EDINBURGH
ALSO IN GLASGOW NEWCASTLE
MANCHESTER AND LEEDS

ORDERS FOR SAT 7th APRIL

CAMPBELLS FISH

- 6 x SEA BASS
- 10lb LANGOUSTINES
- 2lb MONKFISH CHEEKS
- 4 LIVE CRAB
- SWORDFISH LOIN
- 3lb SARDINE FILLETS
- 1 SMOKED EEL

BURNSIDE FARM FOODS

- 6 BABY GUINEA FOWL
- BLACK LEG CHICKEN?
- 6 FRESH QUAIL
- 2 PKTS AIR DRIED HAM
- 4lb OSTRICH SAUSAGES

SEA MAGEE

- 2 BAGS MUSSELS
- 2 DOZ OYSTERS
- 6 RABBIT
- 2 FRESH PIKE?
- 1 BOX DISCO SCALLOPS
- BAIN OF TARVES
- 2 x U.K RIB EYE
- 6 x LAMB SHANKS
- 4lb CALVES LIVER
- 1 HAUNCH VENISON
- 10 OATMEAL BEEF OLIVES

KING'S WARK

0131 554 9260

36 THE SHORE LEITH

DANIELS BISTRO

"The most engaging menu I've seen in years"
- The Scotsman

"One of the friendliest bistros ever"
- The Glasgow Herald

Open all day everyday for morning coffee, snacks, lunches and dinner.

88 COMMERCIAL STREET, LEITH, TEL: 0800 698 1459

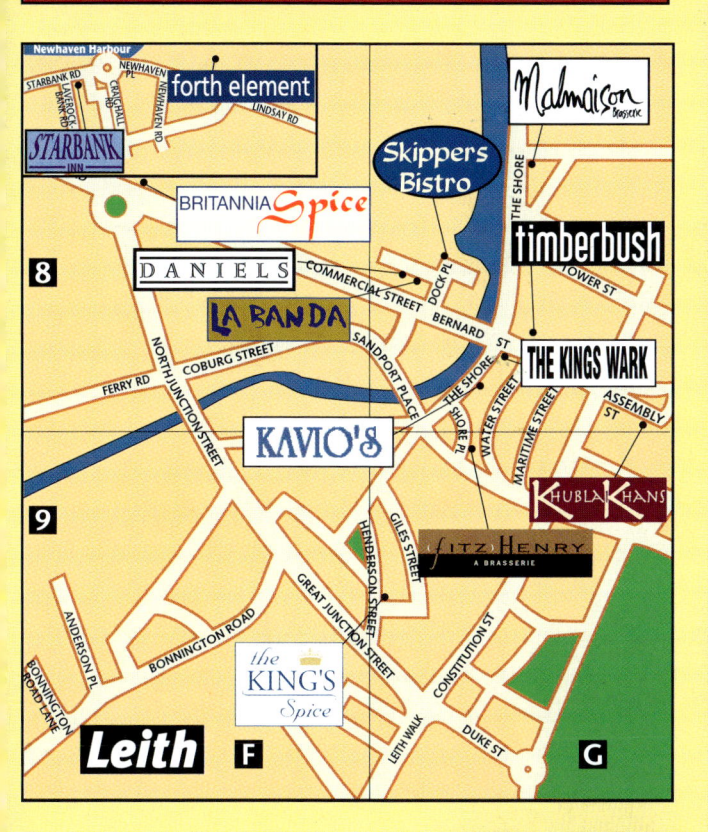

BRITANNIA Spice
Exclusive Exotic Cuisine

Dine in Scotland's Award Winning Restaurant

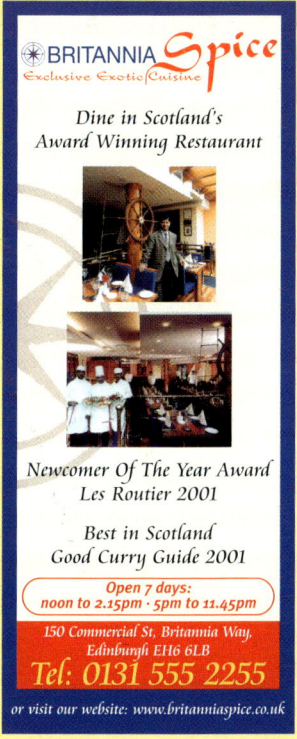

Newcomer Of The Year Award
Les Routier 2001

Best in Scotland
Good Curry Guide 2001

Open 7 days:
noon to 2.15pm • 5pm to 11.45pm

150 Commercial St, Britannia Way,
Edinburgh EH6 6LB
Tel: 0131 555 2255

or visit our website: www.britanniaspice.co.uk

What's on the menu at next generation?

> **Sculpture**: state-of-the-art air-conditioned gym
> **Ace**: indoor and outdoor tennis, squash and badminton courts.
> **Hydrous**: indoor and outdoor pools, plus children's pool.
> **Spa**: relaxing sauna, steam and spa experience.
> **Club Bar and Restaurant**: serving drinks, snacks and meals, from breakfast to dinner.

call: 0131 554 5000

NEXT GENERATION clubs

Malmaison

Where we're serious about produce, serious about cooking, serious about wine, serious about service, but never too serious about ourselves.

Brasserie: 0131 468 5000
1 Tower Place, The Shore, Leith

are subtle and the service relaxed and friendly. We started with deep-fried won tons filled with shrimp and served with a sweet and sour dip (£3.65) and grilled Beijing dumplings stuffed with pork accompanied by some wonderfully gingery Chinese vinegar (£3.45). For a main course I tried sautéed shredded duck with bean sprouts (£6.95) and tomato-flavoured red fried rice (£1.55), whilst my partner enjoyed the more hands-on yellow bean mixed vegetables with pancakes (£7.75). A bottle of well-selected house white, Chateau Planton-Bellevue (£11.55) pleased in complementing the food perfectly. We chose ice cream (£2.25) and banana fritters (£3.35) for dessert but I'm told their speciality home-made green tea ice cream is also well worth a taste (£3.25). Open evenings from 5:30pm and with a take away menu. **DDR**

The King's Spice G9
Situated close to Leith's Shore area, this friendly, comfortable restaurant serves a wide selection of Indian and Bangladeshi cuisine and is very popular amongst locals. This is partly due to the amazing value of its buffet nights, which run Sunday-Thursday, with diners encouraged to eat as much as they like for only £6.95 (or £3.95 for children). A buffet lunch is also available Monday-Friday between 12noon and 2.30pm. However, this popularity is also linked to the high standard of the dishes on offer here. We firstly sampled the samosa (£2.25) and the onion bhajis (£2.25) before being treated further with nurjahan chicken pasanda (£6.10) with basmati palau rice (£2.10), and vegetarian kurmah (£4.50) with fried rice (£2.25). These were accompanied by a soft, sweet nan bread (£1.95) and washed down with the fruity La Fourcade (£8.50), one of the two house whites on offer. Ice cream is always appealing after an Indian meal, and the King's Spice has a fine selection. We chose the coconut half (£2.90) and the pistachio kulfi (£2.75), finishing off a delightful meal in this thoroughly recommended restaurant. **GB**

Skippers G8
Tucked away in a discreet corner of Leith, Skippers is anything but reticent with the fine menu it offers. I began my exploration of the delightful denizens of the deep with smoked salmon and Arbroath smokie roulade (£5.75), the smokie giving a perfect punch to the subtler salmon. My partner's whole king prawns with garlic mayonnaise (£6.20) brought a decent grunt of approval as they were stripped faster than a lap dancer. The Australian Bulletin Place Chardonnay (£12.20) provided an excellent backdrop to roasted monkfish tails with whole roasted garlic and pesto (£14.50). Whilst the marinated fillet of tuna with garlic, chilli and ginger dressing (£12.50) had class washing over my taste buds. To finish off our culinary cruise, warmed white chocolate and raisin cake with orange syrup, and winter berry brûlée (both £3.95) only distinguished Skippers as a superb all-rounder. With Leith now bursting with new eateries Skippers can always be relied upon to give them something to aspire to. **JF**

(fitz) Henry G9
Recently re-launched by new owners, (fitz) Henry has lost none of its exquisite charm but has undergone some changes that undoubtedly enhance its impressive reputation. Now attentive service is coupled with adventurous French dishes, inventively prepared and presented by remaining chef, Hubert Lamort. From the monthly-changing evening menu, I took the vegetarian route. My starter was ravioli of cep with aubergine purée (£6.00), mains were pan-fried potato gnocci with asparagus, spinach, fava beans & petit pois (£10.50), and dessert was peppermint parfait with dark chocolate sauce (£5.50). For meat-eaters, the choice is more diverse. To illustrate, my partner chose dressed crab with celeriac remoulade (£5.50), followed by duck & foie gras torte with sauce rouennaise (£17.50), then toasted broiche with strawberries & peach sorbet (£5.00). An impressive array of wines is available from £11.75, including the aromatic Viognier, Moulin de Ciffre (£22.00). However, if you cannot choose by name alone, short descriptions and recommendations are provided on the list. Classic décor and candlelight ensure that the atmosphere is relatively formal but friendly, while at lunchtime the restaurant exudes a brighter, more airy ambience and offers a weekly-changing menu with set prices from £9.50. **GB**

Forth Element F8
The Forth Element is a cylindrical oasis tucked away in Newhaven and its coastal setting brings spectacular views across the Firth of Forth. At an exceptional £14.50 for 2 courses and £17.50 for 3, I can assure you that the journey out of town is well worth such a breath of fresh air. After we selected a fine Sauvignon Blanc from the extensive list, we began with fresh lobster served with lime and coriander dressing, galia melon with pink grapefruit drizzled in honey and apple syrup. Exquisite. To follow I ordered the honey grilled duck suprême enhanced with Chinese five spices, enoke mushrooms and soy sauce essence, whilst my partner delved into a cutlet of veal with capsicums and citrus sauce. To complete the full circle we choose deserts designed to make you attend the gym out of guilt;

(fitz)Henry
A BRASSERIE

Lunch 12 - 2.30pm
Mon - Fri Set Price Menu

Dinner 6.30 - 10pm
Mon - Sat A La Carte Menu

19 Shore Place, Leith, Edinburgh, EH6 6SW   Tel: 0800 698 1460   Fax: 0131 555 0025   www.fitzhenrys.com

"Tucked away in a quiet corner of Leith, Skippers is a cosy, atmospheric bistro waiting for your discovery. The seafood orientated menu is selected daily and is subject to the day's catch of the Scottish fishing fleets. Look no further out to Sea."

SKIPPERS BISTRO

"the best real bistro in town" Sunday Times

for reservations 0131 554 1018

"THE place to eat seafood in Edinburgh" Where Magazine

1a Dock Place, Leith

chocolate velvet torte with amaretto chantilly cream and toasted almonds, and the curiously named Paris breast with tropical fruit and caramel sauce. Coming up for coffee we basked in the unobtrusive service and charm that the Forth Element encapsulates. **CSR**

Starbank Inn F8
To step into The Starbank is to go back to the days when pubs were warm, friendly places where neighbours gossiped, enjoyed a few pints, and relaxed in an atmosphere free of blaring music and TV screens. From the extensive selection of cask-conditioned ales and malts to the ship memorabilia covering the walls, this is the real thing. We walked through the bar to a smoke-free conservatory, where the Inn's affordable lunches and dinners are served. To start, we whetted our appetites with tasty Madeira herring salad (£2.50), and prawn salad Marie Rose

(£3.50). Next came roast lamb (£5.50), and roast chicken with tarragon cream sauce (£5.50). Both were served with healthy portions of potatoes and vegetables and washed down with a bottle of Leith Gascogne Blanc (£8.00). Homemade fruit pie, and pears and butterscotch sauce (both £2.50) tempted us from the dessert menu. Unfortunately, all good things must come to an end, and after some friendly banter we said our goodbyes and stepped back into the noisy, hurried 21st century. **JFW**

Britannia Spice F8
Newcomer of the Year, included in this Guide's Top Five New restaurants last year, Best in Scotland and even Best in Britain: if the awards being heaped onto Leith's newest gem, Britannia Spice, don't inspire you, then the immaculate maritime splendour of the restaurant itself will surely leave you impressed. Spacious, yet intimate, due to mini-sails

separating the tables, the décor is exceptional and the staff are extremely helpful. From a menu covering Bangladesh, Northern India, Nepal, Thailand and Sri Lanka, we indulged in vegetable samosas (£2.35), tom kar gai (chicken and coconut milk soup) (£3.75), mughlai vegetables (£5.95), kathmandu murgh (a chicken and lentil dish) (£7.95), popadoms (70p), garlic nan (£2.25), aloo khobi (spiced cauliflower and potatoes) (£3.55), pilau rice (£2.75), a bottle of Britannia Spice's own full bodied Beaujolais (£8.95), a balti pot (kulfi with saffron sauce) (£3.95) and two liqueur coffees (£3.50 each). Every mouthful confirmed what we both expected: Britannia Spice fully deserves every one of its accolades. The food, the restaurant and the service: everything at Britannia Spice is outstanding, on the crest of a culinary wave. **JA**

Daniels Bistro G8
Down by Commercial Quay, home of the Scottish Executive and part of the up and coming redeveloped Shore, rests Daniel's Bistro. This particular Friday evening was surprisingly sunny and Daniel's offers the perfect contemporary setting in which to enjoy the waning sunlight and dream of the Continent. Sitting in the conservatory we pondered over the predominantly French menu which incorporates a Scottish twist. Whilst enjoying a crisp, fresh bottle of house white wine (£9.85) imagining we were on the Riviera we tucked into our vegetable crêpe (£3.85) and selection of Alpine cheeses and ham (£4.65), a pleasantly light and refreshing way to begin a meal. For my main course I opted for Daniel's sausages (£6.95) a selection of Alsacien sausages served with garnish and vegetables, whilst my partner delighted in her monkfish à la Bretonne (£11.85) served on rice with seafood and Cognac sauce. A

DANIELS BISTRO

Open all day everyday for morning coffee, snacks, lunches and dinner.

"The most engaging menu I've seen in years"
- The Scotsman

"One of the friendliest bistros ever"
- The Glasgow Herald

88 COMMERCIAL STREET, LEITH,
TEL: 0800 698 1459

THE STARBANK INN

OVERLOOKING "THE FORTH"

Savour home cooked lunches and evening meals in our comfortable, non-smoking conservatory.

Traditional cask conditioned ales and an excellent selection of malts.
Tea and coffee served daily.

64 Laverockbank Road, Newhaven.
Tel 0131-552 4141

BRITANNIA Spice
Exclusive Exotic Cuisine

Dine in Scotland's Award Winning Restaurant

Edinburgh's stunning multi-ethnic restaurant offers a truly memorable dining experience by the royal yacht Brittania

Newcomer Of The Year Award Les Routier 2001

Best in Scotland Award
Good Curry Guide 2001

Open 7 days:
noon to 2.15pm • 5pm to 11.45pm

150 Commercial St, Britannia Way, Edinburgh EH6 6LB

Tel: 0131 555 2255

or visit our website: www.britanniaspice.co.uk

fitting end to any French meal has to be the crème brûlée (£3.85) and sharing this with Daniel's spicy ice cream and butterscotch sauce was a pleasure I would recommend. **CSR**

Khublai Khans G8
Arriving to the sizzling of food and the swiping of swords upon the hotplate, Khublai Khans recreates an exciting style of cooking and cuisine which is of great delight to all who dine there. The set menu (£15.50) offers a selection of starters and desserts and, here's the clincher, as much as you can eat for your main course. We started the evening with choi han, angel hair vermicelli, chicken and beansprouts in piquant mirin sauce and hogan han, steamed mussels and spicy Thai sauce. Enjoying our bottle of sauvignon blanc (£12.95) we eyed the formidable selection at the buffet. Rice or noodles? Chicken, shark or wild boar? All this enhanced by mix your own spice and sauce concoctions such as Emperor's Delight, Khublai Delight or Hordes Delight? Not only does the interactive element make your evening more fun, you can watch the chefs at work on your creation too. All this and unlimited attempts at finding the perfect dish! We followed up with pi Khan, a sumptuous dark chocolate hazelnut pot and an old favourite banoffee pie. Khublai Khan is perfect for group parties and offers a pre-theatre menu from 6pm-7pm for £7.95. **CSR**

Kavio's G8
With its child-friendly, wheelchair accessible, welcoming attitude the Scottish-Italian Kavio's is a real user-friendly restaurant. Happy to cater for large groups and specific dietary requirements (if made in advance) they also boast a good degree of flexibility, as well as one of the most extensive, diverse and reasonably priced menus I have ever seen. Starters range from soup, to antipasti, to mussels, to chicken wings and start at £2.20, while main courses are divided into a vast array of meat, fish, chicken, veal, pizza, pasta, risotto, crêpes and salad dishes, from £4.60 through to £14.90. As if that wasn't enough, Kavio's also offer a selection of seafood specials, as befits their shore setting, a 3-course lunch for just £5.50 per head, a whole page of desserts and a good selection of wine starting at £9.50. I opted for the light, juicy caprese (£4.40) followed by deliciously creamy gnocchi al cardinale (£5.90) and homemade lemon cheesecake (£2.80), which I just managed to squeeze in! My friend chose crispy, garlicky bruschetta (£2.20), filetto stroganoff (£12.80) and the rich chocolate indulgence of the ciocolato (£2.90) topped off by espresso and amaretto biscotti. **CD**

WE ACCEPT CASH, CHEQUES, CREDIT CARDS OR YOUR FIRST BORN FEMALE

ALSO BEEF, CHICKEN, WILD BOAR, OSTRICH, SHARK AND SEAFOOD

43 ASSEMBLY STREET, LEITH, EDINBURGH.
TEL: 0131 555 0005.

KHUBLAI KHAN
MONGOLIAN RESTAURANT

26 CANDLERIGGS, MERCHANT CITY, GLASGOW.
TEL: 0141 400 8090.

www.khublaikhan.co.uk

KAVIO'S
ITALIAN RESTAURANT

CREATES THE TASTE OF ITALY

Business lunch menu
à la carte dinner

most major credit cards welcome
63 The Shore, Leith 0131 467 7746
www.italian-restaurant.com

look good enough to eat

join today and receive food and beverage vouchers worth £2[5]
Edinburgh's premier health and fitness clu[b]

Stop stressing and start living at Next Generation. Keep in shape in our great fitness studio. Or try a refreshing dip in our pool. Join today and you will receive £25 worth of food and beverage vouchers to spend in our fantastic waterside restaurant.* Simply quote the Edinburgh Food Guide. Who said the gym's all about hard work?

call: 0131 554 5000 for informatio[n]

*offer ends 31/12/01

Newhaven Harbour, Newhaven, Edinburgh   www.nextgenerationclubs.co.uk

NEXT GENERATI[ON]

CAFÉ-BARS, PUBS, CAFÉS & COFFEE HOUSES

Eating Out in Café-Bars, Pubs, Cafes & Coffee Houses

Edinburgh is renowned for the quality of its social scene and the cosmopolitan nature means there really is something for everyone. The wealth of establishments offering quality, affordable food has long since dispelled the traditional view of greasy pub-grub, and with this revolution, eating and drinking out has never been so good.

Close to the University, Native State is one of Edinburgh's busiest bars, with a menu that incorporates fine cuisine and affordability it proves to be a real lunchtime hot-spot. Tiles on Saint Andrews Square proves ever-popular with hungry office workers and shoppers in need of refuelling. Kariba Coffee House is a new addition to the Royal Mile, serving paninis and cappuccinos to MSPs from the new Parliament and sample-sized portions of haggis to adventurous tourists.

Highly recommended comes the Elephant House with its delightful home-cooked selection and gourmet coffees. Further along the road is the Bookstop Café, serving literary nourishment and refreshing fayre. Edinburgh's best kept secret remains the Doric Tavern on Market Street, this delightful bistro and wine bar serves fine food in the most romantic setting.

Old Town

Negociants D5
Negociants is a Continental style café and a very relaxed and friendly place to eat. Situated opposite Bristo Square it is a favourite with students due to its generous portions at great value. Its late opening hours also make it popular for a late bite, available from 10pm, there's Nachos, garlic bread and platters. It is also offers an excellent breakfast menu with choices from muesli to a full Scottish breakfast. Instead of starters there are side orders, soup and salads available. We chose bruschetta, garlic bread topped with tomatoes and herbs (£2.25), and carrot and coriander homemade soup served with bread and butter (£2.30). While we drank the house white wine, Sommelier Dry (£9.50) we wondered whether we would actually be able to fit in another course. However, I went on to have peppercorn steak with salad and fries (£9.50) and my partner had Negociants chicken fajitas (£8.95). We definitely couldn't manage dessert, but assorted cakes, muffins and ice-cream are available from £1.50 to £2.45. With outside seating this is also the place to head when the sun is shining! **MJ**

Caffe Lucano D5
Perched on George IV Bridge, straddling the Old Town and South Side, Caffe Lucano, like many of Edinburgh's past worthies, leads a double life. Open most of the from 7am until late, this is, by day a lively, bustling café, with huge windows overlooking one of the city's busiest thoroughfares. The all-day food menu offers breakfast, pasta, pizzas, sandwiches and various specials such as pasta and a glass of wine for £6.50. A treats menu of ice creams, sundaes and got and cold drinks caters for the Scottish sweet tooth and there is a separate children's menu (£3.25). By evening Lucano becomes a relaxed and stylish bistro, boasting an impressive à la carte menu of meat, poultry, fish and vegetable dishes. Particularly good value are the massive t-bone steaks for £13.95, but on the chef's recommendation we opted instead for beautifullt presented galia melon and Parma ham with red cabbage (£5.95). We followed this with petto di pollo balsamico (£8.95), a picquant chicken dish, washed down with a deliciously chilled Frascati (£13.50). Both Doctor Jekyll and Mr Hyde would have been greatly impressed. **IB**

Plaisir du Chocolat E4
Entering a place called 'the pleasure of chocolate' is warning that a little indulgence must be endured for the sake of a good review. The pleasure begins

---

caffè **lucano**

"The coffee, with an accompanying nibble of chocolate, is the best in Edinburgh"

CONRAD WILSON

Open 7 days

Non Smoking
Seventy percent Vegetarian
ALL GM-free foods
Children Very Welcome

37-39 George IV Bridge
Edinburgh EH1 1EL
Tel: 0131 225 6890

CAFÉ-BARS, PUBS, CAFÉS & COFFEE HOUSES

immediately with a beautiful array of chocolates and gateaux, that even make your eyes water. But it's not all chocolate. Ushered into the elegant café, we patiently munched a traditional Croque Monsieur (£9.50) and savoury tartlets of mushroom and salmon (£8.50). These were delicious and came with the largest assortment of bread, imported daily from Paris. The main course swiftly followed - heavenly chocolate mousse (£3.50), and a divine hot, caramelised apple tart (£5.00). Plaisir pride themselves in using only the best ingredients, importing what Scotland can't provide and creating all dishes and chocolate in-house. The menu has ten pages of world-wide teas, but tipsy on house wine (£10 bottle) and chocolate-induced endorphins, we sought out hot chocolate - the Madagascar (£3), thick, milky and just sweet enough, and the exotic 'infinite extravagance' (£3.50); 99% cocoa content infused with chillies! After a finger-licking tour of the basement chocolate factory, we stumbled out, happy. Mr Wonka, eat your heart out - the pleasure was all ours! **KH**

Canons' Gait   E4

For traditional Scottish pub food in the centre of Edinburgh, look no further than the Canons' Gait pub, situated half way down the Royal Mile. The pub's restaurant is always busy at lunchtime, with all its cosy little booths and alcoves occupied by locals and tourists alike. For liquid refreshment the horseshoe bar stocks an impressive selection of ales and whiskies. The restaurant menu is simple but varied, and vegetarians are well provided for. To start we tried the delicious tomato and orange soup (£1.95) and garlic bread (£1.95), followed by traditional haddock and chips (£5.50) and lentil and cashew nut bake with vegetables (£5.95). Wash it all down with a glass of Chardonnay (£2.25), and finish off with a dessert such as death by chocolate if you still have room. The Canons' Gait is a great place to visit for its relaxed atmosphere, genuinely friendly staff and tasty pub fare. **CR**

Native State   E5

Native State lies in the heart of Edinburgh's fashionable student area. With an offbeat Americana theme, the interior exhibits a fusion of aesthetic styles drawing on all aspects of North American culture. Happily, the menu takes this and adds a European twist. My partner and I began by sharing a generous portion of chilli nachos (£3.45), smothered in sour cream, cheese and enough jalapeno peppers to make wine a necessary luxury. Luckily the delicious Australian Shiraz Cabernet (£9.50) did more than simply mellow our

"Chocolate heaven, bar none!"
THE SUNDAY TIMES

PLAISIR DU CHOCOLAT
— EDINBURGH —

251-253 CANONGATE, EDINBURGH EH8 8BQ. TEL: 0131 556 9524
FAX: 0131 556 6553   E-mail: sales@plaisirduchocolat.co.uk

CANONS' GAIT

Lunches Served 12.00 - 3.00
International Menu
12 World Wines By The Glass
Excellent Range Of Malt Whiskies
Cellar Bar Available For Private Hire

NO. 232 CANONGATE ROYAL MILE
TEL: 0131 556 4481
JUST UP FROM NEW STREET

CONTEMPORARY
TRADITIONAL

Lunches Served 12.00 - 2.30
Quality Bar Food
Outstanding Range Of Real Ale
Best City Bar 1999 - Evening News Award
Included In CAMRA 2000 Good Beer Guide

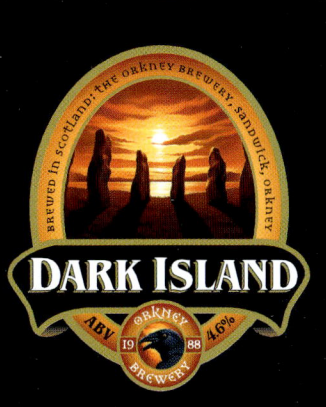

NO. 1-5 WEST REGISTER STREET
EAST END OF PRINCES STREET
TEL: 0131 556 4312

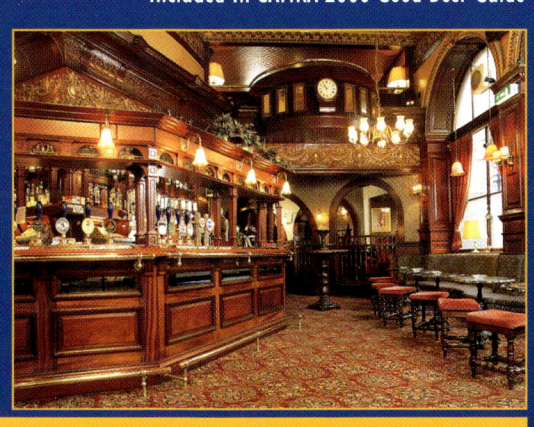

GUILDFORD ARMS

CAFÉ BARS & PUBS

DARK ISLAND
BREWED IN SCOTLAND: THE ORKNEY BREWERY SANDWICK, ORKNEY
ABV 4.6%
ORKNEY BREWERY 1988

THE RED MACGREGOR
ABV 4%
ORKNEY BREWERY 1988

Skull Splitter
ABV 8.5%
ORKNEY BREWERY 1988

ORKNEY BREWERY

♦

award winning cask
ales available at

CANON'S GAIT &
GUILDFORD ARMS

CAFÉ BARS & PUBS

@ alphabet

HOTEL BAR RESTAURANT

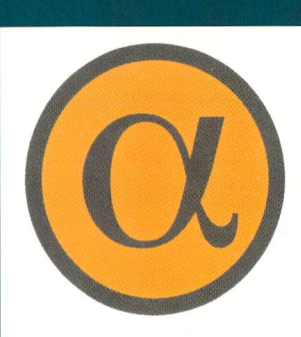

Open from 11am serving a superb selection of wines, beers, cocktails, juices and smoothies.
No-Smoking Area
Fully air conditioned

Tel: 316 4466
92 St. Johns Road
Edinburgh

EDINBURGH'S FINEST SELECTION OF

Kariba COFFEE

'SAMPLER SIZE' HAGGIS, NEEPS & TATTIES

COFFEES, SMOOTHIES, SANDWICHES,

OPEN SEVEN DAYS 8AM 'TIL LATE

160 High Street, Royal Mile
Tel: 0131 220 1818

HOT FILLED PANINI, BEERS & WINES

---

www.thebasement.org.uk
0131 557 0097

freshly prepared meals at surprisingly reasonable prices
served in the lively atmosphere of a bar
seven days 12 noon - 10.30p.m.

again voted one of the top 3 restaurants in edinburgh
by readers of the list magazine

the basement
10a-12a broughton street,
edinburgh, eh1 3rh

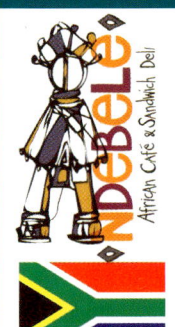

NDEBELE African Café & Sandwich Deli

"I Love it!" – Most often heard words at Edinburgh's only Southern African Café and Deli!

Come in and see for yourself. We do Biltong, Boerewors Rolls, Ouma Rusks and Mrs. Ball's, to name a few. Hot meals, cool sandwiches and cold Smoothies too!

We cater for Parties, Outside Catering and do Mail Order of South African goodies.

Open from 10am to 10pm, 7 days a week.
We can deliver to the local area.
Find us at 57 Home Street, Edinburgh
0800 698 1436   www.ndebele.co.uk

palates! To follow, my partner devoured tagliatelle in a blue cheese and walnut sauce (£4.95), while I sampled flame-grilled beef pinchos with a flavoursome red wine and caramelised onion sauce (£5.95), served with wild rice, sautéed vegetables and salad. Desserts are available, but having indulged enough we instead opted for coffees (from £1.10) to finish the feast. The menu is served all day by an extremely friendly waiting staff, and there is a very tempting breakfast menu too! If you're looking for great pub grub in a friendly environment then look no further. This place would please the natives anywhere! LJT

Kariba Coffee   D4

People-watching has always been popular in Edinburgh: an eighteenth century tourist observed that you could stand in the High Street and see fifty men of genius pass within half an hour. Today there are less strenuous vantage points – Kariba for example. Watch the world go by comfortably installed behind the huge window overlooking the Royal Mile, whilst sipping a speciality coffee. "User-friendly" and "value for money" is how Paul Wightman describes his new venture. "We're independent, not part of a chain, so people come first." The décor is contemporary and uncluttered, the music unobtrusive and relaxing. The menu, is simple but adventurous, using fresh, local ingredients to produce an international range of sandwiches, salads, pasta and pastries, even offering a "tourist sampler-sized" haggis, neeps and tatties dish (£2.95). We chose tortilla wrap with cheese, salsa and sour cream (£2.25) and warmed panini crammed with succulent chicken (£2.75), followed by tea (£1) and hot chocolate (£1.80). "What you

CAFÉ-BARS, PUBS, CAFÉS & COFFEE HOUSES

Edinburgh
Food Guide

see is what you get," declared Paul, just as I spotted a particularly enticing chocolate muffin (95p), so I happily obliged. And those fifty geniuses? Well, the Parliament is just up the road. **IB**

Doric Tavern   D4

Unchanged in decades, the Doric has become an institution. Like the rest of the establishment, its separate dining area is traditional in décor - all dark wood furnishings, warm red walls and muted lighting. Serious about satisfying, quality fare which leans towards the traditional, the Doric's à la carte menus and 2 or 3 course set lunches and dinners (£11 or £14.25 and £16.50 or £19.35 respectively) feature a plethora of meat, seafood and vegetarian dishes made from fresh local produce. Our visit saw us sampling the set option. Rich, velvety cream of spinach soup and beautifully moist stuffed tomato Moroccan formed our starters. My companion then delved into a generous portion of roast haunch of roe deer with port and juniper whilst I enjoyed duck breast accompanied by black pepper and deliciously sweet preserved ginger. After a brief rest, we squeezed in banana crumble with custard and pineapple, and rum sponge with cream. Food this good means the Doric will no doubt be a favourite on Edinburgh's bistro scene for many more years to come. **DK**

Elephants and Bagels E5

Close to the University, it isn't unreasonable to expect that Elephant and Bagels would be filled with students. While this is to some extent true, the clientele crosses age barriers, extending to a colouring competition for kids. The food, as one might expect, consists primarily of bagels, of which they have fourteen different varieties of bagel alone (with breakfast bagels from £1, others £1.95-£3.10) but they also serve baked potatoes, soup, cakes and pastries for tea or the usual selection of bread and rolls for the less adventurous. Unlike the elephant house, there is no licence here, but the good coffee and selection of fruit juices ensure that you don't go thirsty. My partner and I enjoyed a late afternoon snack of a bagel with sundried tomatoes, pine nuts and cream cheese, and one with smoked salmon and cream cheese respectively (both £3.10). Almost everything is available to takeaway at a slight discount and, as almost all of the seats are taken at lunchtime, this is often a good idea, especially on a warm day. **CK**

Elephant House   D5

Open until 11pm every night, The Elephant House is the perfect choice for high quality food within a relaxed and friendly

The DORIC TAVERN
ATMOSPHERIC BISTRO AND WINE BAR

"The menu speaks for itself with an inspired choice of dishes, put together with innovative skill and flair."
Edinburgh Good Food Guide 1999/2000

Set price and à la carte menus.

Seafood, meat, game, vegetarian choices and sumptuous home made desserts. Everything freshly made on the premises from local produce. You may have one course, two courses or three courses as you wish from either menu. Well balanced and well priced wine list with some excellent bin end bargains.

Set Lunch: 2/3 Course £11.00/£14.25 Set Dinner: 2/3 Course £16.50/£19.35

Opening Hours from 12.00 to 01.00:
May to September - open 7 days   October to April - open Mon to Sat
Restaurant from 12.00 to 23.00
Wine Bar Hot snacks available.

The Doric Tavern and McGuffies Bar, (just beside Waverley Station)
15/16 Market Street, Edinburgh, EH1 1DE   Tel: 0131 225 1084   Fax: 0131 220 0894   www.thedoric.co.uk

Edinburgh's first & foremost authentic bagel & sandwich shop

elephants & bagels

www.elephants.bun.com

NICOLSON SQUARE
EDINBURGH   EH8 9BJ
Tel: 668 4404 Fax: 668 4420

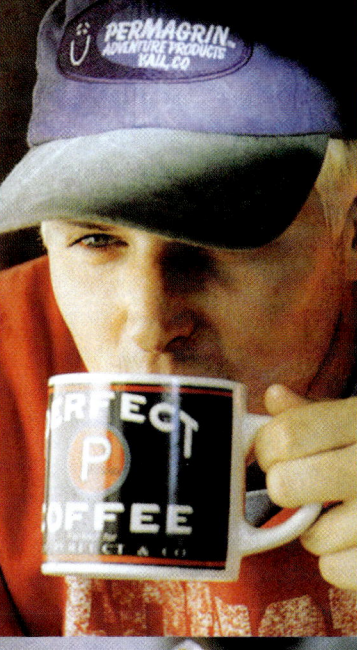

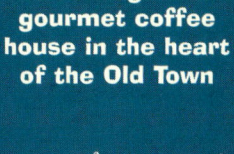

The Unforgettable gourmet coffee house in the heart of the Old Town

the elephant house

www.elephants.bun.com

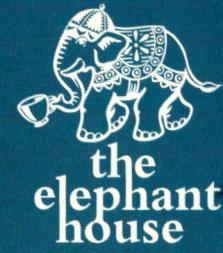

21 GEORGE IV BRIDGE
EDINBURGH   EH1 1EP
Tel: 220 5355 Fax: 220 4272

WE ALSO DO OUTSIDE CATERING!
0131 553 5755

CAFÉ-BARS, PUBS, CAFÉS & COFFEE HOUSES

environment. Situated in the heart of the city, it attracts a wide variety of people, from students to local residents, all attracted by the wide selection of snacks, hot drinks and early evening meals. We began our meal with gourmet pizza (£5.25) which came with a choice of toppings including mushrooms, peppers and salami. We also tried chicken fahitas (£5.75) topped with generous helpings of sour cream and spicy Mexican salsa. To accompany our meal we sampled the house white at (£2.25) per glass. For dessert we had the hot pudding of the day (£2.95), served with fresh cream and hot sauce. We also sampled the healthy option, exotic fresh fruit salad (£2.50) surprisingly indulgent when topped with cream. The Elephant House also serves a wide selection of rolls, baguettes and panini from (£1.90) and a wide range of cocktail pitchers (£12.00). For added atmosphere there is live music every Thursday and an 'open mike' every second Thursday where anyone is welcome to take centre stage. **VI**

New Town

Tiles D3

The casual atmosphere of Tiles comes as a welcome contrast to the commercial arteries of Princess Street and George Street. Upon arrival, we were greeted by a relaxed and informal atmosphere. Décorwise, the large vertical space is wallpapered in ceramic tiles, a relic of the New Town's more illustrious past. From a comprehensive menu I chose the wild mushroom frittatas (£3.45) while my colleague chose the more traditionally Scottish dish of haggis creatively wrapped in filo pastry (£3.95). From the specials menu we selected our next course. Balanced well with the first, the chicken and mango salad (£5.50) proved to be refreshing and light, while the tian of pan seared shark, swordfish and tuna (£5.95) was equally tasty and well presented. The strawberry cheesecake (£2.95) comes highly recommended but for a savoury end to the meal the cheese board and oatcakes (£3.50) allowed a more indigenous conclusion. On Thursday nights there is live music from 6pm and drinks promotions including wine (£5.50), cocktails (£2.00), and beer (£1.50). Judging by the welcoming nature of both staff and clientele, I am sure this would be a lively occasion. **DS**

The Basement D2

Broughton Street has developed a reputation as a place to see, and be seen, housing a number of stylish watering holes, The Basement being no exception. Here, you find a marriage of modern chic and murky charm laced with an industrial edge, most noticeable in the caterpillar track tables and gothic candlesticks. The smokey oranges and blues of the walls are delicately lit, and the overall air is one of vibrancy, a fact reflected in a menu juggling Mexican, Scottish and international dishes with apparent ease. The bruschetta (£2.25), and smoked salmon with oatcakes (£2.80) were tasty precursors to our main courses of roast duck breast with a red peppercorn sauce (£4.75), and chicken burritos with rice and salad (£4.50), accompanied by a bottle of house red (£8.00). The size of the portions was matched only by the quality of the cooking and the produce used, and we finished off with sticky toffee pudding (£2.50), and Mr Boni's ice cream (£1.95). Open all day (two-course lunch £5.95), you can enjoy this remarkably reasonable retreat at any time. **JW**

Theatre Royal E2

If the name conjures up images of bygone elegance, you won't be disappointed. The Theatre Royal boasts a traditional island bar, massive chandeliers and stately red and green décor. If you don't fancy the dramatic grandeur of the interior though, you can sit outside and savour the atmosphere of lively Leith Walk – and (unusually for Edinburgh) at a safe distance from those nasty car exhausts! There's nothing staid about the menu either, which is up-to-date, inventive and cosmopolitan, We began with warm bacon vinaigrette over

tiles

open 11am - till late
food served 11-5 winter, 11-8 summer
comprehensive full menu ranging from snacks & pastries to quality main courses
serving an extensive selection of tea & coffees
a large variety of wines from around the world
an excellent choice of beers & cask conditioned ales
Terrace overlooking historic Georgian Square in summer months
1 st. andrew square, edinburgh eh2 2yp,
tel: 0131 558 1507 www.caley-heritable.demon.co.uk

CAFÉ-BARS, PUBS, CAFÉS & COFFEE HOUSES

mixed leaves (£2.95) and brushetta heaped with chopped tomatoes (£2.25). Massive plates of vegetable chilli nachos smothered in mozzarella, salsa, sour cream and guacamole (£4.25), and grilled Cajun chicken with pitta bread, salsa and sour cream (£5.25) almost made us regret our substantial starters...but not quite. We conquered our marathon meal, sustained by several glasses of a refreshing house white (£2.10 per glass) and frisky wine spritzers (£2.20). There is a theatre next door, though rather confusingly (we thought), it's called something entirely different. A pre-theatre menu is available on performance evenings, but remember to leave room for those interval drinks. **MB**

Guildford Arms D3
Situated a shopping bag's throw away from Princes Street, this is an ideal place to warm yourself after some intensive retail therapy. The sunken table in the corner of the main room reflects the general mood of this opulent bar – you'll have difficulty pulling yourself to your feet to leave. The food in the gallery is served 12-2 except on Sundays and offers an excellent position to view the hordes supping from over twenty malt whiskies and the ever-changing guest ales, such as Jock Frost (£2.30). The food is warming too, and the vegetable soup (£2.20) – like the décor – was traditional but stylish. The smoked salmon with a selection of olives (£3.95) was also impressive. I had the scampi (£5.65) with chunky chips and salad and also on offer was a very filling cheese and ham foccacia (£4.95), which literally melted in the mouth. We topped it off with a very reasonably priced and excellent house red - Marquis de Carceres (£10.70). After all that the cold outdoors didn't seem quite so necessary. **NH**

West End

Patisserie Florentin C2
With its yellow sunflower exterior Florentin oozes French sophisticated sunshine. Once inside you have to fight your way past the tempting small cakes and patisseries, so popular they sell over 500 a week from this café alone. From the lunch menu I opted for the filled croissant (£2.80) with tuna and egg mayo delicious and served with a side salad. My companion chose the pizza (£3.40) again with salad, which she just loved. After sipping our Earl Grey tea (£1.15) we decided to try the famous cakes (all under £2) but when faced with such a display of culinary art it is hard to choose just on, so we opted for the mousse passion, mousse de banana et chocolat and the chocolate tart. All were delicious, and although full it was hard to stop ordering more.

THEATRE ROYAL
♦♦♦♦♦♦♦♦

From a light snack for the interval to the splendour of a theatrical main course and, of course, delicious dessert encore

♦♦♦♦♦♦♦♦

23 - 27 Greenside Place
Edinburgh EH1 3AA
Tel: 557 2142

Florentin also operate a popular outside catering service and have a great reputation for designer French wedding cakes. If you are looking for a great café in which to relax and enjoy great cuisine, there's none to match Florentin, apart from their sister café on St Giles Street. Open 7 days, from 7.30am to 7pm. **BO'R**

Henry J. Beans B4
The newly refurbished Henry J Beans is usually known for it's busy cocktail atmosphere, however it also offers an excellent American themed menu away form the bustle at the bar. For starters we had the chicken satay with spicy peanut relish, toasted sesame seed and Thai cucumber (£4.95) and the deep fried potato skins loaded with cheese and sour cream (£4.75) which was a meal in itself. For main course I had a grilled chicken sandwich served in a ciabatta roll with Monterey jack cheese, bacon and French fries (£7.25) and my partner

Vittoria
ITALIAN RESTAURANT & CAFFÉ BAR
Breakfast • Lunch • Dinner
All Day • 7 Days

Feeding all your fantasies, the restaurant is open 10am till late for breakfast, lunch & dinner or a genuine cup of Italian coffee.

113 Brunswick Street, Leith Walk
FREEPHONE: 0800 698 1454
Fax: 0131 478 7004
E-mail: vittoriaed@aol.com
www.vittoriarestaurant.com

opted for the 14oz ribeye steak on a bed of mashed potato with beer battered onion rings, £11.95. This tasty meal was washed down with the house white, a light Australian wine, Kirkton Vale dry (£8.85 per bottle). We gave in to temptation and managed to force down Belgian waffles and cheesecake with a strawberry coulis for dessert both at £3.95. The restaurant also offers an early bird special from 4.30-6.30, Mon to Thurs with 2 courses for £10.00 and 3 courses for £12.00. **DH**

Newington

Bookstop Café D5
One of a cluster of lively cafés and bistros skirting the university, the Bookstop Café is more relaxed than most. It's popular with students who can plug in their laptops and there's internet access too. Even better, for old timers like myself, are the books: classic novels,

---

The Bookstop Café
4 Teviot Place
226 6929

Weekdays: 8am – 7pm
Saturdays: 10am – 6pm
Sundays: Noon – 6pm

Far from the Madding Crowd
Thomas Hardy

Our reputation for muffins and carrot cakes is only part of the story.

We believe in using fresh ingredients. We love to delight customers with unusual salads and soups.

Try our freshly squeezed juices, our sandwiches, ... and see for yourself why people return again and again...

"Bookstop – A delicious addiction"

Scottish periodicals, even board games for bored kids. And best of all, there's food. Soups sandwiches, salads and home baking can all be found. The emphasis is on choice and flexibility with fresh ingredients prepared to order. My companion had his bagel (£2.15) exactly as he wanted; toasted (15p), with cream cheese, (25p) cucumber and olives (10p each). Whilst I indulged in the spinach and sun-dried tomato tarte served with a salad more imaginative than most (£4.50). Both the kiwi smoothie (large £2.30) and apple juice (small £1.60) were freshly blended and delicious. We completed our postgraduate research with a couple of coffees (large £1.45), but the honey and banana scone (£1.30) and massive wedge of carrot cake (£1.95) were just unqualified gluttony. There's even a free coffee with all book purchases. Now there's an offer I can't refuse! **MB**

Metropole E7
Metropole coffee house provides welcome respite for students, office workers and local shoppers. Brightly decorated, it has a relaxing, tranquil air thanks to the sound of water from its bubbling fountain. Its genuine Art Deco style is no pastiche, but reflects origins as a 1920's Bank. Its easy access is good for families with pushchairs, while seating booths are clubby and inviting. Offering more than just their speciality coffee, teas and sandwiches, the focus is on fresh produce with a wide choice to satisfy all tastes. Newly added to the extensive selection are delicious breakfasts based around authentic Belgian waffles (from £3.75), and an expanded selection of Mexican offerings. Prices are great value, with hot dishes starting at around £3.50, with side dishes of beans, rice, salad etc from £1.45. Our quiche was great, fluffy and light with the red peppers still crisp. The baked potatoes were large, like they should be, and the mature cheese filling more than ample. The cakes (mostly homemade, from £1.75) were irresistible and would grace any German or Austrian café. The proprietor's personal touch shines through and lifts the Metropole above the run of the mill, justifying its popularity. **BM**

Human Be-In E6
A new addition to the south side on West Crosscauseway, Human Be-In's low lighting, candles and earthy colours create a relaxed atmosphere oozing with understated style. The menu is equally stylish with an interesting and inviting selection. I chose smoked duck breast served with salad leaves and raspberry reduction (£4.25) to start and my friend went for roast peppers, egg plant and courgette terrine with balsamic reduction (£4.25). Both were delicious, especially the raspberry reduction, and just enough to keep us happy until our main course. We had a bottle of the house red, Selection of Somellier (£7.50) with salad of watercress, new potato and avocado with paprika and yoghurt dressing (£6.50) and a big bowl of linguini (£6.95) which was really lovely with feta cheese melting through and roast sweet potato. This really filled me up but I left room for chocolate marquise (£2.50), the most wicked chocolate cake ever, while my friend enjoyed her butterscotch and walnut gateaux (£2.50). The full menu is served from 11am until 9pm with a snack menu available for the pre-club crowd served after 9pm. **AL**

Bierex E7
Bierex is a favourite with both students and local residents, attracted by its friendly environment, good music and a

www.humanbe-in.co.uk

photography olivia

in association with
Gordons

the human be-in
bar kafé

2/8 West Crosscauseway, Edinburgh   0131 662 8860   Open 7 days   Full Menu Available 11am until 1am

Food Served
Sun-Thurs 10am-9pm
Fri & Sat 10am-8pm

THE WAITING ROOM

0131 452 9707

7 Belhaven Terrace
Edinburgh
(end of Balcarres St,
nr. Morningside Clock)

Food Served
Sun-Thurs 10am-9pm
Fri & Sat 10am-8pm

0131 667 2335

bierex

132 Causeyside
Edinburgh

CAFÉ-BARS, PUBS, CAFÉS & COFFEE HOUSES

range of special offers running throughout the week. These include a wide selection of shooters, pitchers and cocktails. They also have a large selection of continental beers on draft. Bierex serves a varied menu ranging from snacks such as club sandwiches and filled bagels to meals including fajitas and vegetable lasagne. We started our meal with tortilla chips with vegetarian chilli (£3.90) which came in a massive portion topped with sour cream and guacamole, and pâté served with toast or oatcakes and onion marmalade (£2.70). To follow we enjoyed a ciabatta filled with feta and grilled Mediterranean vegetables (£3.95) and a crispy chicken burger with salad and fries (£4.50). Hot chocolate fudge cake (£2.75) and frozen banana and amaretto cheesecake (£2.75) provided a perfect end to our evening. We accompanied our meal with a bottle of house white wine (a bargain at £4.95 before 7pm). Bierex is highly recommended, excelling in its combination of varied menu, generous portions and friendly staff, all at excellent value for money. **VI**

Babylon Café E5

Babylon Café is a small and friendly eaterie where you can pop in for a quick bite to eat or take away. The best bacon rolls in the capital, as voted by Edinburgh experts last year, is a mainstay of their business. All day breakfasts are available, as are omelettes, burgers, baked potatoes and toasties with a wide range of fillings. From the main dishes menu I chose roast chicken (£3.60) and my partner selected breaded scampi (£4.20). Both dishes came served with generous portions of chips and salad and bread and butter. We received a very quick and efficient service and agreed that our tasty meals had revived us for the shopping activity ahead! As we drank our tea (75p) and fresh orange (£1.20) we watched a stream of regular customers come in for nourishment and a chat, testament to the café's popularity. The wood clad and mirrored interiors make for a light and airy atmosphere, especially on a sunny day. For those wishing some sweets, scones and jam (90p) or ice cream (£1.40) are available. Open all day. **JJF**

Susie's Diner E6

This popular academic haunt works much like a standard canteen, where you look at the menu board on the wall, grab a tray then await service at the counter. I chose a large plate (£4.95), which entitled me to three hot choices and one salad portion. As all options are visible at the counter, it was difficult to decide, but I plumped for spinach and ricotta flan, courgette and mushroom quiche and roasted tomato stuffed with red pepper and mushroom risotto. Opting for a medium plate (£3.95), my partner sampled two hot choices and one salad. The pincholada stuffed with mushroom, spinach and chickpeas was mildly-spiced and came with an optional yoghurt sauce. This, together with rice and celery, apple and walnut salad, proved delightful. Bottles of organic wine (£9.95) are available, as are imported biers (£2.40) and 'smoothies' (£1.95). For dessert, the unusual courgette and poppy seed cake (£1.75) was tastier than it may

SUSIE'S DINER Wholefoods

Serving a great selection of vegetarian & vegan hot dishes & salads

Mon: 9am - 8pm
Tues - Sat: 9am - 9pm
(open Sun during Festival)

No need to book
Licensed & BYOB

51 - 53 West Nicholson St
Tel: 667 8729

Babylon Cafe

Traditional all-day breakfast, fish+chips, hot-filled rolls and ice-cream

Open 8am - 5pm Seven days

26 Nicholson Street
0131 662 7142

Fully Licensed

sound, while the banoffi pie (£2.00) was the highlight. Don't expect to be wined-and-dined at Susie's, but do expect rustic décor, an unpretentious atmosphere and, above all, quality vegetarian and vegan food. **GB**

Tollcross

The Waiting Room B7
Whether you choose to eat, drink or do both at this vibrant bar-restaurant, it's certainly worth seeking out. Besides offering special deals on cocktails, pitchers and shooters, the food menu extends beyond typical 'pub grub' to encompass dishes of Greek, Mexican and Italian orientation. To start, the feta cheese salad (£2.95) was delicious and generously proportioned, as were the nacho chips with sauces (£3.45), leaving little room for our mains of vegetable fajitas with guacamole, salsa, sour cream and cheese (£5.25), and penne pasta with chorizo & spicy tomato sauce (£4.95). Again, both were excellent value for money and mouth-watering too. Although the sweet menu is fairly limited, the possibilities were enticing enough for me to try the Belgian apple pie & cream (£2.75). For those too full for dessert, coffees are available from £1.15, as is tea and frothy hot chocolate (£1.65). Also, if you dine here between 5pm and 8pm, you can enjoy a bottle of house wine at half-price (£4.95). Add to this the lively atmosphere and appealing breakfasts on offer 10am-noon (Mon-Fri) and 10am-4pm (weekends) and it's no surprise that the Waiting Room attracts regular custom of all age groups. **GB**

Filmhouse Café Bar B5
Open from noon to 10 pm, you don't need the excuse of seeing a film to visit The Filmhouse Café. A large open dining space incorporates a huge amount of tables and booths for versatile eating as well as a large bar. Although not specifically a vegetarian café, The Filmhouse does seem to favour wholefoods. They do however also cater for the carnivores amongst us. You can opt for a salad or humous to start but we decided to jump right in. I enjoyed deep-fried stilton, nut and spinach nuggets, which where moist and tasty, served with a light garlic mayo dip and a mixed salad (£4.00). My partner chose filo parcels filled with generous amounts of feta cheese, spinach and pine nuts, and came served with an Italian salad featuring olives and sun-dried tomatoes (£5.50) . To accompany our vegetarian feast, we savoured a delicious bottle of Australian Chardonnay (£9.50). For our finale we chose a slice of cake from the large homemade selection available (£1 - 1.95)

FILMHOUSE CAFÉ BAR

Much more than a movie experience!

Fresh imaginative and affordable food available 10am till 10pm daily

www.filmhouse.demon.co.uk
88 Lothian Road   229-5932

and a rich fresh ground coffee (£1-2) and left entertained, without seeing a film! **AMcC**

Ndebele `C6`
Pronounced in-de-bell-lay this immediately welcoming African café and sandwich deli is named after a Southern African tribe. Small, cheery and unstuffy, almost every inch of its walls are adorned with geometric, tribal art. In addition to meals and snacks, African groceries, deli products, jewellery, pieces of art (there's a gallery downstairs) and cards are also on offer. Its customers are a mix of Tollcross locals, theatre-goers, students and tourists who flock there to enjoy an eclectic menu which, as well as a an unconventional and enticing selection of sandwich fillings, also lists a selection of dishes from all over Africa. We had thick, creamy mango smoothies £1.80. After these my fellow diner enjoyed a spicy boerewors (a large, South African beef, pork and coriander sausage), samp 'n' beans and miele meal £4.50, whilst I chose the hot dish of the day: succulent pork bredie with mango which was served with a healthy portion of rice and salad £5. On finishing, we left Ndebele's warmth and went into the cold, wet night extremely full and happy. **DK**

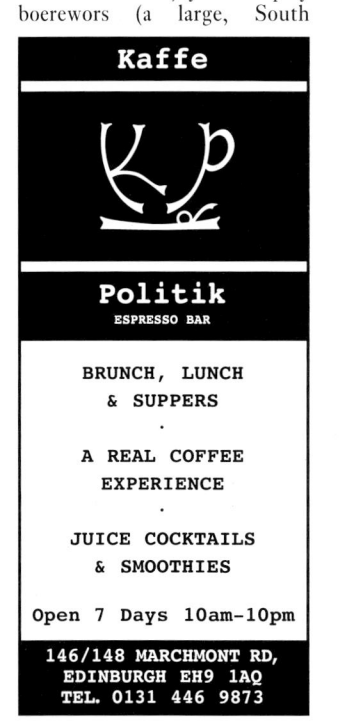

Kaffe Politik `C7`
This brightly decorated, smartly staffed and cleverly devised eatery has an awful lot to offer at any time of day. The political figures and quotes on the wall may range from Boris Yeltsin to Edwina Currie, but the menu is far more harmonious. A gratifying range of pasta and panini caters perfectly for either a planned meal or a last minute bite to accompany the bar's wide selection of coffees, juices and alcohol. We voted for pasta: blue cheese, baby spinach and cream (£5.45) and pesto and parmesan (£5.25), both of which were a winning party for eye and mouth. The house white (£9.75 a bottle, £1.85 a glass) was a lively Australian dry that made a bold comrade to the food. For dessert we nominated banana and chocolate cake (£1.50) and a thoroughly electable Florida key lime pie (£2.10). Marchmont is certainly a better place for this venue, whose constituency is sure to grow! A brunch menu (£2.25-£5.95) is also available until noon on weekdays and all day at weekends. **DDR**

Bruntsfield Links Hotel `C7`
This well-stocked bar overlooking the Bruntsfield Links is informal, relaxed and friendly. The extensive menu of hearty cuisine features burgers, all day breakfasts, traditional pub meals and international choices, all served from 12- 9pm. We started with generous portions of Tuscany bread (£3.65); garlic bread topped with roasted vegetables and cheese, and veggie nachos (small £4.85, large £5.95). For the main course my partner chose the bullburger for £4.85, served on a sesame bun with a mountain of golden fries and fresh salad. I had the excellent fajita (£5.95); succulent spicy chicken wrapped in a tortilla and served with salad, rice, salsa, guacamole and sour cream. A wide choice of desserts including Belgian waffles with ice cream and fresh fruit salad are available for £1.95. There is also a comprehensive student menu, (£3.25 with student I.D., £4 without) including bangers and mash, spicy Mexican pizza and vegetable curry. If you are looking for filling food, friendly and efficient service, lots of vegetarian options and sport on a wide-screen, this is the place to come. **HS**

Kaffe

Politik
ESPRESSO BAR

BRUNCH, LUNCH
& SUPPERS
·
A REAL COFFEE
EXPERIENCE
·
JUICE COCKTAILS
& SMOOTHIES

Open 7 Days 10am-10pm

146/148 MARCHMONT RD,
EDINBURGH EH9 1AQ
TEL. 0131 446 9785

**BRUNTSFIELD
LINKS HOTEL**

Bar Menu
12-9pm

Night Menu
10-12pm
Thurs, Fri, Sat

Whitehouse Loan
Edinburgh
0131 229 3046
www.brunstfieldlinkshotel.co.uk

Eating Out in the Outskirts

With the wealth of attractions in the city of Edinburgh it is easy to overlook what lies on the fringe. Visit Edinburgh Zoo, famed for their penguin parade, and pop into Alphabet who marched their way into our new places to eat serving a range of fine cuisine. Alternatively, if you're after a coffee or a hearty meal St Johns Restaurant has an affordable range and is a favourite with children.

The Hilton at the airport will provide welcome relief from airport food, offering an international range of food so sample before you fly!

At the other side of town is Portobello. In times gone past it was the Scottish Marbella and the rich and famous flocked to its parade year in year out. Now it is host to Inn Over the Green a brand new establishment that serves fine Sunday lunches and has a menu that caters for all ages and tastes. If you fancy something a little exotic spice it up at the Prince Balti House, memorable Indian cuisine perched overlooking the Firth of Forth.

Rottiserie   K11

Situated within the Holiday Inn, Rotiserie offers panoramic views of west Edinburgh and the Pentland Hills beyond - and the food is equally impressive. We started with a remarkable mushroom & mozzarella bake served with sundried tomatoes (£4.25), and a Seattle combo (£4.00 for one; £8 for two), which comprised BBQ spare ribs, chicken wings, deep-fried Cajun mushrooms and onion rings. As portions were generous, it was a relief to find that the staff allowed us to relax with a glass of wine and take in the contemporary décor before our main courses. From the diverse menu, we chose pumpkin & pecorino ravioli with olive oil and rich tomato sauce (12.95), and salmon fillet (£13.95). The former had a refreshingly unusual sweet but herb-tinged flavour, while the latter was of moist and tender texture. After finishing our bottle of house Chardonnay (£12.95) ahead of schedule, we were served toffee pecan pie coated with caramel and banana sauce (£4.25), and a chocolate pyramid with ice cream (£3.45); both deliciously sweet and impeccably presented. The quality of food, together with a friendly, unobtrusive service and a laid-back atmosphere, makes the Rotiserie a very pleasant place to dine.   **GB**

Sampans   K11

A beautiful crimson interior welcomes you to a Thai-Malaysian-Chinese experience fit for an empress. Jasmine tea and prawn crackers get you into the mood for the menu, a bewildering array of Eastern delicacies. Luckily the staff are helpful and willing to tell you about any of the dishes, as well as issuing warnings about the spicier dishes! I started with hot and sour soup (£3.80), whilst my partner enjoyed a tasty chicken satay (£4.45). To follow, I risked trying mee hoon goreng; Malaysian style fried egg noodles with fresh chillies and tiger prawns (£9.95), and the gamble paid off, it was delicious. Despite the warnings, my companion went for the hottest dish on the menu, Thai red keang; chicken cooked in coconut milk, chilli and kaffar lime leaves (£8.95). To cool things down, he had a side order of egg fried rice with coriander and pine kernels (£4.10), and at least one Tiger beer (£2.50) and most of a bottle of French Chablis (£19.95). To finish I enjoyed banana fritter and toffee sauce (£3.95), whilst my partner had some home made ice cream (£3.95), still trying to get over the Thai red keang!   **AMcC**

The Gathering Bistro & Bar   K11

The perfect place to take your clan is hidden in an old stable block behind Norton House. It is family friendly, and has lots of open space outside for the kids to play. Inside, it is a shrine to Scottish heraldry, decorated with various clan tartans and family crests. The menu has a light bistro feel, but is dominated by traditional fare. I began with prawn cocktail (£4.95), whilst my dinner partner tried the tasty Thai spiced chicken with salad greens and yoghurt (£3.95). I urged my companion to order the haggis, but he swayed towards chump of lamb stewed in root vegetables with braised potatoes (£7.95). I was no Braveheart either, and enjoyed a delicate baked cod topped with a lime and herb crust, with salad and new potatoes (£6.95). To accompany our meal, we enjoyed a bottle of Rioja Blanco Marqués de Cáceres (£13.95) which had a beautiful fresh flavour. To round the evening off, I opted for hazelnut meringue with ice cream and apricot compote (£2.75), whilst my friend enjoyed a devilishly rich banoffee pie (£3.22), washed down with unlimited top-ups of tea and coffee (95p). **AM**

The Ritz K11
This spacious restaurant and bar is situated in the centre of South Gyle, and contains a large conservatory and al fresco dining. The ideal place for a business lunch, the service is quick and discreet, and the meals are light and simple. Although we weren't discussing a take-over, we enjoyed the pleasant atmosphere and view of the canal. To begin we shared spicy potato wedges, served with sour cream and salsa (£2.50) and garlic bread with cheese (£2.50). To follow, I opted for the cheese and bacon steak burger, which came with fries and coleslaw (£6.50), and my companion enjoyed a minute steak covered in a peppercorn sauce and served with salad and fries (£5.95). Dessert followed: a selection of ice cream, and banoffee pie (£2.95 each). We shared a bottle of the house white, a dry Vin du Pays du Gers (£8.95 per bottle). The restaurant offers a single menu from 12pm until 10pm, as well as a large bar, lounge area and extensive parking facilities. **AMcC**

Alphabet K11
Set close to Murrayfield Stadium and the zoo, Alphabet is a large but friendly restaurant with a modern, bright interior and helpful, attentive staff. The menu is varied and is twinned with a large delicatessan menu (10am-7pm). After some consideration, I chose goat's cheese parcel (£4.50) to start, while my companion tried the terrine of duck, flavoured with bacon and garlic (£5.20). For my main course, I was satisfied by the St. John sirlion, a 6oz sirlion steak, topped with braised onions, mushrooms, and served sizzling with its own roast potatoes (£8.90). My partner was certainly not dissatisfied by his lamb Wellington, a tender loin of lamb wrapped in pastry and topped with a minted savoury stuffing, served with a redcurrant jus and a timbale of vegetables and potatoes (£10.90). We could just about manage baked apple cheesecake (£2.90) and some homemade ice cream (£2.50) before it was time to feed the penguins. **AMcC**

The Prince Balti K11
The cool, airy elegance of the eating experience at The Prince Balti creeps up on you as you dine. Perfect, as the body needs time to fully appreciate the large portions of exquisitely prepared Bangladeshi and Indian dishes on offer. Choose from an extensive list of Eastern delicacies made with day-fresh ingredients, and bask in the delightful attention to detail the staff put into their service. To begin my partner had a balti lamb kebab (£2.75) which I'm told was as delicious as it was filling. I plumped for balti chana puri (£2.60), which was delicately blended and very tasty. For the main meal I fortunately chose balti Jaipuri chicken (£5.95). This dish comes specially recommended, I need say no more. For her main meal my partner indulged her penchant for the sweeter side of Indian cooking and chose the balti chicken tikka kurma (£5.95), taken to a new level by the almond and cashew mix. This dish is also a must try as part of your visit to this Prince among restaurants. **PD**

```
THE
RITZ
BAR & GRILL
EDINBURGH

2 LOCHSIDE PLACE, EDINBURGH PARK,
EDINBURGH  EH12 9DE
TEL: 0131 317 8800  FAX: 0131 317 1106
```

alphabet
BAR RESTAURANT HOTEL

Bar open from 11am serving a superb selection of wines, beers, cocktails, juices and smoothies.

Delicatessen offering a range of freshly prepared sandwiches, wraps and salad bowls.

Innovative design, friendly and relaxed atmosphere.

Purpose built children's indoor play area.

Outdoor seating on heated timber decks.

Restaurant great for executive lunch or intimate dinner.

OPENING TIMES:
Deli 9am-7pm, Restaurant 10am-10pm

92 St. Johns Road, Edinburgh Tel: 0131 316 4466

The Ultimate Millennium Eating Experience

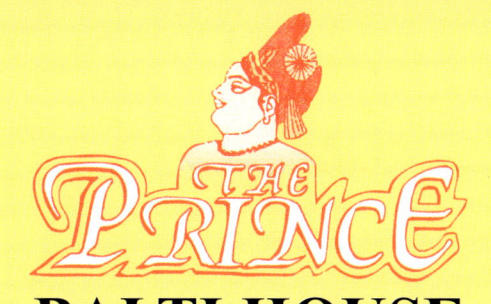

THE PRINCE
BALTI HOUSE
BANGLADESHI & INDIAN CUISINE

The very best Indian restaurant, located by Portobello beach • highly recommended
Edinburgh's finest classic Indian restaurant • highly skilled staff

Here at The PRINCE BALTI HOUSE you can rest assured that the warmth of greeting to you will be ever warm, courteous, cheerful and helpful. We at The PRINCE BALTI HOUSE are proud to claim that we KNOW OUR FOOD and HOW TO PRESENT IT, – even to the most discerning of palates. This area is well served by public transport and car parking facilities are excellent all day.

FULLY LICENSED • OPEN 365 DAYS • Free Home Delivery Service • Special Childrens Menu • Huge fish tank for family attraction • Fully air conditioned • FREE HOME DELIVERY SERVICE (Minimum order £10)
Banquets and set menu from £7.95 • Lunch Specials from £4.95 • Outside Catering • Good Service
Friendly atmosphere • ALL MAJOR CREDIT CARD ACCEPTED

11/12 SEAFIELD ROAD EAST, EDINBURGH, EH15 1EB TEL: 0131 657 1155 FAX: 0131 657 1122

St John's Restaurant K11

Situated near Murrayfield Stadium, and Edinburgh Zoo, St John's Restaurant is well located, warm and welcoming. The menu has a definite Italian slant, the decor cosy and intimate, with separate booths for each table. A BYOB establishment, it's conveniently close to an off license, and we weren't charged the cheeky corking fee that most restaurants incur. I chose melanzane parmigiano to start (£4.50), sliced aubergine baked in a tomato and cream sauce, topped with mozzarella, served sizzling fresh from the oven. My partner made a mess with fresh corn on the cob in a garlic butter and cream sauce (£3.50). To follow, I opted for a delicious scaloppina Milanese (£12.50), veal, pan-fried in breadcrumbs served with a light and tasty spaghetti Napoletana. Fillet steak with a pepper sauce (£12.95) was my companion's choice, served with patate fritti (that's chips to you and me), and home made garlic bread (£1.80). Sweets are freshly delivered each day and cost between £2-£3, and coffees between £1-£2. Lunchtimes are catered for by the adjoining chip shop, and the restaurant opens at 6.30pm. **AMcC**

Hilton at the Airport J11

Literally 5 minutes walk from Edinburgh Airport, this restaurant is ideal if you want to eat before you fly, and avoid those horrible in-flight meals! A large eating area allows privacy and space for each table, and the service is prompt and personal. I began with tiger prawns lightly grilled with garlic, lime juice, herbs and olive oil, served with salad leaves on a chargrilled crostini (£5.50), whilst my co-pilot opted for an antipasti plate, heaped with air-dried ham, salami, olives, tapas and salad (£5). To follow, I enjoyed a rich and delicious chicken breast, filled with a pocket of cream cheese, herbs and garlic, wrapped in proscuttio ham served on a bed of crushed potatoes, caponata and caramelised onion, with a warm balsamic dressing. My co-pilot however went for the more straightforward, but none-the-less delicious prime fillet steak (£15.75) served with salad, and fries (£2.25). South African Silver Sands Chardonnay (£14.25) washed down our delightful dinner, and to round things off, we dabbled in a little apple tarte tatin (£3.60) and banana and toffee sponge pudding (£3.30). After all that food there was no chance of taking off. **AMcC**

Inn Over The Green K11

A leisurely Sunday lunch is what we sought and the newly opened Inn Over the Green served the perfect setting. The floor to ceiling windows mean light streams in whilst the peach and green décor complements blond wood and makes for a serene setting in which to enjoy fine cuisine elegantly presented. We began with soup of the day, and melon and Parma ham with an ingenious twist of lemon sorbet and ginger sauce. Traditional roast beef with wild mushrooms, Yorkshire pudding and a selection of vegetables, were light and tender. Deliciously pink pan-fried salmon garnished with vegetable ribbons and new potatoes was devoured eagerly by my partner. Both main courses, although filling, were not too heavy, allowing room to enjoy sticky toffee and pecan pie. The set price feast (£12.50 for three courses) was accompanied by a bottle of house Chardonnay (£8.50). The adjoining Ryons Bar accommodates a wide selection of drinks and serves a selection of light snacks during the day and into the evening. Rounding our afternoon off with a leisurely coffee (£1.10) we reflected on the excellent standard of service and food that makes Inn Over the Green a must for anyone seeking quality, affordable cuisine. **CSR**

ST JOHN'S RESTAURANT

CORSTORPHINE'S BEST KEPT SECRET
BYOB NO CORKAGE CHARGE

259-261 ST JOHN'S ROAD
CORSTORPHINE, EDINBURGH
EH12 7XD

☎ 0131 334 2857
☎ 0131 539 7022

DELIVERY SERVICE AVAILABLE

Hilton
Edinburgh Airport

Café de Havilland
Bistro Specialising in prime Scottish Steaks and the best dishes from around the world.

Café Cino
Continental café serving speciality coffees, filled breads and mouth-watering pastries.

Edinburgh International Airport Tel: 519 4400

Inn over the Green

The Ultimate Dining Experience in a Relaxed Atmosphere

Simply Fresh Food
Prepared Using
the Finest
Scottish Ingredients

Exquisite surroundings, superb food, with views over the East Lothian countryside.

Dinners • Business Lunches • Celebrations

24 Milton Road East. Tel: 0800 698 1428 Fax: 0131 657 0201

LOTHIANS, BORDERS AND FIFE

Eating out in Lothians, Borders and Fife

People flock to Edinburgh in their millions but many never venture out of the capital, even the locals can forget that the countryside surrounding the city is some of the most impressive, beautiful landscape. Set a day aside to escape the city, enjoy the country and complement your day with some outstanding cuisine.

For an introduction to life beyond the capital venture west towards Newhaven or South Queensferry and sample the delights of the Sealscraig whilst overlooking the forth rail bridge, or cross it and investigate idyllic Fife where Taurasi and Santa Lucia await your tastebuds.

Alternatively, wind your way east down the coast road and enjoy the stunning views and rolling hills. The Old Aberlady Inn makes seafood its speciality whilst Gifford's Goblin Ha' Hotel is a bustling country pub with diversions for the children allowing you to relax and enjoy the delicious fare.

Whitecraig

The Dolphin Inn   K11

The Dolphin Inn, situated in Whitecraig, just outside Edinburgh, is a friendly hotel which has both a bar and restaurant area. There is a strong focus on the family with an outdoor play area, junior menu, baby dinners and changing area. We began our meal with prawn cocktail (£3.35) and salmon brochettes (£3.45), pieces of salmon coated in crispy batter served on a wooden skewer. We followed up with a special for the day, stuffed salmon with white wine sauce (£6.50), accompanied by potatoes, mange tout and carrots. We also had Jacobean chicken (£6.95) which was chicken breast filled with haggis, accompanied by a whisky and cream sauce and a portion of chips. Stuffed, we declined dessert but were very tempted by a wide range of ice cream sundaes (£2.95). We accompanied our meal with a bottle of soave (£9.25). The Dolphin Inn has an excellent menu offering a great deal of variety to suit all tastes including a curry of the day, pasta, steak and burgers and they also serve a variety of lunchtime options.   **VI**

Musselburgh

Shish Mahal   K11

Established in 1979, the family-run Shish Mahal in Musselburgh is an Indian restaurant worth venturing out of the city centre to experience. Its extensive menu caters equally well for vegetarians as it does for meat eaters and includes an impressive number of traditional and speciality dishes. Upon entering, it is apparent that the tasteful décor and subdued lighting combine to create a warm, homely environment while the general atmosphere is relaxed and intimate. Then came the food: the chicken pakora (£2.75) and mushrooms cooked in medium spiced garlic sauce (£2.75) set the standard high, before the prawn rogan josh (£6.95) with pilau rice (£1.95), and mixed vegetable lahore (£5.95) with special fried rice (£2.25) confirmed the culinary excellence of this popular restaurant. Following that, we cooled down with a coconut half (£2.95) and a crème de menthe bombe (£2.49), just two of the many ice cream selections on the dessert menu. Another big attraction is the weekly buffet (Tuesdays 7pm-10pm), where customers can eat as much as they like for only £8.99, and with dishes of this quality, it comes highly recommended.   **GB**

Armadale

The India Cottage   J11

While soaking up the stylish décor and perusing the menu, we enjoyed a glass of the house white, Niersteiner Guttes Domtal (£7.95 per bottle). For starters my partner had succulent charcoal grilled tandoori emperor prawns (£4.95), while I had a tasty lentil pancake (Dosa), filled with fiery looking chick peas (£3.55). Our appetites whetted, my partner enjoyed a mild pasanda, chicken tikka served in a beautiful blend of fresh cream, yoghurt and coconut cream with flaked almonds (£7.25), while I was lured by one of the speciality kormas, the sharabi, which featured added Galiano liqueur, a real pleasure to taste. This magnificent spread was accompanied by saffron pilau (£1.75) and a coriander nan (£1.90) which was just one of the many types of nan on offer. Thoroughly sated, we each still managed a portion of the traditional Kulfi ice cream, which was smooth and creamy, in mango and pistachio flavours

SHISH MAHAL
Fully Licensed Indian Restaurant & Takeaway

Established since 1979

THE HIGHEST RANGE OF EXCELLENCE IN QUALITY & SERVICE

Experience the best curry in Edinburgh

Open 7 days, 5pm till Midnight

Home Delivery Service
10% discount on meals when collected

Try our eat as much as you like Buffet Night every Tuesday

We accept all major credit cards

Tel: 0131 665 3121
63A High Street, Musselburgh

THE DOLPHIN INN
CONSERVATORY - RESTAURANT

Freshly prepared dishes at very reasonable prices

Mon-Fri Lunch served 12-2.30,
Dinner 5.30-9.30 (5-9.30 Fri)
Food served all day Sat & Sun

Tel: 0131 665 3354   Fax: 0131 665 2002
Whitecraig • Musselburgh

OUT OF TOWN

THE INDIA COTTAGE
FULLY LICENSED - FINE INDO-PAK CUISINE

GOURMET NIGHT
MON-THURS 5 TO 10PM
EAT AS MUCH AS YOU LIKE FOR £9.95 PER PERSON

SUNDAY BRUNCH
ONE CHILD UNDER 12 ACCOMPANIED BY ADULT EATS FOR FREE

MASTER CHEF WINNER 1999
QUALITY FOODS WINNER 2000

www.indiacottage.co.uk

ENJOY A LA CARTE CUISINE IN WEST LOTHIAN'S MOST POPULAR INDIAN RESTAURANT

47/49 SOUTH STREET ARMADALE EH48 3ET
TEL: 0800 698 1426   FAX: 01501 734 009

Caerketton Restaurant

"The Caerketton Restaurant deserves top marks for food and style"
BILL CLAPPERTON, EDINBURGH EVENING NEWS

Warm, Friendly Atmosphere, Excellent Cuisine • Situated In Relaxed Country Setting • Modern Scottish Fayre • Courtesy Transport Available Extensive Parking Available • Full Disabled Facilities

Tel. 0800 698 1406

Taste of Scotland Member   www.caerketton.com

Mauricewood Mains, Mauricewood Road, Penicuik, EH26 0NJ
Email: caerketton@mains72.freeserve.co.uk

---

the SEALSCRAIG RESTAURANT

Open noon till 10pm every day

Offers terrific views of firth of forth & its bridges

Easy access from Fife, Edinburgh & Lothians

Good Food. Good Views. Good Value.

23 Edinburgh Road
South Queensferry
Tel: 331 1098

LOTHIANS, BORDERS AND FIFE

(£2.50). The India Cottage thoroughly deserves its Masterchef Five Star rating, offering too many intriguing dishes to try in one visit, this restaurant is well worth going out of your way for. **CP**

Penicuik
Caerketton Restaurant K11
Situated three miles outside Edinburgh, off the A702, Caerketton is a must for diners looking for quality food in the countryside. We were welcomed to the reception area and allowed time to study the exquisite menus and wine-list before being shown to our table. After much deliberation my partner decided to start with the superb lobster and sea-food chowder (£2.95), whilst I selected the chicken and vegetable terrine (£3.95), which was encased in braised leeks. These mouth-watering starters were complemented with the smooth house red wine (£11.95), an Australian shiraz cabernet. We looked forward in great anticipation to our main courses, mine the char-grilled highland sirloin steak 'Castle Stewart' (£15.95), was smothered in molten blue Lanark cheese, accompanied by a garden of fresh vegetables. My partner savoured the delights of spiced winter vegetable casserole (£11.75), a wonderful medley of vegetables. The desserts crowned a wonderful meal, with the breathtaking cheeseboard and the hot chocolate soufflé (both £5.15). The evening surpassed our expectations and we looked forward to the next time we would dine at the Caerketton. **EdM**

Ratho
The Bridge Inn K11
In the Bridge Inn you can hardly move for award plaques and photographs of famous visitors on the walls. This Ratho establishment, a converted 18th century farmhouse beautifully situated next to the re-opened Union canal, has such a reputation for quality that our visit came the night after the entire Scottish rugby squad were catered for, and its standing is complemented by excellent service and wonderful food that justifies the prices. We began with the fresh sautéed mushrooms and red onions, served with tangy lime and ginger mayonnaise (£5), and the smoked salmon and prawn potato cake, rolled in oatmeal and deep fried, served with horseradish crème fraîche (£5.50). From an excellent steak menu I plumped

---

The BRIDGE INN
Ratho
1971-2001 • 20 years of quality

Much more than just an out of town restaurant. To find out about the full canalside experience visit our website or call for a full colour brochure.

0131 333 1320
info @ bridgeinn.com
www.bridgeinn.com

143

for the prime grilled Glenfarg fillet (£15.50) with "Ratho" sauce (£1.50 extra), while my companion chose baked monkfish with a herby lemon crust, served with tiger prawn tails and a light lemon and tarragon yoghurt (£13.50). This was washed down by a bottle of house red (£11.50), and desserts of light creamy lemon parfait and American-style caramel apple cheesecake (£3.75 each) finished off a quite exceptional meal. **JC**

South Queensferry
The Sealscraig J10
Not getting enough iron in your diet? A meal at the Sealscraig will soon change that. Located in South Queensferry, the Sealscraig boasts one of the finest views available of our great monuments to Scottish engineering – The Forth Rail and Road Bridges. It affords such romantic views of the bridges and river, that it's only the even keel of the floor that reminds us we are firmly moored to land. Under new management, the Sealscraig's delicious new menu and the view makes for a very enjoyable evening. We began with scallop feuillantine in a spicy onion compote and lime butter sauce (£7.20) and a luxurious crab veloute with salmon dumplings (£7.50). Accompanied by a South African white wine from the international wine list (£10.25), we followed with grilled sea bass fillets served with asparagus, cherry tomatoes and pepper risotto (£14.95), and duck breast and wild mushrooms marinated in cognac with boulangere potatoes (£14.75). Traditional chocolate fudge cake, a tasty banoffee roulade (both £3.50) and fresh coffee rounded off a perfect trip. The Sealscraig is open daily 12noon-10.30pm and the menu changes quarterly. **PM**

Gifford
Goblin Ha' Hotel L11
Situated in the heart of the East Lothian countryside the Goblin Ha' Hotel in Gifford is a perfect choice for a high quality meal within a friendly environment. The hotel provides the choice of a pub menu including the goblin burger, 'made by goblins' and a more extensive restaurant menu. We started our meal with homemade chicken liver pâté and oatcakes (£4.75) and deep-fried camembert with cranberry relish (£3.95). Both came served with a fresh side salad. To follow we had roast shank of lamb with a caper and mustard sauce (£8.75) and medallions of pork on Chinese noodles and chef's own szechuan sauce (£9.25). Both were accompanied with a selection of seasonal vegetables a and a bottle of house wine (£10). To complete our meal we had crêpes with caramel ice cream and maple sauce (£3.25) and a 'jungle jive' (£3.25) which was a combination of fresh bananas and banana ice cream, chosen from a large ice cream menu. Both provided a perfect end to an excellent value meal within a friendly and scenic environment. Our meal was well accompanied with. **VI**

Aberlady
The Old Aberlady Inn L10
Summer is a coming in – or so the calendar says! If you're heading beach-wards down East Lothian then you must seek refreshment, and a good warming-up, at The Old Aberlady Inn. A pub, a B&B and a superb dining restaurant, this family-friendly Inn serves lunch 12-2pm and dinner 6-9pm. With the option to eat al fresco in the patio garden, we chose to enjoy summer's progress from the warmth of the sunny conservatory. We lunched on feta cheese salad with black olives and garlic croutons (£3.50) and salmon and chive fish cakes in a spicy tomato sauce (£3.75). We followed with baked filo parcels of curried vegetables, served with pilau rice and chilli dressing (£5.00), and roast Scottish salmon marinated in chilli oil (£6.75). Being party to the fact that a Scottish summer ensures a big appetite, we pushed the yacht out with desserts of fruit sorbet and a dark chocolate and Cointreau cheesecake (both £3.85). With so much to offer, The Inn makes a great holiday spot itself, any time of the year. **PM**

North Berwick
Deaveus at the Open Arms Hotel L10
Named after the medieval family who lived in the castle opposite, Deaveus is the award-winning

THE OPEN ARMS

Traditional family run country inn with excellent hospitality, fine food & wines, situated in one of Scotland's prettiest villages.

Deveau's Brasserie – friendly, informal atmosphere with bistro style menu and daily specials.

The Library – intimate fine dining with a Scottish flavour.

The Open Arms, Dirleton, East Lothian, EH39 5EG
Tel:01620 850241 Fax: 01620 850570 www.openarmshotel.com

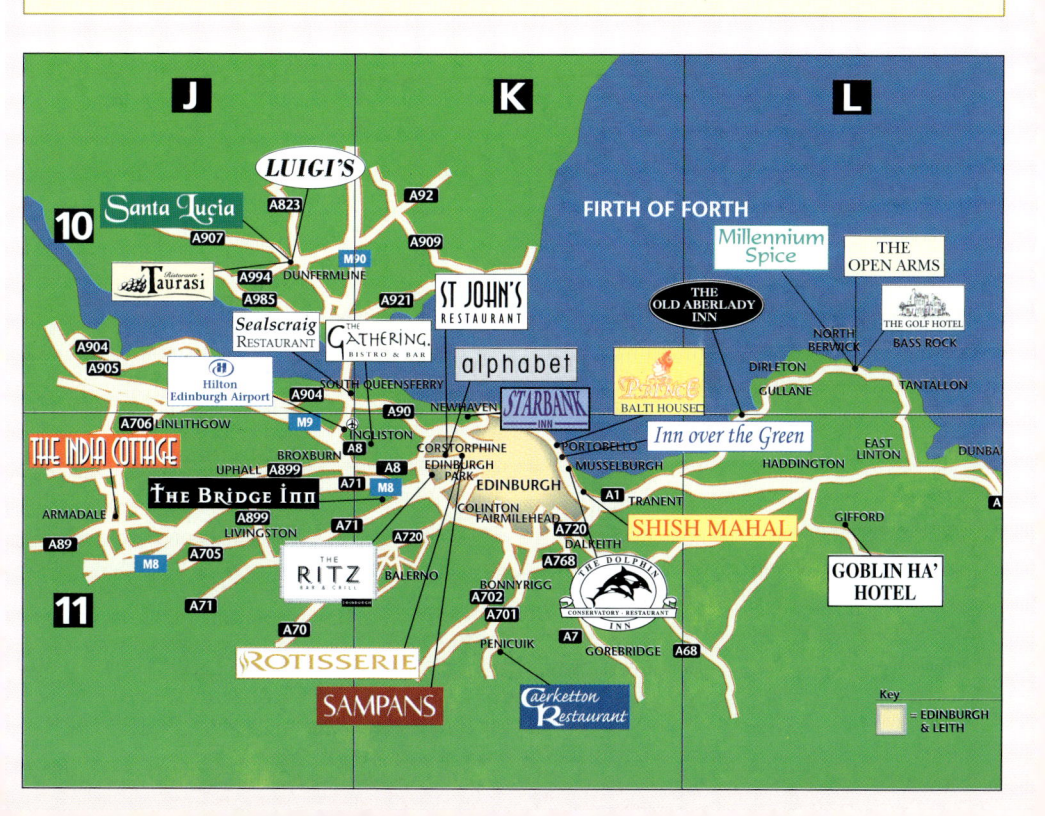

restaurant at the Open Arms Hotel, located within a picturesque village setting. Serving an extremely varied and innovative lunch and dinner menu we began our lunch with mussel and onion stew (£3.75), a restaurant favourite using their traditional 30-year-old recipe. We also had Arbroath smokie and spinach fishcakes in a light sesame crumb with a caper and cucumber dip (£3.50). To follow we enjoyed chicken, leek and smoked cheese crêpe glazed with brie, served with salad and garlic bread (£8.95), and venison and beef casserole on a bed of haggis, neeps and tatties, garnished with grilled potato scone (£9.95). To accompany our meal we enjoyed a quality house white wine (£3.50) per glass and (£11.50) per bottle. The restaurant also serves a wide variety of desserts for around (£3.50) and has a wide range of daily chef specials. The Deaveus combined excellent service and high quality food within a friendly and quiet location. Definitely worth a visit! **VI**

The Golf Hotel L10
North Berwick is a golfer's haven, with courses on the doorstep and many more just a short drive along the scenic winding road overlooking the East Lothian coast. The Golf Hotel caters for many of these golfing visitors and casual tourists alike, providing sensibly priced lunches and dinner served in the bar or the quieter dining room alongside. We started with liver pâté served with hot herb bread (£2.50) and smoked mackerel pâté served with brown toast (£2.60). We then moved on to venison sausage casserole with onions and served with mashed potatoes (£4) and a fillet of haddock served with chips (£4.90). All thoughts of heading home vanished when we spied the vast list of puddings on offer. All homemade, we toyed with treats such as lemon and ginger crunch or marmalade bread and butter pudding but eventually chose a fudge and almond flan and a chocolate steam pudding with hot chocolate sauce (both £2). Like so many of the enthusiastic golfers trying their luck on North Berwick's testing courses, our lunch at the Golf Hotel was well above par. **KH**

Dunfermline

Luigi's Ristorante J10
Luigi's is an authentic Italian restaurant, with a Mediterranean feel. We were welcomed to our table where we savoured complimentary garlic bread whilst we decided on starters. After much deliberation, I chose funghi ripieni (£3.90), a lovely array of mushrooms stuffed with pate. My partner started with pepperoni ripieni (£4.00), a wonderful serving of green peppers stuffed with sea-food and rice. For main course, I decided to take up Luigi's offer and try the tortellini Luigi (£5.75), a superb pasta combination with creamy mushroom, tomato and ham, whilst my partner chose wisely with pollo diavolo (£8.95), chicken with chilli, olives, white wine and red peppers. These fine selections were washed down with the house red, a lovely Merlot, at £8.50 for the bottle or £1.95 a glass. My partner declined dessert, preferring to finish off with cioccolata romano (£2.50), a hot chocolate laced with vodka, and I ended with tartufo (£2.75) (ice-cream coated with nuts and chocolate). We passed on coffee and lumbered out into the night feeling like the starters – stuffed! **EdM**

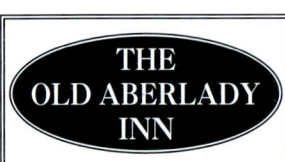

THE OLD ABERLADY INN

Excellent Scottish cuisine, nestled among golf courses, nature reserves, historic sites and beaches, only 16 miles east of Edinburgh

Main Street, Aberlady
01875 870503

RISTORANTE LUIGI'S PIZZERIA

FOR ALL THE FAMILY
~
BIRTHDAYS · WEDDINGS
CHRISTENINGS
~
COMPANY & CORPORATE
OCCASIONS
~
ADVANCED BOOKINGS
ACCEPTED

01383 726666

24 KINGSGATE
SHOPPING CENTRE,
DUNFERMLINE
(OPP. THE MAIN
POST OFFICE)

THE DOLPHIN INN
CONSERVATORY - RESTAURANT

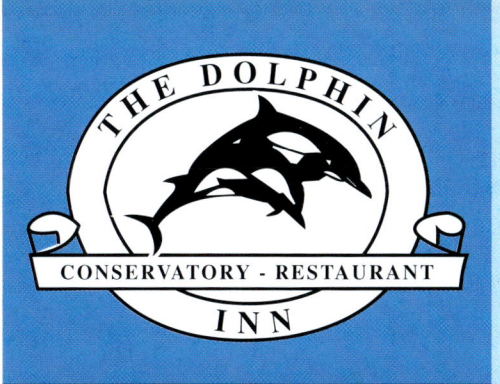

Freshly prepared dishes at very reasonable prices

Mon-Fri Lunch served 12-2.30,
Dinner 5.30-9.30 (5-9.30 Fri)
Food served all day Sat & Sun

Tel: 0131 665 3354
Fax: 0131 665 2002
Whitecraig • Musselburgh

Ristorante Taurasi

01383 623 798
21 Carnegie Drive, Dunfermline

Taurasi Ristorante J10

Taurasi is a very welcoming, family-owned restaurant, not to be missed whenever you are in Fife. There is an extensive menu, with a wide range of vegetarian selections and all dishes made personally by Carmine, the owner. I started with funghi trifolate (£3.50), a delightful medley of wild and cultivated mushrooms cooked in a creamy tomato sauce. My partner chose the New Zealand mussels (£5.70), oven-baked in a white wine cream sauce, topped with coconut and parmesan, followed by penne agli anacardi, (£5.50), a mouth-watering combination of pasta quills in a pesto sauce, with cashew nuts and red peppers. I savoured the pollo erotica (£9.80), fillet of chicken breast, cooked in white wine, cream, asparagus and prawns, served with rice. Our superb meal was well accompanied by the lovely house red, a dry red wine at £1.80 a glass or £8.50 for the bottle. For dessert, we had the wonderful gorgonzola alle mandorle, (slices of gorgonzola cheese with toasted almonds, drizzled with honey and home-made chocolate and malteser cheesecake, both only £3.00. We then said goodbye, eagerly anticipating our return to this very friendly restaurant. **EdM**

Santa Lucia J10

The kingdom of Fife tempts the discerning traveller with royal heritage aplenty, but this gem, nestled in a quiet Dunfermline street, is a hidden treasure. We enjoyed quite simply the best Italian cooking we've experienced north of Milan! Riccardo Ciciriello has created a bustling, lively ristorante with a loyal clientele. Despite the immense range of the main menu, I was tempted by the specials board, and opted for the delicious salmon steak Santa Lucia (£12.95) which involved a tomato, onion, cream, brandy and nutmeg sauce. My companion began with a fine flavoursome lobster soup (£3.50) and continued with pollo al carbonara, as much tender breast of chicken as it was spaghetti (£10.95). We somehow managed to squeeze in Riccardo's Bignolata, 'Granny's cake', swimming in cream (£3.00), and a wicked lemon sorbet with vodka (£4.00). Special menus are offered at various times, presenting incredibly good value, including £6.95 for 3 courses and coffee! It is time for Dunfermline to share this gem with us all, and I for one will be headed north again soon. The conviviality, the welcome, Riccardo's gregarious charm, and not least, the excellent cuisine. **NG**

Ristorante Santa Lucia

"...great hospitality, atmosphere and most importantly excellent food."
Edinburgh Food Guide.

for reservations call
01383 624 462

25 Chapel Street Dunfermline Fife KY12 7AW

SUPPERS

	Supper	Single
Fish	£4.20	£3.20
Special Fish (in Breadcrumbs)	£4.60	£3.60
Steak Pie (Home-made)	£2.60	£1.60
Mince Pie	£2.50	£1.50
Sausage	£2.50	£1.50
Hamburger	£2.50	£1.50
Rump Chipsteak	£2.80	£1.80
King Rib	£2.80	£1.80
Cheese Burger	£2.50	£1.50
Haggis	£2.50	£1.50
White Pudding	£2.50	£1.50
Black Pudding	£2.50	£1.50
Smoked Sausage	£2.60	£1.60
Garlic Sausage	£2.60	£1.60
Spring Roll	£2.50	£1.50
Fish Cake	£2.40	£1.40
Chicken	£3.50	£2.50
Chicken Nuggets	£2.60	£1.60
Chicken Kiev	£3.50	£2.50
Chicken Burger	£2.50	£1.50
Pizza	£2.60	£1.60
Pakora	£2.70	£1.70
Chicken Pakora	£3.80	£2.80
Vegetable Burgers	£2.50	£1.50
Scampi	£3.50	£1.50
Portion of Chips	£1.00	£1.40

PIZZA

All Pizzas listed below contain Mozzarella Cheese, Tomatoes and herbs.

	10 inch	12 inch
Cheese	£2.80	£3.80
Cheese & Mushroom	£3.30	£4.50
Cheese & Onion	£3.30	£4.50
Cheese & Peppers	£3.30	£4.50
Cheese & Ham	£3.60	£4.80
Cheese & Pepperoni	£3.60	£4.80
Cheese & Seafood	£4.00	£5.20
Cheese & Chicken	£4.00	£5.00
Central Special (includes most toppings)	£5.50	£6.50
Turkish Style (Doner Kebab & Mixed Salad)	£5.50	£6.50
Vegetarian (Mushrooms, Onions, Peppers, Sweetcorn)	£3.80	£4.80
Ham & Pineapple	£4.00	£5.10
Ham & Mushrooms	£4.00	£5.10
Spicy Sausage & Mushrooms	£4.00	£5.10
Spicy Sausage & Peppers	£4.00	£5.10
Chicken & Sweetcorn	£4.40	£5.20
Chicken & Pineapple	£4.40	£5.20
Tuna, Onion, Peppers & Sweetcorn	£3.80	£4.80
Anchovies, Black Olives & Artichokes	£4.00	£5.10
Bacon & Onion	£4.00	£5.10
Smoked Sausage & Onion	£4.00	£5.10
Garlic Bread	£1.90	£2.90
Garlic Bread with Mozzarella	£2.60	£3.80

KEBABS

	Small	Large
Doner Kebab	£3.20	£3.90

Minced and seasoned Lamb, served with Pitta Bread, Mixed Salad and Chilli Sauce.

Shish Kebab	£3.20	£4.20

Marinated chunks of Lamb, Onion and Peppers cooked on a charcoal grill, served with Pitta Bread, Mixed Salad and Chilli Sauce.

Chicken Kebab	£3.20	£4.20

Marinated pieces of Chicken, Onion and Peppers cooked over a charcoal grill, served with Pitta Bread, Mixed Salad and Chilli Sauce.

Mixed Kebab £5.50
A taste of all the Kebabs served with Pitta Bread, Mixed Salad and Chilli Sauce.

Vegetable Kebab £1.90
A selection of vegetables served with Pitta Bread, Chilli Sauce and Salad Dressing.

PAKORA

Chicken Pakora Served with Chilli Sauce and Salad	£2.80
Vegetable Pakora Served with Chilli Sauce and Salad	£1.90

BAKED POTATOES

Potato and Butter	£1.10
Coleslaw	£1.80
Baked Beans	£1.80
Cheddar Cheese	£2.20
Cottage Cheese	£2.20
Egg & Cheese	£2.20
Egg Mayonnaise	£2.20
Mushroom & Garlic Salad	£2.20
Sweetcorn	£2.00
Coleslaw & Ham	£2.30
Ratatouille (Home-made)	£2.40
Pasta Salad	£2.40
Tuna Salad	£2.60
Greek Salad	£2.60
Chicken Salad	£2.60
Prawn Cocktail	£3.20
Hot Filling Of The Day	£2.80

Special Offer
Two Half Portions of any filling (excluding Seafood) £2.70
Two Half Portions of any filling (including Seafood or Hot Filling) £3.20

BURGERS

Burger	£1.40
Double Burger	£2.20
Cheese Burger	£1.70
Cheese Burger with Bacon	£2.20
Cheese Burger with Egg	£2.20
Double Cheese Burger	£2.50
Double Cheese Burger with Bacon	£3.00
Triple Cheese Burger with Bacon	£4.10
Chicken Burger	£1.50
Chicken Burger with Cheese	£1.80
Chicken Burger with Cheese and Bacon	£2.30
Chicken Burger with Cheese and Egg	£2.30
Double Chicken Burger with Cheese	£2.70
Double Chicken Burger with Cheese and Bacon	£3.20
Bacon and Egg Double Decker	£1.50

BOOZE
Wines Available For Delivery

White Wine
Lambrusco (sparkling)
Liebfraumilch (medium dry)
Soave (medium dry)
Jacobs Creek (dry or medium)
Frascati (dry)

Red Wine
Lambrusco (sweet, sparkling)
Valencia (dry) Jacobs Creek (dry)
Chianti (dry)

Beers
Tennents Lager, Holsten Pils,
Red Stripe Lager McEwans Export, Becks

CENTRAL
THE BEST TAKE-AWAY IN TOWN

OPEN 7 DAYS

LUNCHTIME:
MON-FRI 11.30am-2pm

EVENINGS:
SUN-THURS 4.30pm-2am
FRI-SAT 4.30pm-3am

DELIVERY SERVICE
5.30PM-12.30am EVERY NIGHT
PLEASE NOTE THAT PRICES ARE SUBJECT TO CHANGE WITHOUT NOTICE

15/16 TEVIOT PLACE, EDINBURGH

0131 226 6898

MADE IN ITALY

Made In Italy 42 Grass Market Edinburgh EH1 2JU

FOR REAL ITALIAN PIZZA CALL

Tel: 0131 622 7328
Fax: 0131 622 7329

SIDE ORDERS

Garlic Mushrooms - Whole mushrooms covered with our own Crispy Italian Garlic Coating, served with dip. (V)	£2.75
Potato Skins - The best part of the potato, deep fried until golden and crispy, served with dip. (V)	£2.75
Mozzarella Sticks - Fresh Mozzarella Sticks covered with a specially seasoned Italian coating, served with dip. (V)	£2.75
French Fries - Deep fried until golden brown. (V)	£1.75
Chillie Poppers - Fresh tangy Jalapeno peppers halves, filled to the brim with rich creamy cheese, submerged in a light potato breading & fried to a golden brown, served with dip. (V)	£3.30
Chicken Fillet Strips - Choice fillets of chicken, served with dips.	£3.50

PIZZA (we use only 100% mozzarella)

	10" Small	12" Medium	16" Large
Cheese & Tomato	£3.25	£4.60	£7.30
Additional Toppings	£0.60	£0.80	£1.30

Full portions are given on half 'n' half pizzas, Double Dough - For extra thick base (charged as an extra toping)

TOPPINGS

Meat: Chicken, Ham, Salami, Pepperoni, Spicy Beef, Spicy Pork, Meatballs, Mortadella (+30p), Parma Ham (+30p), Bacon, Spicy Chicken, Bolognese Beef, Smoked Sausage, Frankfurter Sausage.

Vegetable: Onion, Mushroom, Sweetcorn, Peppers, Black Olives, Green Olives, Artichokes, Fresh Garlic, Chillies, Sliced Tomato, Sun Dried Tomato, Capers, Roasted Peppers, Roasted Aubergines, Hot Jalapeno Peppers.

Seafood: Prawn, Anchovy, Cockles, Tuna, Calamare, Mussels.

Cheese: Mozzarella, Gorgonzola, Brie, Cheddar, Jarlsberg.

PASTA

Mix 'n' Match Spaghetti, Penne or Fusilli with:

	hot	cold
Bolognese - tomato & Meat sauce	£2.90	£2.50
Carbonara - creamy egg, parmesan & ham sauce	£2.90	£2.50
Napoli - tomato, onion & herb sauce (V)	£2.90	£2.50
Funghi - creamy mushroom sauce (V)	£2.90	£2.50
Arrabbiata - napoli sauce with chilli & black olives (V)	£2.90	£2.50
Pesto - creamy basil sauce (V)	£2.90	£2.50

GARLIC BREADS & BRUSCHETTA

Garlic Bread (V)	£1.30
Garlic Bread with Mozzarella (V)	£1.60
Bruschetta - garlic bread, fresh tomatoes, basil & olive oil (V)	£1.70
Focaccia - pizza base, topped with olive oil, garlic & herbs (V)	£2.20
Focaccia Pomodoro - pizza base, topped with olive oil, garlic, fresh tomato & basil (V)	£2.50

SALADS

Green Salad - lettuce, cucumber, onions, green peppers & olives (V)	£1.50
Caesar Salad - lettuce, croutons, parmesan cheese & Caesar salad dressing (V)	£1.70
Caprese Salad - fresh mozzarella, tomato, basil (V)	£1.70
Insalata Siciliana - lettuce, cucumber, tuna, olives, egg & anchovies (V)	£1.95

DESERTS & ICE CREAM

We have a large selection of tempting desserts, just ask what's available when phoning your order.
Also we have Eight different flavours of creamy Italian Ice Cream.

WINES & BEERS

At Made In Italy we have one of Edinburgh's largest selections of Italian wines and beers, we can deliver a selection of Merlot's, Chardonnay's, Soave, Chianti, Montepulciano and sparkling wines. Beers available - Budweiser, Miller, Peroni, Bud-Ice, Stella, etc.

Please note that prices may change with no prior notice

(V) suitable for vegetarians

☎ **call for current special offers** ☎

mex2go

Mouthwatering mexican take-out & home delivery

56 South Clerk Street
Edinburgh EH8 9PS
Freephone: 0800 698 1497

19 Dalry Road
Edinburgh EH11 2BQ
Freephone: 0800 698 1496

SMALLS !

Wedges — 1.45 *Max it! 1.95*
Potato wedges in a spicy coating served with sour cream.

Nachos — 1.95
Corn tortilla chips served with mex2go's special nacho cheese sauce, topped with jalapeno chillis.

Turnovers — 2.45
A flour tortilla filled with melted cheese, dry fried & served with freshly made salsa - very tasty!

Burrito — 3.45 *Max it! 3.95*
A soft flour tortilla with your choice of filling - Chicken, Chilli Beef or Veg, topped with cheese & freshly made salsa. Rolled up & ready 2go...

Mexiburger — 3.45
Prime steak burger coated with mex2go spice, served on a toasted roll with freshly made salsa, mayo & lettuce.

Quesadilla — 3.45 *Max it! 3.95*
Soft flour tortilla filled with melted cheese, roasted peppers and onions, dry fried & served with freshly made salsa and sour cream.

Extra portions — 0.95
Guacamole, salsa, "hot" salsa, sour cream, cheese, jalapeno chillis, refried beans, mex2go's cheese sauce, flour tortillas (x2)
Mexican rice (1.25)

Mexican Beers
Compliment our tasty food with a cool chilled beer straight from Mexico!

Sol or Corona   (330ml)   1.75
as a 6 pack (with free lime!) 8.95

Soft Drinks
Coke, Diet Coke, Fanta, Irn Bru,
Diet Irn Bru, Sprite   (330ml)   0.75
Still Mineral Water   (500ml)   0.75
Coke, Diet Coke, Fanta,
Irn Bru, Sprite   (2 litre) 1.75

MAINS !

Burrito Supreme — 4.95
The Supreme has it all ! flour tortilla stuffed with your choice of filling (chicken, chilli beef or veg) and freshly made salsa, guacamole, cheese & sour cream..

Chicken Quesadilla Supreme — 4.95
Flour tortilla packed with tender pieces of spiced chicken, melted cheese, roasted peppers & onions. Dry fried & served with freshly made salsa, sour cream & guacamole.

Chilli — 4.95
Spicy beef or vegetarian chilli served on a bed of mexican rice with salsa and sour cream. Accompanied with corn tortilla chips.

Nachos Supreme — 4.95
Corn tortilla chips with your choice of filling - Chicken, Chilli Beef or Veg - served with mex2go's special nacho cheese sauce, jalapeno chillis & our freshly made salsa.

Enchiladas — 5.95
Soft flour tortillas filled with your choice of marinated chicken, chilli beef or vegetables, served on a bed of mexican rice with mex2go's red sauce, guacamole and sour cream.

Fajitas — 5.95
Your choice of marinated chicken, vegetables or steak (add 50p) served with soft flour tortillas and individual portions of salsa, sour cream, guacamole & cheese. Just roll them !

Tacos —
3 crispy corn tortillas with beef or veg chilli & served with lettuce, cheese & freshly made salsa.

Ben & Jerry's Ice Cream (Made in the USA)

Finish off your meal with a tub of the funkiest ice-cream available....various flavours..

500ml tubs   3.95
100ml tubs   1.35

mex2go meal deals

Meal for 1 — 4.95
Burrito or Mexiburger or Quesadilla
+
Nachos or Wedges
+
Soft Drink

Meal Supreme for 1 — 6.45
Burrito Supreme or Chilli or Quesadilla Supreme
+
Nachos or Wedges
+
Soft Drink

Meal for 2 — 13.95
Fajitas
+
Nachos Supreme
+
Quesadilla
+
2 Soft Drinks

Family Meal Deal (serves 3 or 4) — 24.95
2 Fajitas + 2 Quesadilla
1 Nachos Supreme
2 Potato Wedges
& 2 ltr bottle of soft drink

Delivery orders must be over £10 in value & within restricted radius

PIZZA Primo

FREE DELIVERY*
0800 298 3417
If our line is busy your call will be diverted

OPEN FRI-SAT TILL 2AM | SUN-THUR TILL MIDNIGHT

Knives, forks & paper napkins can be provided
244a Morrisons Street, Haymarket EH3 8DT

MasterCard · Switch · VISA

MEAL DEALS

- A Large (12") Pizza with up to 3 regular toppings, 1 coleslaw, 1 chocolate fudge cake & 2 cans — **£9.90**
- An Extra Large (14") pizza with up to 3 regular toppings, 1 coleslaw, 2 chocolate fudge cakes & 1.5l of coke — **£12.90**

FREEPHONE

"For the best Pizza in Town"

	DEEP PAN			THIN CRUST			Pizza
	9"	12"	14"	9"	12"	14"	
	3.90	5.90	7.90	3.70	5.70	7.70	**CHEESE & TOMATO**
Extra toppings	55p	75p	95p	55p	75p	95p	EXTRA TOPPINGS can be added to any Pizza on our menu or used to create your own! CHEESE · FETA CHEESE · ONION · MUSHROOM · GREEN PEPPERS · JALAPENO PEPPERS · SPINACH · PINEAPPLE · SWEETCORN · HAM · SMOKED BACON · FRANKFURTER SAUSAGE · PEPPERONI · SPICY CHICKEN · SPICY BEEF · SALAMI · TUNA · PRAWN · CAPERS · ANCHOVIES · BLACK & GREEN OLIVES · HOT CHILLIES · AUBERGINE · FRESH TOMATO · FRESH GARLIC · ARTICHOKE · SUN DRIED TOMATOES
	5.45	7.85	9.95	5.25	7.65	9.75	**CHICKEN EATER:** Spicy chicken, mushroom, onion **BEEF EATER:** Spicy beef, mushroom, onion **MEDITERRANEAN:** Spinach, green olives, feta cheese [V]
	5.80	8.10	10.80	5.60	7.90	10.60	**VEGETARIAN:** Green pepper, mushroom, onion, sweetcorn, fresh tomato [V] **SEAFOOD:** Tuna, prawn, mushroom, fresh tomato **MIXED GRILLL:** Smoked bacon, mushroom, fresh tomato, frankfurter sausage
	6.15	8.55	11.35	5.95	8.35	11.15	**HOT & SPICY:** Pepperoni, spicy beef, green pepper, onion, hot chillies 🌶 **VEGETARIAN PLUS:** Aubergine, green pepper, onion, fresh tomato, fresh garlic [V]
	6.40	8.90	11.80	6.20	8.70	11.60	**MEAT FEAST:** Pepperoni, spicy beef, ham, salami, smoked bacon **SICILIAN:** Artichoke, sun dried tomato, fresh garlic, green olives [V] **VEGETARIAN HOT:** Jalapeno peppers, green olives, green peppers, sweetcorn, fresh garlic, fresh tomato [V] 🌶
	6.75	9.05	12.05	6.55	8.85	11.85	**MEAT INFERNO:** Hot chillies, pepperoni, ham, smoked bacon, frankfurter sausage, onion 🌶 **SPECIAL:** Pepperoni, spicy beef, ham, green pepper, mushroom, onion, sweetcorn
	7.55	9.95	13.45	7.35	9.75	13.25	**SUPRIMO:** Pepperoni, spicy beef, anchovies, capers, ham, green pepper, mushroom, fresh tomato, fresh garlic

[V] = Suitable for vegetarians   🌶 = Hot Chillies

FREE DELIVERY FREEPHONE 0800 298 3417

SALADS AND SIDE ORDERS
FRESH MIXED SALAD	1.70
CLASSIC COLESLAW	80p
GARLIC BREAD & CHEESE	1.20
GARLIC BREAD	80p

DESSERT AND DRINKS
CHOCOLATE FUDGE CAKE	1.50
COKE, DIET COKE, FANTA, SPRITE, LILT, IRN BRU, DIET IRN BRU – 330ml cans	50p
COKE, DIET COKE – 1.5 litre bottles	1.50

CONDITIONS: *FREE delivery with Pizza orders over £5.00. Limited delivery area. Surcharges payable outside our specified FREE delivery area. Prices subject to change without prior notice. All prices include VAT. Offers subject to availability

THE PIZZA FACTORY

223 CAUSEWAYSIDE
FREEPHONE 0800 698 1460

FREE DELIVERY 0800 698 1460

Home of the 18" Party Pizza

Accepted: MasterCard, VISA, SWITCH, DELTA

ORIGINAL CHEESE & TOMATO

THIN CRUST (FOR DEEP PAN, ADD THE COST OF A STANDARD TOPPING)

Size	9" REG 1	12" LG 1–2	14" X-LG 2–3	16" FAM 3–4	18" PARTY 4–5	CAL-ZONE
Price	£4.25	£6.25	£8.25	£10.35	£13.25	£6.90

CREATE YOUR OWN

STANDARD TOPPINGS: mushroom, sweetcorn, onions, spinach, pineapple, peppers, egg, black olives, sliced tomato, jalapeno peppers, extra cheese, smoked pork sausage, smoked bacon, spicy meatballs, pepperoni, smoked salami, chicken, garlic sausage, spicy beef, chilli beef, ham, spicy pork, spicy chicken, anchovy, mussels, prawns, smoked salmon, tuna

Topping prices	80p	£1.00	£1.20	£1.50	£1.80	£1.00

Speciality Pizza	9"	12"	14"	16"	18"	Cal
OLD FAVOURITE: Juicy ham & freshly sliced mushrooms	£5.25	£7.65	£9.55	£11.85	£15.25	£8.10
HAWAIIAN DELUXE: Ham, pineapple, mushroom, fresh garlic	£6.15	£8.15	£11.05	£13.75	£16.95	£8.60
PEPPERONI EXPERIENCE: Double pepperoni, mushrooms						
SICILIANA: Black olives, anchovy, Italian sun dried tomatoes, garlic						
J.A.'s SPECIAL: Mushrooms, green & red peppers, sweetcorn, pepperoni,						
COUNTRY SPECIAL: Mushroom, green & red pepper, onion, s'corn, pineapple						
SON OF A GUN: Spicy beef, onion, mushrooms, pepperoni	£6.30	£8.30	£11.15	£14.35	£17.99	£8.90
SEAFOOD SPECIAL: Anchovies, prawns, mussels						
CHICKEN SPECIAL: Spicy chicken, chicken, sweetcorn						
INFERNO – HOT: Pepperoni, onions, jalapenos, chilli beef, dried chilli						
THE ITALIAN JOB: Mushroom, green & red peppers, pepperoni, black olives, onion						
MEATPACKER: Ham, spicy beef, spicy pork, pepperoni, onion	£6.95	£9.15	£11.95	£15.70	£18.65	£9.80
GIANT MEGA MIX: Spicy beef, spicy pork, ham, pepperoni, mushroom, green & red peppers, onion, sweetcorn, pineapple	£7.45	£10.05	£12.75	£16.95	£19.95	£10.55

MEAL DEALS

The Match!
We will match any up to date offer of our local competitors on receipt of their coupon/flyer. (subject to availability and restricted to items on our menu)

FAMILY FEAST
£15.95 NORMAL PRICE ~~£20.44~~
(exc. speciality) 12" pizza with 3 toppings 9" pizza with 3 toppings 9" garlic bread with cheese 1.5 L soft drink

THE DESTROYER
£29.95 NORMAL PRICE ~~£38.68~~
Any 18" speciality pizza, 1 x nachos deluxe, 1 x chicken wings, 12" bruschetta, 500ml Luca's ice cream, 1 x crema caramellata ice cream, 2L soft drink (serves 5-6)

Buy any large speciality pizza and get another large pizza HALF PRICE
(second pizza cannot exceed value of first)

SIDE ORDERS

Nachos Deluxe £3.50
Corn Tortilla chips with cheese, jalapenos, salsa, sour cream & guacamole.

Potato Skins £2.45
7 pieces topped with cheese, served with sour cream and chive dip.

Chicken wings, salads & garlic bread available. Please ask.

DESSERTS
Danish Pastries 65p, Tiramisu £1.99
Luca's ice cream £1.10/£3.75
Crema Caramellata ice cream £1.99

SOFT DRINKS
Cans = 65p, 500ml = 89p,
1.5L = £1.59, 2L = £1.79

Biggest PIZZAS
FREE* DELIVERY

Lunch Time Specials

OPEN:
TUES-FRI 11.30am-2.30pm
SUN-THURS 5pm-midnight
FRI & SAT 5pm-1am

OPEN 7 DAYS

Knives, forks & paper napkins can be provided. Please ask.

*within specified radius & amount. Last delivery 30 mins before close.

COOKING SINCE 1973

THE GY CHINESE TAKE OUT
AND HOME DELIVERY SERVICE
26/27 ROSENEATH PLACE,
MARCHMONT, EDINBURGH EH9 1JD
Tel: 0800 298 3414
Fax: 0131 229 7799

COOKING HOURS
OPEN 7 DAYS
5pm till LATE
Special set dinner available
Where possible non M.S.G in our cooking

FREE LOCAL DELIVERY FOR FOOD ORDERS OVER £12

SOUP

Gy Special Soup	£1.90
Wan Tun Soup	£1.90
Hot and Sour Soup Gy Style	£1.90
Crab Meat and Sweetcorn Soup	£1.90
Chicken and Sweetcorn Soup	£1.70
Chicken Noodle and Mushroom Soup	£1.70
Chicken and Mushroom Soup	£1.50
Chicken and Noodle Soup	£1.50
Vegetable Soup	£1.50
Tomato and Beaten Egg Soup	£1.50

HORS 'D' OEUVRES

Mini platter combination (2 mini s/roll, 2 spare ribs, 2 chicken wings)	£2.80
Crispy Spring Roll/Vegetarian Spring Roll	£1.80
Mini Spring Roll/Mini Vegetarian Spring Roll	£2.20
Barbecued Spare Ribs	£3.50
Spare Ribs in Black Bean Sauce or Sweet and Sour Sauce	£3.70
Spare Ribs Beijing Style/Szechuan Style	£3.90
Honey Chilli Ribs Gy Style	£3.90
Crispy Spare Ribs Canton Style	£3.90
Honey Chilli Crispy Spare Ribs	£3.90
Salt and Chilli Crispy Spare Ribs	£3.90
Wafer Paper King Prawns	£3.90
Spicy Chicken Wings	£3.00
Honey Chilli Crispy Chicken Wings	£3.00
Crispy Chicken Wings Beijing Style/Szechuan Style	£3.10
Open Sesame Prawns on Toast	£2.80
Poisson in Greens (crispy seaweed, dried fish)	£2.30
Prawn Cocktail	£2.40
Beef, Chicken or Pork Sar-dee (skewered meat)	£2.90
King Prawn Sar-dee (skewered meat)	£4.00
Deep Fried Crispy Wantun (sweet & sour dip)	£2.90
Deep Fried Crispy Squid (sweet & sour dip)	£3.60

CHOW MEIN (NOODLES) OR FRIED RICE DISHES

Gy Special Noodles or Fried Rice Canton Style	£5.00
Oriental Spiced Noodles or Fried Rice (mixed meat, cucumber, pineapple, sweetcorn, cashew nuts)	£5.00
Gy Special Noodles or Fried Rice	£4.90
King Prawn Noodles or Fried Rice	£4.90
Roast Duck Noodles or Fried Rice	£5.00
Singapore Style Vermicelli Noodles or Fried Rice	£4.80
Beef or Chicken with Black Bean Noodles	£4.80
Yang Chow Noodles or Fried Rice	£4.60
Chicken and Ham Noodles or Fried Rice	£4.60
Shrimp Noodles or Fried Rice	£4.50
Char Siu Noodles or Fried Rice	£4.50
Beef Noodles or Fried Rice	£4.40
Chicken Noodles or Fried Rice	£4.40
Pork Noodles or Fried Rice	£4.40

CHICKEN, BEEF AND PORK DISHES
(Char Siu and Shrimp Dishes 30p extra, King Prawn Dishes 70p extra) (No Rice or Chips Included)

.....and Bamboo Shoots	£3.70
.....and Mushrooms	£3.70
.....and Beansprouts	£3.70
.....and Onions	£3.70
.....in Oyster Sauce	£3.70
.....and Fresh Tomato	£3.80
.....and Green Peppers	£3.80
.....and Pineapple	£3.80
.....and Sweetcorn	£3.80
.....and Green Peppers in Black Bean Sauce	£3.90
.....and Mushrooms in Black Bean Sauce	£3.90
.....and Almonds	£3.90
.....and Cashew Nuts	£3.90
.....and Young Corn	£3.90
.....and Straw Mushrooms	£3.90
.....in Garlic Sauce	£3.90
.....in Chilli Bean Sauce	£3.90
.....in Satay Sauce	£3.90
.....in Plum Sauce	£3.90
.....and Lychees	£4.00
.....and Cashew Nuts in Yellow Bean Sauce	£4.00
.....and Chinese Mushrooms	£4.00
.....and Chinese Leaves	£4.00
.....and Kung Po Style	£4.00
.....and Pineapples with Ginger	£4.00
.....and Spring Onions with Ginger	£4.00
Chicken and Char Siu Special	£4.00
.....and Pepper with Cucumber and Cashew Nuts	£4.10
.....and Celery in Garlic Sauce	£4.10
.....and Broccoli in Oyster or Garlic Sauce	£4.10
.....and Young Corn and Straw Mushrooms	£4.30

SPECIAL DISHES

Lemon Chicken/Orange Chicken	£4.60
Chicken in Spicy Sauce Beijing Style	£4.70
Grilled Chicken Beijing Style in garlic, ginger and spring onion sauce	£4.70
Chicken Garlic Sauce Harbour Style	£4.70
Shredded Hot Chilli Chicken or Beef	£4.70
King Prawn with Mange Tout in Garlic Sauce	£4.90
Salt & Chilli Crispy King Prawn	£4.90
Golden Crispy King Prawns (sweet & sour dip)	£4.80
King Prawns in Spicy Sause Beijing Style	£4.90
King Prawns in Lemon Sauce	£4.90
Lemon Fish	£5.20
Grilled Fish Beijing Style	£5.40
Drunken Fish	£5.40
Seafood Combination in Garlic Sauce	£5.50
Treasurers Duck	£5.50

Ma Po To Fu	£4.30
Lar Chee Chicken	£4.60
Cheung Bau Chicken	£4.60

EGG FOO YUNG DISHES (No Rice or Chips Included)
Gy Special Egg Foo Yung	£4.30
King Prawn Egg Foo Yung	£4.30
Shrimps or Char Siu Egg Foo Yung	£3.70
Chicken and Mushroom or Chicken and Ham Egg Foo Yung	£3.70
Chicken or Mushroom Egg Foo Yung	£3.60
Vegetable Egg Foo Yung	£3.60

CHOP SUEY DISHES (Mixed Vegetables) (No Rice or Chips Included)
Gy Special Chop Suey	£4.20
King Prawn Chop Suey	£4.20
Shrimps or Char Siu Chop Suey	£3.70
Sweet and Sour Chicken Chop Suey	£3.70
Beef, Chicken or Pork Chop Suey	£3.60

CURRIED DISHES (No Rice or Chips Included)
Gy Curry Special	£4.20
Curry King Prawns	£4.20
Curry Shrimp or Char Siu	£3.60
Curry Beef, Chicken or Pork	£3.50

SWEET AND SOUR DISHES (No Rice or Chips Included)
Sweet and Sour King Prawn	£4.20
or Canton Style	£4.60
Sweet and Sour Chicken	£3.60
or Canton Style	£4.10
Sweet and Sour Pork	£3.60
or Canton Style	£4.10

DUCK DISHES (No Rice or Chips Included)
Roast Duck and Mushrooms or Pineapple	£5.00
Roast Duck and Pineapple with Ginger	£5.10
Roast Duck and Young Corn or Straw Mushrooms	£5.10
Roast Duck and Green Peppers in Black Bean Sauce	£5.10
Roast Duck in Plum Sauce	£5.10
Roast Duck Spring Onions and Ginger	£5.10
Roast Duck and Char Siu	£5.30
Roast Duck Canton Style	£5.30
Lemon Duck/Orange Duck	£5.30
Aromatic Duck and Pancakes with Crudities	
Half	£11.90
Whole	£22.40

SZECHUAN DISHES (No Rice or Chips Included)
Gy Special Szechuan Style	£5.10
King Prawns Szechuan Style	£5.10
Shrimps or Char Siu Szechuan Style	£4.70
Beef, Chicken or Pork Szechuan Style	£4.60

EUROPEAN DISHES (Chips Included)
Deep Fried Chicken or Fish	£4.30
Gy Special Omelette	£4.50
King Prawn Omelette	£4.50
Shrimp or Ham Omelette	£4.30
Chicken, Tomato or Mushroom Omelette	£4.20
Plain Omelette/Vegetarian Omlette	£3.80

VEGETARIAN DISHES
(Rice or Chips Not Included Unless Stated)
Why not add To-Fu *in your Vegetarian Dishes?* - 60p extra

Stir-fried Vegetable Chop Suey	£3.10
Mixed Vegetables in different sauces of your choice.	
1. Black Bean Sauce 2. Curry Sauce 3. Garlic Sauce	
4. Lemon Sauce 5. Oyster sauce 6. Plum Sauce	
7. Satay Sauce 8. Sweet and Sour Sauce	
9. Yellow Bean Sauce and Cashew Nuts	£3.60
Vegetables with Almonds or Cashew Nuts	£3.60
Vegetables and Pineapple with Ginger or Spring Onions with Ginger	£3.80
Vegetables Beijing or Szecheun Style	£3.90
Vegetables and Celery in Garlic Sauce	£3.90
Pepper, Cucumber and Vegetables with Cashew Nuts	£3.90
Fried Aubergines in Black Bean Sauce or Chilli Bean Sauce	£4.00
Vegetable Chow Mein or Fried Rice	£4.00
Vegetable Spicy Chow Mein or Spicy Fried Rice	£4.10
Vegetable Chow Mein and Black Bean	£4.10
Vegetable Chow Mein or Fried Rice with Spring Onions and Ginger	£4.10
Vegetable Chow Mein or Fried Rice and Broccoli in Garlic Sauce	£4.10
Tropical Fried Rice (*cucumber, pineapple, sweetcorn, cashew nuts*)	£4.10
Chinese Monk Vegetables	£4.20
Seasonal Pak Choi or Choi Sum in Garlic/Oyster Sauce	£4.00
Vegetable Cheung Bau Style	£4.00
Vegetables Lar Chee Sauce	£4.00

SIDE DISHES
Straw Mushrooms and Young Corn	£2.60
Fresh Broccoli in Garlic or Oyster Sauce	£2.60
Salt and Chilli Crispy To-Fu	£2.90
Bamboo Shoots/Mushrooms	£1.80
Mushrooms with Garlic	£2.00
Beansprouts/Onions	£1.70
Mange Tout in Garlic/Oyster Sauce	£2.90
Crispy Fried Noodles	£1.90
Soft Fried Noodles	£1.80
Egg Fried Rice	£1.40
Boiled Rice	£1.30
Chips	£1.40
Prawn Crackers	£1.60
Barbecued or Curry or Sweet and Sour Sauce	£1.00
Black Bean or Chilli Bean or Satay Sauce	£1.20

SWEETS AND DRINKS
Fritters in Syrup *(apple, banana, pineapple)*	£1.60
Toffee Apple or Banana or Pineapple	£2.10
Lychees	£1.80
Fried Toast in Syrup	£1.60
Cans/Bottles of Soft Drinks	£0.65/£1.65/£1.95

the KING'S Spice
Indian & Bangladeshi Cuisine

50-54 Henderson Street, Edinburgh EH6 6DE
FREEPHONE 0800 698 1504 Fax: 0131 555 3104

Opening Hours:
Lunch: Mon-Fri 12noon-2.30pm
Evenings: Mon-Fri 5pm-11.30pm, Sat-Sun 4pm-11.30pm

Delivery Service Available

Here at the King's Spice you can rest assured that the warmth of greeting to you would be ever warm, courteous, cheerful and helpful. We at the King's Spice are proud to claim that we KNOW OUR FOOD and HOW TO PRESENT IT – even to the most discerning of palates.
This area is well served by public transport and car-parking facilities are excellent all day.

Appetisers

Papadoms	£0.50

Starters

Sabzi Pakura — £1.70
Gran Mour onion and curd, freshly spiced with ghee served with special salad and sauce

Somosa — £1.90
Pasties stuffed with vegetables, served with salad and sauce

Sheek Kebab — £2.50
Garlic flavoured spicy minced kebab served with salad and sauce

Murgh Kebab — £2.60
Boneless chicken marinated in yoghurt and medium spices cooked in Tandoori, served with salad and sauce

Mughlai Lamb Kebab — £2.60
Diced boneless lamb marinated in yoghurt and medium spices cooked in Tandoori, served with salad and sauce

King's Spice Assorted Kebab — £3.45
Consists of lamb, chicken and Sheek kebab served with salad and sauce

King Prawn Butterfly — £4.75
King prawns fried in batter served with salad and sauce

King Prawn Puri — £4.95
King prawns cooked with medium spices garnished with spring onion and fresh coriander, served with puffed, fried bread

Prawn Puri — £3.50

King's Spice Eastern Prawns — £3.50
Steam cooked mildly spiced prawns with tamarind and coconut chutney

Vegetable Spring Roll	£2.25
Tandoori Chicken	£2.60
Garlic Mushrooms	£2.10
Prawn Cocktail	£2.95
Chicken Pakora	£1.90
Aloo Tok	£1.90
Chicken Tikka Garlic	£2.75
Onion Bhaji	£1.80
Chat on Puri Chicken or prawn	£3.50

King's Spice Tandoori Specialities

Murgh Tandoori — £5.75
Half chicken marinated in yoghurt, aromatic spices and fresh herbs. Barbecued in Tandoor served with salad and sauce

Murgh Tikka — £5.75
Diced boneless chicken marinated in yoghurt and medium spices. Barbecued in Tandoor served with salad and sauce

Mughlai Lamb Tikka — £5.75
Diced boneless lamb marinated in yoghurt and medium spices. Barbecued in Tandoor served with salad and sauce

King's Spice Mixed Tandoori — £8.95
Consists of Tandoori Murgh, Murgh Tikka, Lamb Tikka, Sheek Kebab served with Nan, salad and sauce

Mughlai Tandoori Shaslick — £5.75
Tandoori lamb/chicken with fresh green herbs with medium spices. Garnished with fresh coriander. Barbecued in Tandoor served with salad and sauce

Seafood Legend

Tandoori King Prawn Massallam — £9.95
King prawns cooked in yoghurt based sauce with medium spices, cream, tomatoes and fresh herbs

Mughlai King Prawn Jalfrezie — £8.95
Steamed cooked king prawns with fresh green chillies, tomatoes and coriander, garnished with a touch of fresh garlic. Fairly spicy and hot to taste

Calcutta Prawn Palak — £5.95
Steamed cooked prawns with fresh spinach, garnished with a touch of garlic and fresh coriander. Medium to spiced taste

Chicken Specialities

Nurjahan Chicken Pasanda — £5.45
Chicken breast cooked with ground almonds, fresh cream and ground herbs and spices, garnished with cashew nuts. Very mild and smooth to taste

Chicken Tikka Kurma — £5.45
Breasts of chicken barbecued in Tandoor with mild creamy buttery sauce garnished with almonds and cashew nuts. Mild to taste

Kashmiri Murgh Makhani — £5.45
Barbecued chicken cooked in Tandoor, fairly mild creamy sauce with banana, lychee and pineapple, dressed with almonds. Mild to taste

Shahi Rougan Josh — £5.45
A special preparation of Tandoori cooked chicken garnished with tomatoes, onions and fresh coriander

Persian Murgh Massallam — £5.45
Barbecued chicken cooked in Tandoor. A most popular Persian dish with a beautiful combination of spices, pineapple, lentil and mango chutney, producing a sour, sweet and hot taste. Garnished with fresh coriander.

Katmandu Murgh Tikka Massallam — £5.45
Barbecued chicken cooked in Tandoor with lentils, spring onion, fresh garlic and ginger. Garnished with coriander and a squeeze of lemon

North Indian Chilli-Garlic Chicken — £5.45
Tandoori cooked chicken in green chilli-garlic and garnished with a touch of fresh ginger. Medium hot to taste

East Indian Chicken Jalfrezie — £5.45
Tandoori cooked finely chopped chicken with fresh green chilli and fresh coriander garnished with a touch of fresh ginger. Fairly spicy and hot to taste

Shahi Murgh Tikka Massallam — £5.45
Diced boneless chicken barbecued in Tandoor, cooked in yoghurt-based sauce with medium spices, cream, tomatoes and fresh herbs

Morich Mosalla — £5.45
A traditional madras curry but cooked with hot spices, green chillies and decorated with fresh Dania to give taste that Royalty enjoy

Lamb Delicacies

Mughlai Lamb Tikka Massallam — £5.45
Diced boneless lamb barbecued in Tandoor, cooked in yoghurt-based sauce with medium spices, cream, tomatoes, and fresh herbs

Shajahani Lamb Pasanda — £5.45
Sliced lamb steam cooked with ground almonds, fresh cream and ground herbs and spices. Mild and very smooth to taste

Karai Gosht — £5.45
Tender lamb chops with green herbs and refreshing North Indian medium spices. Medium to taste

Muglai Chana Gosht — £5.45
Tender lamb stewed with Afghan chickpeas in spicy fresh lemon juice. Garnished with a touch of fresh coriander and fresh ginger. Medium and slightly sour to taste

Calcutta Methi Gosht — £5.45
Diced lamb stewed in methi (fenugreek) seeds and fresh methi leaves. Exclusive and delectable, medium hot to taste

Sylheti Achar Gosht — £5.45
Tender lamb in a spicy sauce with fine pickle, green chilli and fresh stewed coriander. Garnished with spring onion. Hot and sour to taste

Madrasi Chilli Palak Gosht — £5.45
Steamed cooked lamb with fresh spinach, garnished with a touch of garlic and fresh green chilli. Hot and spicy to taste

East Indian Lamb Jalfrezie — £5.45
Tandoori cooked diced lamb with green chilli and fresh coriander garnished with a touch of fresh ginger. Spicy and hot to taste

North Indian Chilli Gosht — £5.45
Tender lamb stewed in spicy sauce with fresh methi, fresh green chilli and fresh coriander. Garnished with a slice of lemon and fresh green chilli. Very hot and slightly sour to taste

Harialy Lamb — £5.45
An aromatic dish cooked with ground spinach with extra garlic, ginger, herbs and spices to give a remarkable, fairly hot taste

FREE DELIVERY (within a 2 mile raduis on orders over £12)

King's Spice Biryani Dishes

Please ask for mild, medium or hot to suit your taste
Grand festive dishes prepared from basmati rice, barbecued chicken, lamb cooked in Tandoor includes mixed vegetable curry

Tandoori Chicken Biryani	£7.45
Mughlai Lamb Biryani	£7.45
Murghi Tikka Biryani	£7.45
Curry King Sabzi Biryani	£6.45
Chicken Biryani	£6.95
Lamb Biryani	£6.95
King Prawn Biryani	£9.95

Balti Dishes

Balti's are traditional Kashmiri dishes cooked in authentic spices along with sliced onions and green peppers

Chicken	£5.45
Lamb	£5.45
Prawn	£5.95
King Prawn	£7.95
Mixed Vegetables	£4.45

King's Spice Vegetable Dishes

Bombay Chana Massallam £4.40
Chickpeas stewed in sweet and sour, fairly hot. Garnished with fresh chilli and fresh coriander

Sag Aloo Delight £4.40
Potato and spinach with fresh coriander and mustard seed. Medium spicy to taste

Persian Veg Sambar £4.40
Potato and lentil with fresh coriander garnished with spring onion. Medium spicy to taste

Sabzi Panir Jalfrezie £4.40
Oriental cottage cheese. Mixed vegetables steam cooked with fresh green chilli and coriander garnished with a touch of fresh ginger

Sabzi Bahar £4.40
Mixed vegetables, a speciality of the chef

King's Spice Curry Selection

Here is a selection of age old popular and favourite curries now specially prepared by King's Spice unique style. All these dishes are carefully prepared with fresh ingredients and freshly ground spices and herbs.

Kurmah (very mild)
A delicate preparation of curd, cream and selected spices, producing a very mild flavour

Chicken	£4.45
Lamb	£4.45
Prawn	£5.75
King Prawn	£7.95

Rougan Josh
Lamb, prawn or chicken specially prepared with pimento and garlic garnished with tomato, medium hot

Chicken	£4.45
Lamb	£4.45
Prawn	£5.75
King Prawn	£7.95

Malayan (mild)
A mildly spiced dish prepared with pineapple, fruit juices, coconuts and cream to create a beautifully balanced flavour

Chicken	£4.45
Lamb	£4.45
Prawn	£5.75
King Prawn	£7.95

Bhuna (medium)
Garnished dish with onions, green herbs, tomatoes and selected spices

Chicken	£4.45
Lamb	£4.45
Prawn	£5.75
King Prawn	£7.95

Dupiaza (medium hot)
A large quantity of onions seasoned and freshly treated with dozens of spices and herbs to produce a medium hot taste

Chicken	£4.45
Lamb	£4.45
Prawn	£5.75
King Prawn	£7.95

Dhansak (fairly sweet and sour)
A beautiful combination of spices with lentil mixed with curd producing a sour, sweet and hot taste

Chicken	£4.45
Lamb	£4.45
Prawn	£5.75
King Prawn	£7.95

Pathia (sweet and sour)
A hot and sour tasting dish prepared with garlic, red chilli onion, green pepper and tomato puree, producing a sweet and sour dish

Chicken	£4.45
Lamb	£4.45
Prawn	£5.75
King Prawn	£7.95

Madras (hot)
A most popular dish with rich, hot and sour tastes

Chicken	£4.45
Lamb	£4.45
Prawn	£5.75
King Prawn	£7.95

Ceylon (hot)
A most popular dish that is much hotter than madras and cooked with coconut powder

Chicken	£4.45
Lamb	£4.45
Prawn	£5.75
King Prawn	£7.95

Vindaloo (very hot sauce)

Chicken	£4.45
Lamb	£4.45
Prawn	£5.75
King Prawn	£7.95

Vegetarian Dishes

Vegetarian Kumah	£4.10
Vegetarian Rougan Josh	£4.10
Vegetarian Bhuna	£4.10
Vegetarian Dhansak	£4.10
Vegetarian Pathia	£4.10

Sabzi Side

Sag Panir Spinach	£2.10
Aloo Gobi Cauliflower and potato	£2.10
Khumb Bhaji Mushroom	£2.10
Fresh Okra Ladies Finger	£2.10
Benign Kalia Aubergine	£2.10
North Indian Dal Lentil	£2.10
Bombay Aloo Jeeri Fried potato with a touch of garlic	£2.10
Gobi Bhaji Cauliflower	£2.10
Sag Aloo Spinach and potato	£2.10
Chana Massla Chickpeas	£2.10
Cucumber Raitha	£1.00

Chawal Rice Dishes

Fried Rice	£2.00
Basmati Pulao	£1.80
Steamed Plain Lemon Rice	£1.80
Mushroom Pulao	£2.25
Sabzi Pulao	£2.25

Fresh Bread

Chapati Thin unleavened whole wheat bread	£0.60
Tandoori Unleavened bread baked in our clay oven	£1.30
Nan Leavened bread with garlic	£1.60
Garlic Nan Leavened bread with garlic	£1.70
Sabzi Paratha Stuffed with vegetables	£1.95
Paratha	£1.80
Payazi Nan with spring onion	£1.90
Panir Nan Cheese	£2.10
Keema Nan Mince	£2.25
Peshwari Nan Sweet	£1.90

King's Spice Set Meals

A) 2 Papadoms • Chicken Kurma • Chicken Bhuna.Basmati Pulao • Nan   £11.50 for two

B) Pakura • Chicken Korma • Chicken Rogan Josh • Pulao Rice • Nan   £11.95 for two

C) Pakura • Garlic Chicken • Chicken Tikka Massallam • Pulao Rice • Garlic Nan   £13.95 for two

D) Chicken Kebab • Chicken Tikka Massallam Jaipuri Chicken • Pulao Rice • Garlic Nan   £14.50 for two

E) Pakora & Onion Bhaji • Sabzi Bahar Jaipuri Vegetable • Pilau Rice • Nan   £11.95 for two

For Prawn £3.50 extra, King Prawn £2.50 extra on all meals.

Children's Menu

A) Chicken Korma • Pilau Rice • Drink   £2.95

B) Chicken Tikka Massallam • Pilau Rice or Nan Bread • Drink   £3.50

C) Pakora • Lamb Bhuna or Rogan Josh Pilau Rice or Nan Bread • Drink   £4.95

D) Chicken Pakura • Jaipuri Chicken Pilau Rice or Nan Bread • Drink   £5.95

We are open Xmas Day and New Year.

the KING'S Spice

TEL: FREEPHONE 0800 698 1504   OPEN 7 DAYS

THE BALTI RAJ

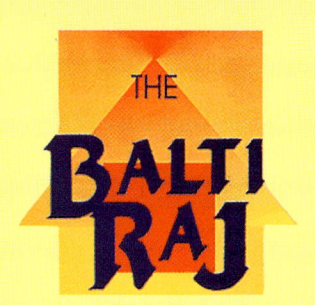

BANGLADESHI & INDIAN CUISINE

OPEN 7 DAYS
SUN-THURS: 5pm - 11.30pm
FRI & SAT: 4pm - 12am
DELIVERY SERVICE AVAILABLE

0800 698 1403

1-2 LIBERTON DAMS, EDINBURGH EH16 6AJ
TEL: 466 7281 FAX: 466 7335

APPETISERS

Popadums	£0.50
Soup of the day	£1.60
Prawn Cocktail	£2.10

STARTERS

Balti Sabzi Pakora — £1.70
Gram flour, onion and curd, spiced with ghee and served with special sauce

Balti Samosa — £1.95
Pasties stuffed with vegetables, served with special sauce

Balti Onion Bhaji — £1.80
Balti Chicken Pakora — £2.50
Balti Chana Puri — £2.50
Chick peas cooked with medium spices garnished with spring onions and coriander leaves served with puffed fried rice

Balti Chana Tikka — £2.60
Chick peas with chicken, cooked with medium spices garnished with spring onions and coriander leaves served with puffed fried rice

Balti Margh Bhaja — £2.60
Chicken Tikka cooked in a special balti with fresh herbs and spices served with chapati

Balti Mixed Bhaja — £3.45
Tandoori lamb and chicken cooked in a special Balti with fresh herbs and spices, seved chapati

Balti Shami Kebab — £2.60
Balti Chicken Kebab — £2.60
Diced boneless chicken marinated in yoghurt and medium spices, grilled in skewers, served with salad and sauce

Balti Lamb Kebab — £2.60
Diced boneless lamb marinated in yoghurt and medium spices, cooked in a tandoor, served with salad and sauce

Balti Sheek Kebab — £2.60
Tender steak mince lamb with onions, fresh mint and herbs grilled on skewers, served with salad and sauce

Balti Mixed Kebab — £3.45
Lamb, chicken and sheek kebab served with salad and sauce

Balti Tandoori Chicken — £2.60
Portion of chicken marinated in spices, cooked in a clay oven, served with salad and sauce

Balti Spicy Wing — £2.50
Chicken wings marinated in spices, cooked in a clay oven, served with salad and sauce

Balti Prawn Pathi — £3.50
Steamed prawns cooked with fresh garlic, ginger and tomato using a special sweet and sour sauce with chapati

Balti Prawn Puri — £3.50
Prawns cooked with medium spices garnished with spring onion and fresh coriander leaves, served with puffed fried bread

Balti King Prawn Butterfly — £4.75
King prawns fried in batter, served with salad and sauce

BALTI SELECTION

BALTI KORMA – VERY MILD
A delicate preperation of curd, cream and selected spices producing a very mild flavour

CHICKEN	£4.65
LAMB	£4.65
PRAWN	£5.95
KING PRAWN	£7.95
VEGETABLE	£4.25

BALTI MALAYAN - MILD
A mildly spiced dish prepared with pineapple, fruit juices, coconut and cream to create a beautifully balanced flavour

CHICKEN	£4.65
LAMB	£4.65
PRAWN	£5.95
KING PRAWN	£7.95
VEGETABLE	£4.25

BALTI BHUNA – MEDIUM
Strongly spiced curry and a special blend of spices, fried together to provide a dish of medium strength

CHICKEN	£4.65
LAMB	£4.65
PRAWN	£5.95
KING PRAWN	£7.95
VEGETABLE	£4.25

BALTI ROGAN JOSH – MEDIUM
Characteristics of this dish are derived from the use of lots of tomatoes, garlic, pimentos and onions, fried in a special oil in a manner, which produces a dish of similar strength to Bhuna

CHICKEN	£4.65
LAMB	£4.65
PRAWN	£5.95
KING PRAWN	£7.95
VEGETABLE	£4.25

BALTI DUPAIAZA – MEDIUM
A method of preparation similar to the Bhuna where raw onions are mixed with spices and fried briskly

BALTI DANASK – FAIRLY HOT & SOUR
Parsee dish sweet hot and sour with lentils and pineapple

BALTI PATHIA - SWEET AND SOUR
A hot and sour tasty dish prepared with garlic, red chilli and onion

BALTI VINDALOO DISHES – VERY HOT
Related to the madras but using a generous use of hot spices

BALTI SRI LANKA – HOT DISH
Sri Lanka curries are made from strongly flavoured spices, which make them hotter, with a coconut flavour

CHICKEN SPECIALITIES

BALTI CHICKEN PASANDA — £5.75
Tender pieces of chicken, marinated with spices, cooked with cream and herbs.

BALTI KASHMIRI MURGH MAKHANI — £5.75
Barbecued chicken cooked in a tandoor, fairly mild creamy sauce with banana, lychee and pineapple, dressed with almonds. Mild

BALTI MURGH MASSALLAM — £5.75
Spring chicken in spices, mixed with special curry sauce and grilled

BALTI KASHMIR CHICKEN — £5.75
Fairly mild, mixed with banana, pineapple and lychee

BALTI CHICKEN JALFREZIE — £5.75
Finely chopped chicken with fresh green chilli, coriander leaves, garnished with a slice of lemon. Very hot, slightly sour to taste

BALTI NORTH INDIAN CHILLI GARLIC CHICKEN — £5.75
Steam cooked in a hot chilli-garlic sauce and garnished with fresh coriander. Hot and spicy to taste

BALTI CHICKEN TIKKA MASSALLAM — £5.75
Boneless chicken grilled on skewers, cooked in a very tasty curry sauce

BALTI CHICKEN TIKKA BHUNA — £5.75
Boneless chicken grilled on skewers, cooked with medium spices, coriander and onions

BALTI CHICKEN TIKKA KORMA — £5.75
Breast of chicken barbecued in a tandoor with mild creamy buttery sauce, garnished with almonds and cashew nuts. Mild

BALTI MURGH SHAHANI — £5.75
Delicious combination of chicken tikka and spinach with onions, coriander sand chillies

BALTI SHAHI ROGAN JOSH — £5.75
Special tandoori chicken, garnished with tomatoes, onions and fresh coriander

BALTI KATHMANDU MASSALLAM — £5.75
Marinated boneless chicken barbecued in clay oven, cooked with garlic and ginger dressed with fried chillies on top

BALTI ZEERA TIKKA MASALA — £5.75
Whole seeds keep their flavour well and in this dish cumin seeds are used along with fresh coriander for a distinctive flavour

BALTI JAIPURI CHICKEN — £5.75
Tender pieces of chicken grilled in the tandoor and cooked with fried mushrooms, onions and capiscums with fresh punjabi masala in a thick sauce. Highly recommended

BALTI CHICKEN PALAK — £5.75
Spring chicken cooked with spinach and a touch of garlic and herbs

BALTI MURGH TIKKA CHANA — £5.75
Spring chicken cooked with Afghan chickpeas in a spicy fresh lemon juice, garnished with a touch of fresh coriander and fresh ginger

BALTI CHASNI MASSALLAM — £5.75
Tender pieces of chicken cooked in the tandoor oven, mixed with a special sauce and grilled

LAMB DELICACIES

BALTI LAMB PASANDA — £5.75
Tender pieces of Lamb, marinated with spices, cooked with cream and herbs. Very mild

BALTI LAMB PALAK — £5.75
Fresh lamb cooked with fresh spinach, a touch of garlic and herbs

BALTI GREEN HERB LAMB — £5.75
Tender lamb in a spicy sauce of tomato, green peppers and fresh coriander leaves, garnished with spring onion and fresh ginger.

BALTI MUGHLAI CHANA GOSHT — £5.75
Tender lamb stewed with Afghan chickpeas in spicy fresh lemon juice, garnished with a touch of fresh coriander and ginger. Medium and slightly sour to taste

BALTI LAMB TIKKA MASSALLAM — £5.75
Boneless lamb grilled on skewers, cooked in a tasty curry sauce

BALTI EAST INDIAN LAMB JALFREZIE — £5.75
Tandoori cooked diced lamb with green chilli and coriander garnished with a touch of fresh ginger. Spicy and hot to taste

BALTI NORTH INDIAN GOSHT — £5.75
Tender lamb stewed in spicy sauce with methi, fresh green chilli and coriander, garnished with a slice of lemon and fresh green chilli. Very hot and slightly sour to taste

BALTI BADAMI GOSHT — £5.75
Fillet of spring lamb steamed in a separate pot and sauce prepared with onions, cream and almonds, which create a unique mild taste

BALTI KATHMUNDO MASSALLAM — £5.75
Marinated boneless lamb barbecued in a clay oven, cooked with fresh garlic and ginger with fried chillies on top

BALTI ZEERA TIKKA MASALA — £5.75
Whole seeds keep their flavour well and in this dish cumin seeds are used along with fresh coriander for a distinctive flavour

BALTI JAIPURI LAMB — £5.75
Tender pieces of lamb grilled in the tandoor and cooked with fried mushrooms, fried onions and fried capsicums with fresh Punjabi masal in a thick sauce.

BALTI METHI GOSHT — £5.75

BALTI BIRYANI DISHES

Please ask for mild, medium or hot to suit your taste. Special preparations of saffron rice treated together with meat prawn or chicken in butter ghee with delicate herbs and spices, served with a vegetable curry sauce.

BALTI VEGETABLE — £6.95
BALTI CHICKEN — £7.20
BALTI LAMB — £7.20

BALTI MEAT AND CHICKEN — £7.25
BALTI PRAWN — £7.95
BALTI MURGH TIKKA — £7.95
BALTI TANDOORI CHICKEN — £7.95
BALTI KING PRAWN — £9.95

TANDOORI SPECIALITIES

Designed for customers who wish to watch their waistline. Recommended with Roti or Nan bread.

BALTI TANDOORI CHICKEN — £5.75
Half spring chicken marinated in yoghurt, tandoori barbecued served with sauce

BALTI LAMB TIKKA — £5.75
Diced lamb marinated with sauces, grilled on skewers, served with salad

BALTI CHICKEN TIKKA — £5.75
Diced chicken marinated with sauces, grilled on skewers, served with salad

BALTI TANDOORI MIXED — £8.75
Tandoori Chicken, Lamb tikka, sheek kebab and drumsticks, served with nan bread and salad

BALTI SHASHLICK — £5.75
Garlic Lamb/Chicken, sauteed with onion, tomato, green pepper, fresh coriander leaves and stewed spring onions, cooked in Tandoor

SEAFOOD LEGEND

BALTI GALDA CINGHI MAKHANI — £8.95
King prawns primarily made in a clay oven with mild delicious sauces

BALTI GREEN HERB KING PRAWN — £8.95
Garlic fried king prawns sauteed with onion, tomato, green chilli, fresh corianderleaves and stewed spring onions.

BALTI MUGHLAI KING PRAWN JALFREZIE — £8.95
Steamed king prawns with fresh green chilli, tomato, coriander and garnished with a touch of fresh garlic. Fairly hot and spicy to taste

BALTI KING PRAWN JAIPURI — £8.95
King prawns grilled in the tandoor and cooked with fried mushrooms, fried onion and fried capsicum with fresh Punjabi masala in a thick sauce

BALTI CALCUTTA PRAWN PALAK — £6.95
Steam cooked prawns with fresh spinach garnished with a touch of garlic and fresh coriander. Medium to taste.

BALTI GREEN HERB PRAWN — £6.95
Garlic fried prawns sauteed with onions, tomato, green chilli, fresh coriander leaves and stewed spring onion.

BALTI VEGETARIAN DISHES

BALTI SABZI PANIR JALFREZIE — £4.45
Oriental cottage cheese and mixed vegetables, steamed cooked with fresh green chilli and coriander, garnished with a touch of fresh ginger. Very hot to taste

BALTI ALLO GUL MIRCH — £4.45
Potatoes cooked with steamed green peppers. Hot to taste

BALTI SABZI BHAR — £4.45
Mixed vegetables consisting of fresh green beans, peas, carrots, sweet corn and courgettes, garnished with garlic, mustard seed and fresh coriander

BALTI FRUITY MASSALLAM — £4.45
Fairly mild creamy sauce, with banana, pineapple, lychees and dressed with almonds

BALTI CHASNI MASSALLAM — £4.45
Mixed vegetables cooked with sweet and sour taste

BALTI SAG ALOO — £4.45
Potatoes and fresh spinach with fresh methi, coriander and mustard seeds. Medium hot

BALTI SABZI PARSI SPECIAL — £4.45
Mixed vegetables in a parsi wedding style, garnished with garlic and daal

SIDE DISHES

BALTI BHINDI BHAJEE (okra)	£2.25
BALTI MUSHROOM BHAJEE	£2.25
BALTI DAAL TARKA (lentil with garlic)	£2.25
BALTI BRINJAL BHAJEE (aubergine)	£2.25
BALTI BOMBAY POTATO	£2.25
BALTI POTATO AND PEA BHAJEE	£2.25
BALTI CAULIFLOWER BHAJEE	£2.25
BALTI AOO ZEERA (potato with cumin seed)	£2.25
BALTI SAG BHAJEE (spinach)	£2.25
BALTI ALOO GOBI (potato and cauliflower)	£2.25
BALTI ALOO CHANA (potato and chickpeas)	£2.25
BALTI SAG DAAL (lentil with spinach)	£2.25

BALTI CHAWAL RICE

STEAM LEMON RICE	£1.70
PULAO RICE (Saffron, basmati rice)	£1.90
FRIED RICE	£2.00
MUSHROOM PULAO RICE	£2.25
KASHMIRI DAHI RAITHI (yoghurt and cucumber)	£1.00

FRESH BREAD

NAN	£1.60
GARLIC NAN	£1.80
PESHWARI NAN (sultanas and almonds)	£1.90
KEEMA NAN (stuffed with mince)	£2.25
PARATHA	£1.90
STUFFED PARATHA	£2.25
CHAPATI	£0.60
TANDOORI ROTI	£1.20

SET MEALS

MEAL A — £7.50
Starters: Chana Puri or Pakora
Main course: Choose any dish from Balti Vegetarian
Lemon Rice or Nan

MEAL B — £6.50
Starters: Popadum
Main Course: Choose any dish from Balti selection or Vegetarian
Lemon Rice or Nan

MEAL C — £8.50
Starters: Chana Tikka Puri or Chicken Pakora
Main Course: Choose any dish from Balti selection
Pulao Rice or Garlic Nan

MEAL D — £9.50
Starters: Balti Lamb Kebab or Balti Chicken Kebab
Main Course: Choose any dish from Chicken Tikka or Lamb Tikka or Chicken/Lamb specialities
Basmati Rice or Nan

For Prawn £1.50 extra King Prawn £3.50 extra on all meals.

Chilli Connection
Indian Takeaway

Halal

Tel: 0800 298 3467
47 South Clerk Street, Edinburgh
Free Home Delivery for orders over £10.00 within specified area.

OPENING HOURS
7 DAYS
5pm – Midnight

Vegetarian Starters

Subzi Pakora	£1.45

Deep fried balls of gram flour, onions, mixed vegetables and a variety of spices served with special sauce

Chana on Puri	£1.95

Chick peas cooked in fresh herbs and spices with a sweet and savoury sauce

CC's Vegetable Puri	£1.95

Lightly spiced potatoes served inside a tantalising puri

Vegetable Samosa	£1.95

Crispy pastry filled with mixed vegetables and served with salad and mint sauce.

Onion Bhaji	£1.95

Thin slices of onion fried in our own batter.

Mixed Pakora	£1.95

Assorted vegetable pakoras from our selection.

Garlic Mushrooms	£1.95

Lightly fried mushrooms with a variety of spices CC's style.

Mushroom Pakora	£2.45

Mushrooms fried in our own spicy batter and served with salad and mint sauce.

Non Vegetarian Starters

CC's Kebabs Fresh Meat charcoal grilled and served with salad and mint sauce.

Tandoori Chicken	£2.95
Chicken Tikka	£2.45
Sheek Kebab Minced Lamb	£2.45
Lamb Tikka	£2.45
CC's Special Selection	£2.45

A tasteful combination of lamb and chicken and mouth watering donor kebab

Chicken Chaat	£2.45

Small pieces of succulent chicken cooked with tomatoes and cucumbers in a hot and spicy stew

Prawn or King Prawn Patia on Puri	£2.95/£3.95

King Prawns in a subtle sauce enhanced by fresh coriander in a bed of puffed fried bread.

Chicken Breast Pakora	£2.95

Spiced and battered chicken pieces, deep fried and served with salad and sauce.

Tandoori Dishes

The Tandoori is a beehive shaped top opening earthen oven fired with charcoal. In it we roast or bake various marinated meats, seafood vegetables and breads. Tandoori foods are marinated in mildly spiced yoghurt. They are low in calories, nutritious, delicious and easily digested. All Tandoori dishes are served with mint sauce and salad.

Tandoori Chicken	£5.95

Half spring chicken marinated in yoghurt with delicate herbs and spices, skewered and roasted in our clay ovens.

Chicken or Lamb Tikka	£4.95

Fresh, succulent pieces of chicken or lamb marinated and spiced with fresh herbs and spices, skewered and roasted in our clay oven.

Tandoori King Prawn	£7.95

King-sized prawns marinated in sauce, with an assortment of exotic spices, skewered and charcoal grilled.

CC's Assorted Tandoori	£7.95

Tandoori chicken, lamb tikka, king prawn and sheek kebabs – all prepared in our own special way to produce a succulent and mouth watering main course choice.

Balti Dishes

Charcoal roasted pieces of lamb/chicken or prawn cooked in a medium strength sauce with our chef's special recipe, to create a unique flavour.

Chicken	£5.45
Lamb	£5.45
Prawn	£6.45
King Prawn	£7.95
CC's Special Balti	£6.95

Assortment of chicken, lamb and king prawn cooked in a medium Balti sauce with green pepper, onion and tomatoes.

Chilli Connection's Specialities

Massallam – succulent pieces of chicken tikka and king prawn cooked in a mild flavoured sauce with fresh herbs and spices.

Chicken Tikka Massallam	£5.25
Lamb Tikka Massallam	£5.25
King Prawn Massallam	£7.95
CC's Pasanda – Lamb or Chicken	£5.25

Fresh lean chicken or lamb marinated and cooked in a mild creamy sauce.

Shahi Chasni	£5.25

Chicken tikka coated in a delicate sweet and sour sauce with a touch of fresh herbs and spices. Suggested side dish ALOO MUSHROOM

Garlic Chicken or Lamb	£4.95

Medium strength, cooked with fresh garlic, lentils, spices and fresh chillies

Green Herb Chicken or Lamb	£5.25

Medium strength, tender pieces of chicken or lamb in a spicy sauce of tomatoes, green peppers, coriander, spring onions, ginger and fresh chillies.

Kathmandu Chicken or Lamb	£5.25

Chicken or lamb Tikka deliciously coated with garlic, ginger, whole spring onions, cinnamon and lentils – medium hot.

Ginger Chicken or Lamb	£5.25

A fairly hot chicken or lamb dish cooked in a ginger sauce with lots of coriander

Chicken or Lamb Jalfrezie	£5.25

Freshly chopped pieces of chicken or lamb, green chillies and coriander with a touch of fresh ginger - fairly hot.

Jaipuri Chicken or Lamb	£5.25

Diced pieces of chicken or lamb in a medium flavoured sauce prepared with fresh mushrooms and onions.

Kabuli Gosht or Chicken	£5.25

Chicken or Lamb cooked in a medium strength masala sauce with fresh herbs, coriander & chick peas. Suggested side dish mushroom BHAJEE

Chicken or Lamb Tikka Makhani	£5.25

Spiced with yoghurt, fresh cream and a tikka masala sauce. Suggested side dish DAAL SAAG

Gobi Prawn	£5.25

Prawn with cauliflower, spicy onion & coriander. Suggested side dish Bhindi BHAJEE

Sag Prawn	£5.25

Garlic Prawn with spinach. Suggested side dish Mushroom BHAJEE

Karai Gosht	£5.25

Tender pieces of chicken or lamb coated with green peppers and spices garnished with fresh chillies

Khairabadi Gosht or Chicken	£5.25

Barbecued lamb or chicken marinated and cooked with roast potatoes garlic, onion, coriander, ginger &

a slice of lemon. suggested side dish DAAL SAAG

Saag Gosht £5.25
Tender pieces of lamb with fresh spinach, herbs and spices – medium

Bhindi Gosht or Chicken £5.25
Lamb or chicken cooked with Bhindi, fragrant herbs & spices with fresh coriander to give a delicious medium hot flavour. Suggested side dish CAULIFLOWER BHAJEE

Garlic Chilli Chicken or Lamb £5.25
Chicken or lamb tikka cooked in garlic sauce with green chillies and fresh coriander – hot to taste

Punjab Massala Chicken or Lamb £5.25
Chicken or lamb tikka cooked in a medium strength massala sauce with fresh herbs and green peppers

Afghani Korma Chicken or Lamb £5.25
Roasted pieces of chicken or lamb cooked in a mild sauce with fresh cream, peaches and cashew nuts

Connection Classics

Massallam – succulent fresh lean chicken, lamb, prawns or king prawns served with a classic range of sauces. Please state whether you prefer a thick sauce.

Mixed Vegetable	£3.95
Chicken	£4.25
Lamb	£4.25
Prawn	£4.45
King Prawn	£6.95

Korma – a mild delicate sauce of fresh cream, almonds, coconut and a light assortment of spices

Kashmiri – a mild sauce prepared with fresh lychees and bananas in exotic tropical spices

Malayan – a mild delicate dish prepared with almond, coconut, pineapple fruit juices and cream to create a beautiful balanced flavour

Bhuna – a medium strength traditional dish prepared with onions, herbs, tomatoes and green peppers and selected spices

Dopiaza – of medium strength prepared with plenty of onions, herbs and spices

Rogan Josh – a medium strength dish prepared with garlic, fresh coriander and spices, garnished with fired tomatoes

Madras – a very popular dish with garlic, chilli and lemon juice

Pathia – a hot sweet and sour dish with garlic, red chillies and chopped onion

Dansak – a fairly hot dish prepared with lentils and fresh spices to create a hot and sour flavour

Vindaloo – only for the connoisseur – fresh spices and green chillies to create a sauce rich in flavour and very, very hot

Biryanis

A Biryani is saffron rice prepared with vegetables fried in butter; delicate spices then mixed with the main ingredient of your choice. A separate Vegetable curry is included making this a complete meal in itself. Please state whether mild, medium or hot.

Vegetable Biryani	£4.95
Chicken/Lamb Biryani	£5.45
Chicken tikka/Lamb Tikka Biryani	£6.25
Prawn Biryani	£6.25
King Prawn Biryani	£7.95
CC's Special Biryani	£6.95

Assortment of chicken, lamb and prawn

Kebabs

All kebabs are prepared with our special assortment of spices then cooked on a charcoal grill to produce a tasty and 'finger licking' meal. All kebabs are served with mixed salad and sauce in nan bread

Donor Kebab (small) £2.95 (large) £3.45
This eastern Mediterranean dish consists of freshly made minced lamb flavoured with Turkish herbs and spices cooked uniquely on a revolving skewer

Sheek Lamb Kebab (small) £2.95 (large) £3.45
Minced lamb prepared with onions and spices cooked in our clay oven

Lamb Kebab (small) £2.95 (large) £3.45
Tender cubed pieces of lamb lightly spiced on a skewer and charcoal grilled

Chicken Kebab (small) £2.95 (large) £3.45
Choice pieces of chicken breast lightly spiced on a skewer and charcoal grilled

CC's Mixed Kebab £4.95
An amazingly tasteful assortment comprising of skewer chicken, lamb, sheek and doner kebab

Keema Curries

All our Keema curries are made with minced lamb.

Aloo Keema £4.95
Curried mince with potato

Keema Mutter £4.95
Curried mince with peas

Keema Rogan Josh £4.95
With onion, tomato & green pepper

Keema Dansak £4.95
Curried mince with lentils

Keema Pathia £4.95
A tasty sweet & sour flavour

Vegetarian Main Dishes

Sabzi Jalfrezie £3.95
Mixed vegetables cooked in blend of medium hot sauce

Sabzi Sambar £3.95
A hot rich gathering of mixed vegetables, prepared together with lentils

Sabzi Kurma £3.95
Mixed vegetables prepared in a rich delicate, mild sauce of almonds and coconut

Saag Panir £3.95
Medium strength dish prepared in a delicate tasting surprise with home-made cottage cheese

Mutter Panir £3.95
Medium strength dish containing peas and home-made cottage cheese

Chana Massallam £3.95
Chick peas with lentil, egg, spring onions, fresh coriander, herbs and spices

Mixed Vegetable Massallam £3.95
Mixed vegetables cooked in a mild sauce with fresh herbs and spices

Sabzi – Side Dishes

Saag Aloo *spinach with spiced potatoes*	£2.45
Bhindi Bhaji *spiced okra*	£2.45
Cauliflower Bhaji *spiced cauliflower*	£2.45
Brinjal Bhaji *spiced aubergine*	£2.45
Mughai Saag *spinach*	£2.45
Mixed Vegetable Bhaji *dry mixed vegetables*	£2.45
Aloo Mutter *peas with potatoes*	£2.45
Bombay Aloo *lightly spiced potatoes*	£2.45
Tarka Daal *stewed lentils and split peas*	£2.45

Rice

Boiled Basmati Rice	£1.15
Pilau Saffron Basmati Rice	£1.45
CC's Special Basmati Rice	£1.95
Basmati stir fried with egg, peas and spring onion
| Sabzi Rice | £1.95 |
Basmati stir fried saffron and mixed vegetables
| Mushroom Pilau | £1.95 |
Basmati stir fried with mushrooms

Breads

Nan *flat bread baked in a tandoori oven* £1.45
CC's Special Nan Bread *stuffed with ground almonds and sultanas. Delicious compliment as part of your meal or as a dessert* £1.65
Keema Nan £1.65
Stuffed bread with spiced mince meat
Garlic Nan £1.65
Bread coated with fresh garlic
Paratha £1.45
Fried layered whole wheat bread
Stuffed Paratha £1.95
Fried layered whole wheat bread filled with vegetables
Tandoori Roti £0.95
Wholemeal bread in our clay oven
Chapati £0.55
Thin wholemeal bread
Puri £0.45

Popadums and Chutneys

Plain Popadums	£0.45
Cucumber Raita	£1.45
Lime Pickle	£0.95
Spicy Popadums	£0.55
Mango chutne	£0.95
Green Salad	£0.95
Spicy Onion	£0.95

Soft Drinks

Cans	£0.60
Bottle of Coke 1.5 litre	£1.60
Bottle of Diet Coke 1.5 litre	£1.60
Bottle of Iron Bru 1.5 litre	£1.60

We will be pleased to provide special set menus of your choice for larger parties. Please contact the management with your suggestions.

BANGALORE TANDOORI RESTAURANT

Established since 1984
The Restaurant with a difference

52 Home Street,
Edinburgh EH3 9NA
Tel: 0800 698 1408
Fax: 0131-221 9170

APPETISERS

Papadums (plain or spicy)	£0.50
Prawn Cocktail	£2.45
Soup of the day	£1.25

STARTERS

Sabzi Pakora	£1.95
Chicken Pakora	£1.95
Samosa	£1.95
Aloo Chaat	£2.05
Murgh Chaat	£2.95
Sheek Kebab	£2.95
Shami Kebab	£2.95
Murgh Kebab	£2.95
Mughlai Lamb Kebab	£2.95
Bangalore Assorted Kebab	£3.95
Bangalore Tandoori Chicken	£2.95
King Prawn Puri	£3.95
Bangalore Eastern Prawns	£2.95
Prawn Puri	£2.95

BANGALORE TANDOORI DELICACIES

Murgh Tandoori	£4.95
Murgh Tikka	£4.95
Mughlai Lamb Tikka	£4.95
Tandoori King Prawn	£9.95
Chicken Shashlik	£5.95

SEAFOOD LEGEND

Tandoori King Prawn Massallam	£9.95
Green Herb King Prawn	£8.95
Mughlai King Prawn Jalfrezie	£8.95
Calcutta Prawn Palak	£5.95
Green Herb Prawns	£5.95

CHICKEN SPECIALITIES

Shahi Murgh Tikka Massallam	£5.95
Butter Chicken	£5.95
Nurjahan Chicken Pasanda	£5.95
Chicken Tikka Kurma	£5.95
Kashmiri Murgh Makhani	£5.95
Shahi Rougan Josh	£5.95
Kathmandu Murgh Tikka Massallam	£5.95
North Indian Chilli-Garlic Chicken	£5.95
East Indian Chicken Jalfrezie	£5.95
Chicken Palak	£5.95
Jaipuri Chicken	£5.95
Jeera Tikka Bhuna	£5.95
Chicken Razala	£5.95

BANGALORE BIRYANI DISHES

Grand festive dishes prepared from basmati rice, barbecued chicken, lamb cooked in a Tandoor, includes mixed vegetable curry. Please ask for mild, medium or hot to suit your taste.

Tandoori Chicken Biryani	£7.95
Mughlai Lamb Biryani	£7.95
Murgh Tikka Biryani	£7.95
Bangalore Sabzi Biryani	£6.45
Chicken Biryani	£7.45
Lamb Biryani	£7.45
King Prawn Biryani	£10.96
Prawn Biryani	£7.95

VEGETABLE DISHES

Kurma	£4.50
Rougan Josh	£4.50
Bhuna	£4.50
Dhansak	£4.50
Pathia	£4.50

LAMB SPECIALITIES

Mughlai Lamb Tikka Massallam	£5.95
Shahjahani Lamb Pasanda	£5.95
Punjabi Karai Gosht	£5.95
Maghlai Chana Gosht	£5.95
Calcutta Methi Gosht	£5.95
Sylheti Achar Gosht	£5.95
Madrasi Chilli Palak Gosht	£5.95
East Indian Lamb Jalfrezie	£5.95
North Indian Chilli Gosht	£5.95
Green Herb Lamb	£5.95
Jaipuri Lamb	£5.95
Jeera Tikka Bhuna	£5.95
Lamb Razala	£5.95

BANGALORE VEGETABLE DISHES

Bombay Chana Massallam	£4.60
Sag Aloo Delight	£4.60
Persian Veg Sambar	£4.60
Sabzi Panir Jalfrezie	£4.60

BANGALORE CURRY SELECTION

Kurma (very mild)
A delicate preparation of curd, cream and selected spices, producing a very mild flavour.

Chicken	£4.75
Lamb	£4.75
Prawn	£4.75
King Prawn	£8.95
Vegetable	£4.50

Rougan Josh (medium hot)
Lamb, prawn or chicken specially prepared with pimento and garlic garnished with tomatoes

Chicken	£4.75
Lamb	£4.75
Prawn	£4.75
King Prawn	£8.95
Vegetable	£4.50

Malayan (mild)
A mildly spiced dish prepared with pineapple, fruit juices, coconuts and cream to create a beautifully balanced flavour.

Chicken	£4.75
Lamb	£4.75
Prawn	£4.75
King Prawn	£8.95

Bhuna (medium)
Garnished dish with onions, green herbs, tomatoes and selected spices.

Chicken	£4.75
Lamb	£4.75
Prawn	£4.75
King Prawn	£8.95
Vegetable	£4.50

Dupiaza (medium)
A large quantity of onions seasoned and fresh, treated with dozens of spices and herbs to produce a medium hot taste.

Chicken	£4.75
Lamb	£4.75
Prawn	£4.75
King Prawn	£8.95

Dhansak (fairly sweet and sour)
A beautiful combination of spices with lentils mixed with curd producing a sour, sweet and hot taste.

Chicken	£4.75
Lamb	£4.75
Prawn	£4.75
King Prawn	£8.95
Vegetable	£4.50

Pathia (sweet and sour)
A hot and sour tasting dish prepared with garlic, red chilli, onion, green pepper and tomato puree producing a sweet and sour dish.

Chicken	£4.75
Lamb	£4.75
Prawn	£4.75
King Prawn	£8.95
Vegetable	£4.50

Madras (hot)
A most popular dish with a rich, hot and sour taste.

Chicken	£4.75
Lamb	£4.75
Prawn	£4.75
King Prawn	£8.95

Ceylon
A most popular dish, much hotter than Madras. Cooked with coconut powder.

Chicken	£4.75
Lamb	£4.75
Prawn	£4.75
King Prawn	£8.95

Vindaloo (very hot sauce)

Chicken	£4.75
Lamb	£4.75
Prawn	£4.75
King Prawn	£8.95

EUROPEAN DISHES
(served with salad and French fries)

Sirloin Steak	£7.95
Chicken Salad	£6.95
Roast Chicken	£6.95
Prawn Omelette	£6.95
Chicken Omelette	£6.95

SABZI DISHES
Vegetables served as a side dish only. The following are served with main meals only and are all freshly prepared.

Bindi Bhajee (okra)	£2.60
Vegetable Massallam	£2.60
Mushroom Bhajee	£2.60
Dal Tarka (lentil with garilc)	£2.60
Brinjal Bhajee (aubergine)	£2.60
Bombay potato	£2.60
Potato and Pea Bhajee	£2.60
Cauliflower Bhajee	£2.60
Sag Bhajee	£2.60
Mixed Vegetable Bhajee	£2.60

CHAWAL RICE

Plain boiled rice	£1.75
Pulao Rice (saffron, Basmati rice)	£1.95
Special Fried Rice	£2.10
Vegetable Pulao	£2.25
Mushroom fried rice	£2.25
Dahi Raitha (yoghurt with cucumber)	£1.00

FRESH BREAD

Nan	£1.75
Keema Nan (stuffed with mince)	£1.90
Garlic Nan	£1.90
Peshwari Nan (stuffed with sultanas and almonds)	£1.90
Paratha	£1.75
Stuffed Paratha	£1.90
Chapati	£0.70

BUFFET NIGHT
Every Wednesday and Thursday 6pm-11pm (different menu each day)

VERY IMPORTANT
Should any of our customers have any allergies to any kinds of foods, oils or spices, please let the manager know and we will advise you on the dishes to avoid.

FUNCTION SUITE
Our exclusive Function Suite caters for parties between 24 and 32 persons. The Suite is ideal for office parties, weddings, birthdays, anniversaries and other special occasions.

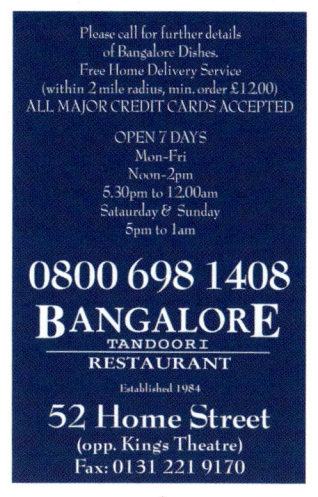

Please call for further details of Bangalore Dishes.
Free Home Delivery Service
(within 2 mile radius, min. order £12.00)
ALL MAJOR CREDIT CARDS ACCEPTED

OPEN 7 DAYS
Mon-Fri
Noon-2pm
5.30pm to 12.00am
Saturday & Sunday
5pm to 1am

0800 698 1408

BANGALORE
TANDOORI
RESTAURANT
Established 1984

52 Home Street
(opp. Kings Theatre)
Fax: 0131 221 9170

The Finest Indian Cuisine in Edinburgh
Awarded by Les Routiers

Ayutthaya

THAI HOME DELIVERY SERVICE

FREEPHONE 0800 698 1402

STARTERS

1. **'Ayutthaya'** £7.00
Mixed Starters as recommended by the Chef (for two)

2. **Por Pea Tord** £3.50
Home made spring rolls made with a mixture of chicken, vegetables and glass noodles, served with spicy plum sauce.

3. **Satay**
Marinated then grilled over charcoal, served with peanut sauce and cucumber dip.

	4 Sticks	6 Sticks
Gai: Chicken	3A £3.95	3B £5.25
Goong: Prawn	3C £4.50	3D £6.25

4. **Angel Wings** £4.10
Boneless chicken wings stuffed with spiced mince, chicken and vegetables, served with a mild chilli sauce.

5. **Tord Mun Pla** £3.75
Thai fish cakes served with home made chilli sauce. Topped with ground peanuts.

6. **Thai Tempura** £3.70
Thai style prawns dipped in a light batter then quick fried. Comes with a chilli / plum sauce.

7. **Kha Nom Jeep** £3.60
Minced pork, prawns and water chestnuts, steamed in a light Thai Style Dim Sum dumpling, sitting in a blended soy sauce mix.

8. **Gradoog Moo Tord** £4.00
Pork spare ribs marinated in honey and spices and quick fried.

9. **Gai Haw Bai Teoy** £4.00
Aromatic chicken marinated, wrapped in pandan leaf, deep fried served with a sesame dip.

10. **Ayutthaya Prawns** £4.15
Marinated king prawns, individually wrapped in a thin pastry leaf, quick fried and served with a spicy plum.

11. **Kanom Pang Nagai** £3.50
Spicy minced chicken on wholemeal bread, topped with sesame seeds, crisp fried with a cucumber dip.

SOUP

12. **Tom Yum**
Thai Soup, distinctive flavour we are confident you will enjoy.
12a. Gai: Chicken £3.70
12b. Goong: Prawn £4.10
12c. Ahan Talay Sea Food £4.10

13. **Tom Kar Gai** £3.90
Chicken in a rich coconut milk soup flavoured with galanga, lemon grass, lime leaves and mushrooms.

14. **Gang Jend Woong Sen** £5.00
Vermicelli noodles with minced pork and prawns mixed in a hot sauce.

15. **Tom Yum Poh Taek (for two)** £7.35
A tangy mixed seafood soup.

YUM THAI THAI (THAI SALAD)

16. **Yum Woon Sen** £5.00
Vermicelli noodles with minced pork and prawns in a hot sauce

17. **Som Tum** £3.55
Northern Thai dish of raw mixed vegetables and shrimp in hot lemon vinegar.

18. **Yum Talay** £6.00
Mixed seafood with thinly spiced tomatoes, onions and mushrooms in a spicy dressing.

19. **Yum Neua** £5.00
Beef, tomatoes, onions and mushrooms, thinly sliced with an average to hot dressing.

NOODLES

20. **Pud Mee** £5.00
Plain fried noodle with bean sprouts and spring onion (not a main course)

21. **Guey Teow Pad (V)** £5.00
Thin yellow noodles with chicken or prawns stir fried with vegetables

22. **Guey Teow Rad Na (V)** £5.00

RICE DISHES

25. **Kao Plao** £1.30
Steamed Thai fragrant rice

26. **Kao Neow** £1.60
'Sticky rice'

27. **Kao Mun Grati** £1.90
Steamed Thai rice in coconut milk

28. **Kao Pud Grati** £3.95
Thai fried rice with chicken, tomatoes and spring onions.

67. **Egg Fried rice** £2.00

SEAFOOD DISHES

29. **Goong Ob Mordin** £6.00
King prawns steamed with ginger and spring onions served with noodles and black bean sauce.

30. **Gratiam Prig Thai**
Seafood stir fried with chilli and basil leaves
30a. Goong: King Prawn £6.50
30b. Plameuk: Squid £6.10

31. **Pad Gra Prao**
Seafood stir fried with chilli and basil leaves
31a. Goong: King Prawn £6.50
31b. Plameuk: Squid £6.10

32. **Preow Wan**
Thai style sweet and sour dish
32a. Goong: King Prawn £6.50
32b. Pla: Fillet of Rainbow Trout £6.10

33. **Pla Neung Bauy** £6.60
Fillet of Rainbow Trout garnished with ginger, spring onions and Vegetables steamed in a spicy plum sauce and flavoured with Thai herbs.

34. **Choo Chee**
Crispy quick fried trout or prawns topped with the chefs own spicy red curry sauce
34a. Goong: King Prawn £6.50
34b. Pla: Whole Rainbow Trout £6.50

35. **Geang Keow Wan Goong** £6.50
King Prawns cooked with Thai herbs and fairly hot green curry paste

36. **Pad Ped Talay** £6.70
Mixed seafood stir fried with red curry paste, fresh chilli, lime leaves and basil

37. **Pla Lad Prig** £6.70
Crispy fried Rainbow Trout with mild chilli sauce and basil

MEAT AND POULTRY

38. **Gratam Prig Thai** £5.95
Beef, Pork or Chicken stir fried with garlic, peppers and fresh chilli

39. **Preow Wan Gai** £5.75
Thai style sweet and sour chicken

40. **Pad Gra Proa** £5.95
Beef, Pork or Chicken stir fried with basil, fresh chilli, onion and garlic

41. **Gai Yang** £6.25
A whole small chicken marinated in honey and spices, charcoal grilled with sweet chilli sauce

42. **Panaeng** £6.00
Chicken or Beef in a medium hot panang curry

43. **Gaeng Panaeng** £5.95
Mild red curry with sliced bamboo shoots and herbs. Beef, Chicken or Pork

44. **Geang Keow Wan** £5.95
Hot green curry, rich in coconut milk with aubergines and vegetables. Beef, Chicken or Pork

45. **Gaeng Phed Ped Yang** £6.25
Roasted duck, sliced and cooked in mild red curry with coconut milk, tomatoes and pineapple

46. **Gaeng Massaman** £6.10
A mild curry dish with potato cubes, onions and peanuts. Beef or Chicken

47. **Gaeng Supparod** £5.90
A mild pineapple curry available with Chicken or Pork

48. **Pad Nam Man Hoi** £5.75
Beef or Chicken stir fried with oyster sauce and vegetables

49. **Ped Yang Ayutthaya** £6.50
Roasted duck with sauce made to the chefs own recipe

50. **Ped Pud King** £6.50
Sliced roast duck, chicken or pork, stir fried with onion, fresh sliced ginger root, spring onion, mushroom and flavoured with a garlic and Soya bean sauce

51. **Gai Pad Prig Haeng** £6.00
Chicken stir fried with cashew nuts snd sun dried chillis

BANQUETS

A. £13.00 / Person (min 2 people)

STARTER
'Ayutthaya'
Mixed starters as recommended by the Chef

MAIN COURSE
Panaeng
Medium hot green curry available with Beef or Chicken

Pud King
Sliced roast chicken stir fried with onions, ginger root, spring onion, mushrooms in a garlic and Soya bean sauce

Geang Keow Wan
Fairly hot green chicken curry, rich in coconut milk with aubergines and vegetables

B. £11.00 / Person (min 2 people)

VEGETARIAN
'Ayutthaya'
Vegetarian mixed starters as recommended by the Chef

MAIN COURSE
Pud Toa Hoo
Bean curd and bean sprouts stir fried with Thai spices and herbs

Gaeng Phed
Mixed vegetables cooked in a mild red curry with sliced bamboo shoots and herbs

Pad Makhew Moung
Aubergine in a Thai style batter stir fried with fresh chilli basil and Soya sauce

C. £13.00 / Person (min 3 people)

STARTER
'Ayutthaya'
Mixed starters as recommended by the Chef

SOUP
Tom Kar Gai
Chicken in a rich coconut milk soup, flavoured with fresh galanga, lemongrass, kaffir lime leaves and mushrooms

MAIN COURSE
Gaeng Phed Ped Yang
Roasted duck, sliced and cooked in mild red curry with coconut milk, tomatoes and pineapple

Gratium Prig Thai
A beef, pork and chicken stir fry with garlic, peppers and fresh chilli

Gai Pad Med Mamuang
Chicken stir fried with cashew nuts

Pud Puk
Fresh mixed vegetables stir fried with blended Soya sauce and garlic

ALL SERVED WITH STEAMED RICE AND PLAIN NOODLES

14b Nicholson St, Edinburgh.   www.leisurenet.co.uk/ayutthaya.htm

Babylon Cafe

0131 229 7793
07811 711307

FRIED FOOD

	Supper	Single
Fish	£3.50	£2.50
Special Fish	£3.85	£2.85
Chicken	£3.20	£2.20
Smoked Sausage	£2.40	£1.50
King Rib	£2.65	£1.85
Rump Steak	£2.65	£1.85
Hamburger (2)	£2.40	£1.60
Sausage (3)	£2.20	£1.40
Jumbo Sausage (2)	£2.50	£1.70
Steak Pie	£2.30	£1.45
Mince Pie	£2.30	£1.40
White Pudding	£2.30	£1.40
Black Pudding	£2.30	£1.40
Haggis Pudding	£2.30	£1.40
Cheeseburger (1)	£2.50	£1.60
Spring Roll (2)	£2.30	£1.40
Deep Fried Pizza	£2.50	£1.70
Half Pizza	£1.80	£1.00
Fish Cakes (2)	£2.50	£1.70
Scampi	£3.20	£2.30
Jumbo Haggis	£2.50	£1.70
Chicken Nuggets	£3.20	£2.30
Chicken Kiev	£2.70	£1.90
Chicken Burger	£2.50	£1.70
Veggieburger	£2.30	£1.40
Chips	(large) £1.20	(small) £1.00
Chips & Curry Sauce		£2.00
Chips & Cheese		£1.80
Chip Roll		£1.20
Burger Roll		£1.20

SIDE DISHES

Onion rings	£1.30
Mushrooms in Batter	£1.30
Vegetable Pakora	£2.20
Chicken Pakora	£2.80
Curry Sauce	£1.20

PIZZAS

	9"	12"	16"
Margherita — Cheese & tomato	£2.90	£3.90	£5.90
Hawaian — Cheese, tomato, ham & pineapple	£3.90	£4.90	£7.90
Pepperoni Feast — Cheese, tomato, pepperoni, mushroom, onion, peppers and olives.	£4.00	£5.00	£8.00
Meat Feast — Cheese, tomato, salami, pepperoni, chicken & ham.	£4.00	£5.00	£8.00
Turkish — Cheese, tomato & doner meat. Served with salad and chilli sauce.	£4.00	£5.50	£9.00
Spicy Chicken — Cheese, tomato & spicy chicken.	£3.90	£4.50	£7.90
Spicy Beef — Cheese, tomato and spicy beef.	£3.90	£4.90	£7.90
Seafood — Cheese, tomato, prawns, mussels, squid & cockles.	£4.00	£5.00	£8.00
Mexicana — Cheese, tomato, spicy beef, sweetcorn, onion, peppers, jalapenos & olives.	£4.50	£5.50	£8.50
Quattro Stagioni — Cheese, tomato, ham, sweetcorn, peppers, mushrooms, tomato & olives.	£4.50	£5.50	£8.50
Super Combo — Cheese, tomato, ham, chicken, salami, pepperoni, mushroom, onion, peppers, tomato, olives, sweetcorn & pineapple	£4.50	£5.50	£8.50
Vegetarian — Sweetcorn, pineapple, mushroom, onion, peppers, tomato & olives.	£4.50	£5.50	£8.50
Calzone — Cheese, tomato, ham, chicken, salami, pepperoni, mushroom, sweetcorn, pineapple, onion, peppers & tomato.	£4.90	£5.90	£8.90
Garlic Pizza (garlic butter)	£2.00	£2.50	£4.50
Pizza with 1 meat topping	£3.90	£4.90	£8.50
Pizza with 1 veg topping	£3.50	£4.30	£7.50
Extra Vegetable topping	£0.50	£0.80	£1.20
Extra Meat topping	£0.70	£1.00	£1.50
Garlic Bread	£1.35		
Garlic Bread with Cheese	£2.60		

Why not make your own pizza from the following toppings: Cheese, Onion, Mushroom, Ham, Chicken, Spicy Chicken, Spicy Beef, Peppers, Pepperoni, Capers, Tomato, Sweetcorn, Pineapple, Jalapeno Chilli, Tuna, Salami, Olives, Anchovies.

KEBABS

	Small	Large
Doner Kebab	£3.00	£3.50
Chicken Kebab	£3.50	£4.20
Shish Kebab	£3.50	£4.20
Mixed Kebab		£5.00
Vegetarian Kebab	£2.00	£3.00
Kebab Roll		£2.00
Kebab Meat & Chips	£3.00	£3.50
Chicken Pakora		£2.60
Vegetable Pakora.		£2.00

BAKED POTATOES

Plain	£1.20
Coleslaw	£1.60
Cheese	£1.70
Cheese & Onion	£2.00
Egg Mayonnaise	£2.00
Tuna Mayonnaise	£2.00
Beans & Cheese	£2.20

AMERICAN STYLE BURGERS

Quarter Pounder	£1.60
Quarter Pounder Cheeseburger	£1.70
Half Pounder Cheeseburger	£2.60
Half Pounder	£2.20
Quarter Pounder Chicken Burger	£1.70
Quarter Pounder Chicken CheeseBurger	£2.00
Half Pounder Chicken Burger	£2.40
Half Pounder Chicken Cheese Burger	£2.90
Quarter Pounder Veggie Burger	£1.70
Half Pounder Veggie Burger	£2.70

Free Delivery on Food Orders over £10.00
Delivery Service: 5pm to Midnight
Open: Sun-Thurs 4pm-1am, Fri & Sat 4pm-3am

Babylon Cafe
25-27 BROUGHAM ST, TOLLCROSS

0131 229 7793

CATEGORY INDEX

Manchester Food Guide

CATEGORY	ADDRESS	TEL	FACILITIES	MAP PG
AA, Michelin & Good Food Guide 2001 Listed				
Atrium	10 Cambridge Street, Lothian Road	228 8882		
Banks	10 Newington Road, Newington	667 0707		
Bar Café	Cambridge Street, Lothian Road	221 1222		
Bonham, The	35 Drumsheugh Gardens, New Town	226 6080		
Cafe St-Honore	34 NW Thistle Street Lane, New Town	226 2211		
Carvers, George Inter-Continental	19-21 George Street, New Town	225 1251		D2 54
Channings Restaurant	South Learmonth Gardens, Comely Bank	315 2225		A2 78
Duck's at Le Marche Noir	2-4 Ayre Place, New Town	0800 698 1411		C1 65
Fishers	11 The Shore, Leith	554 5666		
(fitz) Henry	19 Shore Place, Leith	0800 698 1460		G9 114
Grill Room, Sheraton Grand Hotel	1 Festival Square, Lothian Road	229 6254		B5 98
Hadrian's, Balmoral Hotel	2 North Bridge, New Town	0800 698 1440		D3 36
Haldanes	39a Albany Street, New Town	0800 542 4383		
Holyrood Hotel	Holyrood Road, Old Town	550 4500		
Igg's Restaurant	15 Jeffrey Street, Old Town	557 8184		E4 16
Kalpna	2-3 St Patrick Square, Newington	0800 698 1457		E6 108
Kelly's Restaurant	46 West Richmond Street, Newington	668 3847		
Malmaison Hotel	One Tower Place, Leith	468 5000		G8 111
Marque, The	19-21 Causewayside, Newington	466 6660		
Marriott Dalmahoy	Kirknewton, Lothian	333 1845		
Martin Wishart	54 The Shore, Leith	553 3557		
Martins	70 Rose St North Lane, New Town	0800 542 4363		
Norton House Hotel	Ingliston, Outskirts	333 1275		
Number One, Balmoral Hotel	1 Princes Street, New Town	0800 698 1439		D3 36
Rhodes & Co.	3-15 Rose Street, New Town	220 9190		D3 40
Rock, The	78 Commercial Street, Leith	555 2225		
Shore	3-4 The Shore, Leith	0800 542 4368		
Skippers	1a Dock Place, Leith	0800 542 4385		G8 115

Maison BJEUE — a unique dining experience

Map Ref: D4

lunch special — 3 courses £4.90
pre-threatre — 3 courses £9.90

open 12 noon - 12 midnight
bookings welcome
large parties catered for

36-38 Victoria Street
Tel/Fax: 0131 226 1900

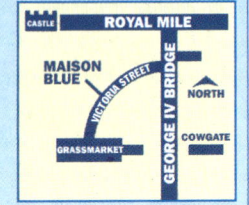

CATEGORY INDEX

AA, Michelin & Good Food Guide 2001 Listed continued

Terrace, Sheraton Grand Hotel	1 Festival Square, Lothian Road	221 6423		
Tower, The	Museum of Scotland, Chambers Street	0800 698 1485		D5 15
Tuscan Square	30 Grindley Street, Lothian Road	229 9859		
Valvona & Crolla Caffe Bar	19 Elm Row, Leith Walk	556 6066		
Winter Glen	3A1 Dundas Street, New Town	477 7060		
Yumi Japanese Restaurant	2 West Coates, Haymarket	337 2173		

African

Nile Valley Restaurant	6 Chapel Street, Newington	667 8200		E6 101

All Day Menus

Bank Hotel	1 Southbridge, Old Town	556 9940		D4
Beluga	30a Chamber St., Old Town	0800 698 1404		D5 22
Park Bar	4 Alvanley Terrace, Bruntsfield	229 3834		
Royal Ettrick Hotel	13 Ettrick Road, Stockbridge	228 6413		
Three Sisters	139 The Cowgate, Old Town	662 6801		D5

American

Hard Rock Café	20 George Street, New Town	260 3000		D3 44
Henry J. Beans, Caledonian Hilton Hotel	Caledonian Hotel, Princes Street	459 1999		B4 129
TGI Fridays	26 Castle Street, New Town	0800 197 3527		C3 66

Bar Meals

Au Bar	101 Shandwick Place, Edinburgh	228 2648		B4 74
Bruntsfield Links Hotel, The	3 Alvanley Terrace, Whitehouse Loan	229 3046		C7 134
Canons' Gait	232 Canongate, Royal Mile	556 4481		E4 122
Goblin Ha Hotel	Main Street, Gifford	01620 810 244		L11 144
Golf Hotel	34 Dirleton Avenue, North Berwick	01620 892 202		L10 146
Guildford Arms	1-5 West Register Street, New Town	556 4312		D3 129

Bistro

A Room in the West End	69 William Street South, East Lane,	226 1036		

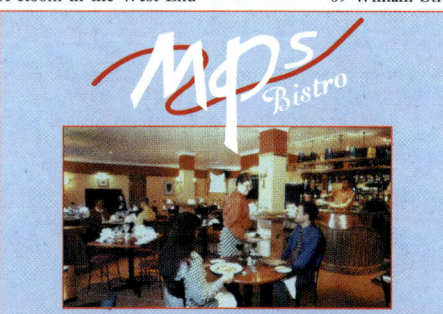

MPs Bistro
GREAT FOOD, RELAXED ATMOSPHERE
OPEN 7 DAYS 7-9.30pm (LAST ORDERS)
15 CALTON HILL
RESERVATIONS: 0131 478 4000

COOKING SINCE 1973
EUROCARD MasterCard VISA
THE GV CHINESE TAKE OUT AND HOME DELIVERY SERVICE
Tel: 0131 229 9922 Fax: 0131 229 7799
OPEN 7 DAYS – 5pm till LATE
Special set dinner available
26/27 ROSENEATH PL, MARCHMONT
Where possible no M.S.G. in our cooking

Haddows Caterers

With a range of experience in catering & event management, we strive to provide the perfect environment for any function/event.

- corporate hospitality
- marquees
- weddings
- barbeques

0800 698 1503

W ← Edinburgh → E
N / S

24-7ltd.co.uk
catering and events

FRESH

t: 0131 538 8676   f: 0131 538 8675   w: 24-7ltd.co.uk   e: info@24-7ltd.co.uk

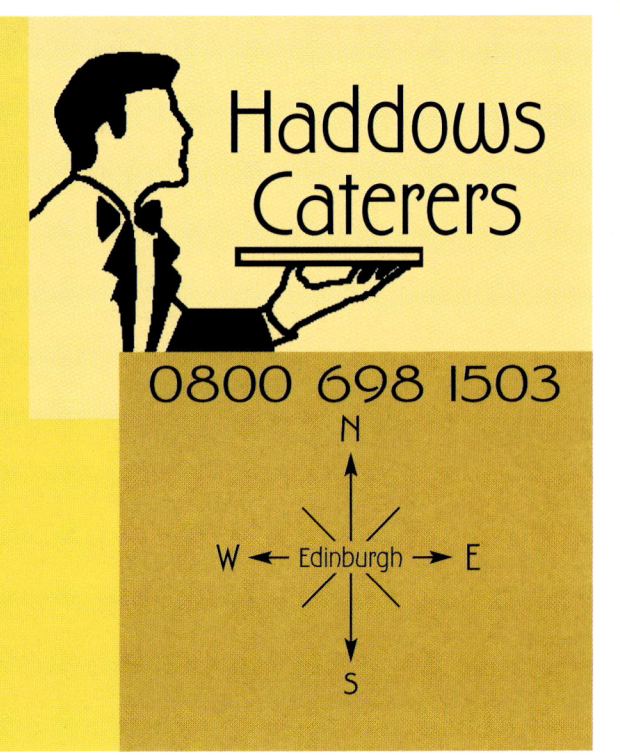

We exceed your expectations for all catering & event managment function.

0800 698 1503

Haddows Caterers

CEC|Catering

- Weddings • Garden Parties •
- Funerals • Exhibitions, Marquees •
- Trade Fairs • Corporate Hospitality •
- Bar-B-Q's • Sporting Events •
- Boardroom Lunches •

0800 698 1470

E-mail: info@cec-catering.co.uk
491 Queensferry Road
Edinburgh EH4 7QD

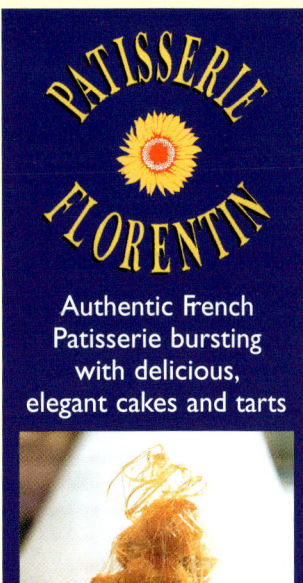

PATISSERIE FLORENTIN

Authentic French Patisserie bursting with delicious, elegant cakes and tarts

5 Nth. West Circus Place, Stockbridge Tel: 220 0225
www.florentin.co.uk

CATERERS

CATERERS

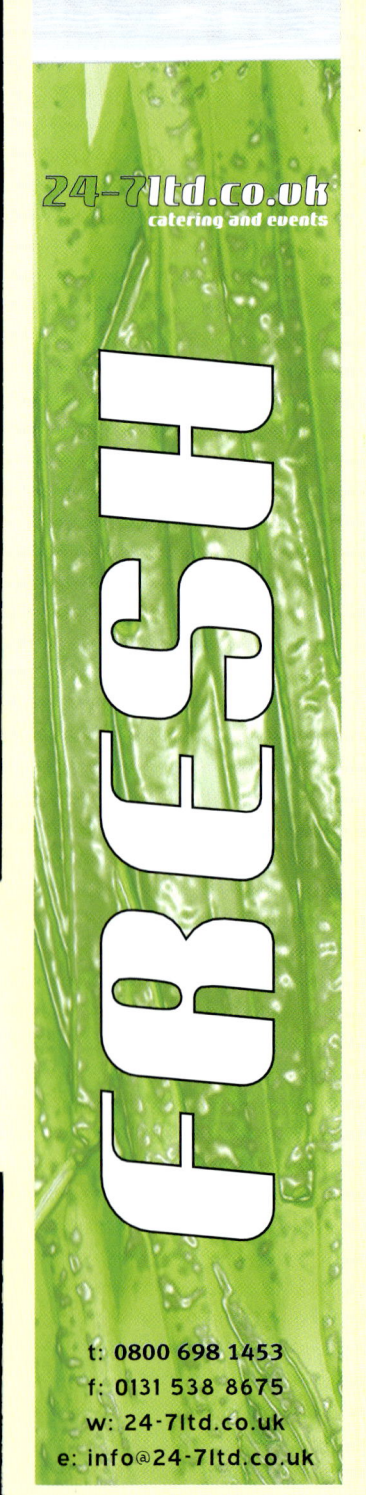

24-7ltd.co.uk
catering and events

FRESH

t: 0800 698 1453
f: 0131 538 8675
w: 24-7ltd.co.uk
e: info@24-7ltd.co.uk

EDINBURGHCATERING.COM

from sushi buffets and thai banquets
to traditional wedding dinners and
sumptuous barbecues

innovative outside catering
provided by the award winning
basement bar and smoke stack restaurant

large events and licensed bars a speciality.
check web site or call for details

BANQUETS   BUFFETS   BARBECUES   BARS

0800 6981412
FAX: 01315578097
WWW.EDINBURGHCATERING.COM
E-MAIL: INFO@EDINBURGHCATERING.COM
53-55 BROUGHTON STREET, EDINBURGH, EH1 3RJ

ABSOLUT CATERING

Buffets to Functions - We Do It All

- ✔ Private & Business Catering
- ✔ Daily Trolly Service
- ✔ Food Vending
- ✔ Sandwich delivery
- ✔ Weddings
- ✔ Private Functions

www.absolutcatering.com
or call Jim for a sample menu

0800 698 1401

10 Stewart Gardens, Edinburgh

Edinburgh
Food Guide

CATERERS

24-7 Catering & Events ltd.

Not only is our food fresh so is our attitude!

Our experienced and enthusiastic team, work closely with our clients in skilfully designing & producing unique entertainment & catering packages to suit.

24-7 also have a very experienced team of classically trained French Chefs and we pride ourselves on the quality, innovative presentation, style, flavour and freshness of our cuisine. We design exclusive bespoke menus for each individual client and event. We have many delighted customers as a result.

Not only does 24-7 offer innovative and stylish catering solutions, our event team have access to some of Edinburgh's more exclusive & unusual venues, which we cater at regularly. 24-7 also co-ordinate with other professionals, including florists, musicians and performers, enabling 24-7 to offer a complete package of entertainment.

From Large Corporate Events, Bars, Conferences, Weddings, Ship Launches, Private Parties, Product Launches, contact 24-7 for an assured, professionally run event with flair, style and superbly crafted fresh food.

ELEPHANT HOUSE CATERING

Client and Director lunches, hot & cold buffets. If you need sandwiches for the office or formal dinner from 6 to 600, give us a call.

EDINBURGH'S ONLY 24 HR CATERERS!

0131 553 5755
07980 060615

www.elephant-house.co.uk

CEC|Catering

• Weddings • Garden Parties •

• Funerals • Exhibitions, Marquees •

• Trade Fairs • Corporate Hospitality •

• Bar-B-Q's • Sporting Events •

• Boardroom Lunches •

0800 698 1407

E-mail: info@cec-catering.co.uk

491 Queensferry Road

Edinburgh

EH4 7QD

CATEGORY INDEX

Manchester Food Guide

Bistro continued

Bierex	1 Grange Road, Southside	667 2335	☺	E7 130
Café Provencal	34 Alva Street, West End	220 6105	☺	B4 70
Daniel's Bistro	88 Commercial Street, Leith	0800 698 1459	♿ WC V ☺ ✖	G8 114
Gathering Bistro & Bar, The	Norton House Hotel, Ingliston	333 1275	♿ WC V ☺ ✖	K11 135
Hilton Edinburgh Airport	100 Eastfield Road, Outskirts	519 4400		J11 138
Hilton Edinburgh Grosvenor	5-21 Grosvenor Street, Haymarket	226 6001		A5 74
Human Be-In, The	2/8 West Crosscauseway, Newington	662 8860	V ☺	E6 130
MP's Bistro	15 Calton Hill, New Town	478 4000	V	E3 35
Native State	32-34 Potterow, Old Town	662 9788	♿ WC V	E5 122
Rick's	29 Queensferry Street	226 1370		C3 56
Ryan's Bar	4 Hope Street, West End	226 6669	♿ WC V ✖	B4 84
Starbank Inn, The	64 Laverockbank Road, Newhaven	552 4141	V ☺ ✖	F8 116
Waiting Room, The	7 Belhaven Terrace, Morningside	452 9707	♿ WC V	B7 133

Bistro/Bar

Basement, The	10a-12a Broughton Street, Broughton	557 0097	V	D2 66
Caley Ale House, The	1/3 Haymarket Terrace, West End	337 1006	V	A5 80
Doric Tavern & McGuffies Bar	15/16 Market Street, Old Town	225 1084	V	D4 126

Bistro/Restaurant

Old Aberlady Inn, The	Main Street, Aberlady	01875 870 503	♿ WC V ☺ ✖	L10 144

Brasserie

Browns Restaurant	131-133 George Street, New Town	225 4442	♿ WC V ☺ ✖	C3 42
Café Hub	The Hub, Castlehill, Royal Mile	473 2067	♿ WC V ☺ ✖ ✖	D4 20
Chisolms, Caledonian Hilton Hotel	Caledonian Hotel, Princes Street	200 9941		B4 69
Deveaus at Open Arms Hotel	The Green, Dirleton	01620 850 241	♿ WC V ☺ ✖	L10 144
Dome, The	14 George Street, New Town	624 8624	WC	D3 48
(fitz) Henry	19 Shore Place, Leith	0800 698 1460	♿ WC V	G9 114
The Terrace, Sheraton Grand Hotel	1 Festival Square, Lothian Road	221 6422	♿ WC V ☺ ✖	B5 98

Breakfast/Brunch

City Restaurant, The	33-35 Nicolson Street, Old Town	667 2819	V ☺	E5 30

Burgers and Steaks

Bell's Diner	7 St Stephen Street, Stockbridge	225 8116	♿ V ☺	B2 74

BYOB

A Room in The Town	18 Howe Street, New Town	225 8204	V	C2 40
A Room in the West End	69 William St South, East Lane, West End	226 1036	V	B4 68
Susie's Diner	51-53 West Nicolson Street, Southside	667 8729	V ☺ ✖	E6 104

Café

Susie's Diner	51-53 West Nicolson Street, Southside	667 8729	V ☺ ✖	E6 132

KEY:
- ♿ Disabled Access
- WC Disabled Facilities
- V Vegetarian-Friendly
- ☺ Child Friendly
- ✖ Non-Smoking Area
- ✖ Separate Non-Smoking Room

CATEGORY INDEX

Café-Bar

Alphabet	92 St Johns Road, Corstophine	316 4466	♿ WC ✓ ☺ ✂	K11	136
Elephant House, The	21 George IV Bridge, Old Town	220 5355	♿ WC ✓ ☺ ✂	D5	128
Elephants & Bagels	Nicholson Square, Newington	668 4404	♿ ✓ ☺ ✂	E5	126
Filmhouse Cafe Bar	88 Lothian Road, West End	229 5932	♿ WC ✓ ☺ ✂	B5	133
Kaffe Politik	146/148 Marchmont Road, Marchmont	446 9873	♿ WC ☺	C7	134
Kariba Coffee	160 Royal Mile, Old Town	220 1818	✂ ✗	D4	125
Metropole	33 Newington Road, Newington	668 4999	✓	E7	130
Nexus Café Bar	60 Broughton Street, Broughton	478 7069	✓ ☺ ✂	D2	60
Plaisir du Chocolat	251-253 Canongate, Royal Mile	556 9524	✓ ☺ ✂ ✗	E4	121

Café-Bistro

Loopy Lorna's	24 Dean Haugh Street, Stockbridge	332 4476	✓ ☺	B2	86

Café-Restaurant

Vittoria Restaurant & Italian Coffee Bar	113 Brunswick Street, Leith Walk	556 6171	♿ ✓ ☺ ✂ ✗	E1	67

Cantonese

Great Wall Chinese Restaurant	105/109 Lothian Road, Lothian Road	229 7747	✓	B5	95
Kweilin	19-21 Dundas Street, New Town	0800 698 1430	✓	C2	58

Chargrill

Podricious	192 Rose Street, New Town	0800 698 1442 ♿	✓ ☺	C3	58
Smoke Stack	53-55 Broughton Street, Broughton	556 6032	✓	D2	61

Chinese

Dragon Way	74/78 South Clerk St, Newington	0800 298 3413		E7	102
Dragon Way	27 Links Road, Port Seaton	01875 813 551 ♿	✓	E7	102
Jasmine Chinese Restaurant	32 Grindlay Street, Lothian Road	0800 698 1429 ♿	✓ ☺	B5	100
Ping On	32 Deanhaugh Street, Stockbridge	332 3621	✓ ☺	B2	56
Rainbow Arch	8-16a Morrison Street, Lothian Road	0800 698 1443		B5	88

Coffee Shop

Annabelle's	27 Sciennes Road, Southside	667 0700	♿ WC ✓ ☺ ✂ ✗		

Contemporary British

Sealscraig, The	23 Edinburgh Road, South Queensferry	331 1098	✓ ☺	J10	144

Country Cuisine

Dolphin Inn	10 Whitecraig Road, Whitecraig	665 3354	♿ WC ✓ ☺ ✂	K11	140

Delivery Service

Absolut Catering	10 Stewart Gardens, Outskirts	0800 698 1401			168
Ayutthaya	14b Nicholson Street, Old Town	0800 698 1402		E5	164
Babylon Takeaway	25-27 Brougham Street, Tollcross	229 7793	✓		165
Balti Raj, The	1-2 Liberton Dams, Liberton	0800 698 1403			158
King's Spice	50-54 Henderson Street, Leith	0800 698 1504 ♿ WC ✓ ☺			156
New Bangalore	52 Home Street, Tollcross	0800 698 1408 ♿ WC ✓ ☺ ✂			162

173

CATEGORY INDEX

European
Bonham, Restaurant at the | 35 Drumsheugh Gardens, West End | 623 9319 | ♿ ♿WC ✓ ✗ | A3 78

Family Restaurant
Est Est Est | 135a George Street, New Town | 225 2555 | ♿ ♿WC ✓☺✗ | B3 38
Taurasi Ristorante | 21 Carnegie Drive, Dunfermline | 01383 623 798 ♿ ♿WC ✓☺ | J10 146
Vine Leaf, The | 22a Nicolson Street, Newington | 662 9191 | ♿ ♿WC ✓☺✗ | E5 24

Filipino
La Commedia (Pearl of the Orient) | 20 Leopold Place, London Road | 556 6748 | ✓☺✗✗ | E2 62

Fine Dining
Pompadour, Caledonian Hilton Hotel | Caledonian Hotel, Princes Street | 200 9941 | | B4 69
Potters Fine Dining Restaurant | Salisbury View Hotel, 64 Dalkeith Road | 662 9010 | ✓ ✗✗ | E7 106

Fish & Seafood
Mussel Inn | 61-65 Rose Street, New Town | 225 5979 | ♿ ✓☺ | C3 48
Skerries | 4 West Coates, West End | 0800 698 1448 | ✓☺ ✗ | A5 73
Skippers Bistro | 1a Dock Place, Leith | 0800 542 4385 ♿ ♿WC ✓☺ | G8 115

French
Café Marlayne | 76 Thistle Street, New Town | 0800 698 1462 | ✓☺ | C3 51
Jacques | 8 Gillespie Place, Tollcross | 229 6080 | ✓☺ | C6 96
La Bagatelle | 22a Brougham Place, Tollcross | 0800 698 1431 ♿ | ✓☺✗ | C6 96
La P'tite Folie | 61 Frederick Street, New Town | 225 7983 | ✓☺ | C3 44
Lafayette | Tudor House, 9 Randolph Place, West End | 225 8678 | ✓☺ | B3 36
Maison Bleue | 36-38 Victoria Street, Old Town | 226 1900 ♿ | ✓☺ | D4 21
Malmaison Brasserie | 1 Tower Place, Leith | 468 5000 ♿ ♿WC ✓☺ | G8 111

French/Delicatessen
Made in France | 5 Lochrin Place, Tollcross | 221 1184 ♿ | ✓☺✗ | C6 90

French/Scottish
Duck's at Le Marché Noir | 2/4 Eyre Place, New Town | 0800 698 1411 ♿ ♿WC ✓☺ | ✗ C1 65

Maison BJeue

36-38 Victoria Street
0131 226 1900
Map Ref: D4

innovative, funky dining

the new style of eating

lunch special
3 courses £4.90

pre-threatre
3 courses £9.90

open 12 noon –
12 midnight

CATEGORY INDEX

French/Scottish continued
(fitz) Henry	19 Shore Place, Leith	0800 698 1460 ♿ WC ✓		G9	114
La Gavotte	8 Union Street, New Town	557 8451 ♿	✓ ☺	E2	44
Le Chambertin at George Hotel	19-21 George Street, New Town	240 7181	✓	D3	54
Theatre Royale Bar	23-27 Greenside Place, New Town	557 2142	✓	E2	128
Tiles	1 St Andrews Square, New Town	558 1507	✓ ☺	D3	128

Functions
CEC Catering	491 Queensferry Road, Outskirts	0800 698 1407			171
Susie's Diner	51-53 West Nicolson Street, Southside	667 8729	✓ ☺ ✗	E6	104

Fusion
Alphabet Hotel Bar	92-98 St Johns Road, Corstorphine	316 4333 ♿ WC ✓	✗	K11	136
Iguana	41 Lothian Street, Old Town	0800 698 1425		D5	24
Indigo Yard	7 Charlotte Lane, West End	0800 298 3416 ♿ WC ✓	✗	B3	72

Gay Friendly
Nexus Cafe Bar	60 Broughton Street, Broughton	478 7069	✓ ☺ ✗	D2	60

Hotels
Christopher North House Hotel	6 Gloucester Place, New Town	225 2720	☺	F8	116

Indian
Bay of Bengal	164 High Street, Royal Mile	225 2361 ♿	✓ ☺	D4	28
Britannia Spice	150 Commercial Street, Ocean Drive	555 2255 ♿ WC ✓ ☺ ✗		F8	116
116 Golden Bengal	5a Johnston Terrace, Old Town	225 6633 ♿ WC ✓ ☺ ✗		D4	11
India Cottage, The	47-49 South Street, Armadale	0800 698 1426 ♿ WC ✓ ☺		J11	140
Indian Cavalry Club, The	3 Atholl Place, West End	228 3282	✓ ☺ ✗	A5	74
King's Spice	50-54 Henderson Street, Leith	0800 698 1504 ♿ WC ✓ ☺		G9	114
Modern India	20 Union Place, New Town	556 4547 ♿	✓ ☺	E2	38
Mountains of India	146 Dundas Street, New Town	556 9862	✓ ☺	C1	58
Namaste North Indian Frontier	41-42 West Preston St, Newington	0800 698 1435	✓ ☺	E7	106
New Bangalore	52 Home Street, Tollcross	0800 698 1408 ♿ WC ✓ ☺ ✗		C6	98
Pataka Restaurant	190 Causewayside, Southside	668 1167 ♿	✓ ☺	E7	105
Prince Balti House	11-12 Seafield Road East, Portobello	657 1155 ♿ WC ✓ ☺ ✗ ✗		K11	136
Shalimar Indian Restaurant	29 West Maitland Street, West End	220 0603	✓ ☺	A5	86
Shezan Tandoori	25 Union Place, New Town	557 5098 ♿ WC ✓ ☺		E2	65
Shish Mahal	63a High Street, Musselburgh	665 3121 ♿	✓ ☺	K11	140
Suruchi	14a Nicolson Street, Old Town	0800 298 3418	✓ ☺	E5	22

International
La Commedia (Pearl of the Orient)	20 Leopold Place, London Road	556 6748	✓ ☺ ✗ ✗	E2	62
Maison Bleue	36-38 Victoria Street, Old Town	226 1900 ♿	✓ ☺	D4	21
Negociants	4 Hope Street, Old Town	225 6313 ♿	✓ ☺ ✗	D5	121
Ritz Bar & Grill, The	2 Lochside Place, South Gyle	317 8800 ♿ WC ✓ ☺ ✗ ✗		K11	136

Italian
Bar Roma	39a Queensferry Street, West End	226 2977 ♿ WC ✓ ☺		B3	42
Bella Pasta	54-56 North Bridge, Off Royal Mile	225 2044		D4	38

175

CATEGORY INDEX

IItalian continued

Bella Pasta	9 Hanover Street, New Town	225 4808		D3 18
Bellini Fine-Dining	8b Abercromby Place, New Town	476 2602	♿ ✓ 🚭	D2 46
De Niros	140 Nicholson Street, Newington	0800 698 1481	✓ ☺	E6 104
Est Est Est	135a George Street, New Town	0800 698 1413	♿ WC ✓ ☺ 🚭	B3 38
Giuliano's	18/19 Union Place, Broughton	0800 698 1415		
Giuliano's on the Shore	1 Commercial Street, Leith	0800 698 1416		
Gordon's Trattoria	231 High Street, Royal Mile	225 7992	✓ ☺	D4 16
Il Castello	36 Castle Terrace, Old Town	229 2730	♿ WC ✓ ☺	C5 28
Kavios	63 The Shore, Leith	467 7746	♿ WC ✓ ☺	G8 118
La Lanterna	83 Hanover Street, New Town	226 3090	✓	D3 60
La Piazza	97/99 Shandwick Place, West End	0800 698 1432	✓ ☺	B4 84
Lazio's	95 Lothian Road, Lothian Road	229 7788	♿ ✓ ☺	B5 96
Lorenzo's	5 Johnston Terrace, Old Town	226 2426	♿ WC ✓ ☺ 🚭	D4 26
Pasquale's	169 Gilmore Place, Tollcross	228 3115	♿ WC ✓ ☺	B6 92
Patio Restaurant	87 Hanover Street, New Town	226 3653	♿ ✓ ☺	C3 64
Sambuca	103-105 Causewayside, Southside	667 3307	♿ WC ✓ ☺ 🚭	E7 104
San Marco	10-11 Marys Place, Stockbridge	332 1569	♿ WC ✓ ☺	B2 72
Santa Lucia Ristorante	25 Chapel Street, Dunfermline	01383 624 462	✓ ☺	J10 148
Santini	8 Conference Square, Lothian Road	229 9131	♿ WC ✓ ☺	
St John's Restaurant	259 St John's Road, Corstophine	334 2857	♿ WC ✓ ☺	K11 138
Taurasi Ristorante	21 Carnegie Drive, Dunfermline	01383 623 798	♿ WC ✓ ☺	J10 146
Ti Amo	16 Nicholson Street, Newington	0800 698 1482	✓ ☺	E5 12
Vittoria Restaurant & Italian Coffee Bar	113 Brunswick Street, Leith Walk	0800 698 1454 ♿	✓ ☺ 🚭 ❌	E1 69

Italian/Scottish

City Restaurant, The	33-35 Nicolson Street, Old Town	667 2819	✓ ☺	E5 30
Est Est Est	135a George Street, New Town	0800 698 1413	♿ WC ✓ ☺ 🚭	C3 38

Japanese

YO! Sushi	Hanover Buildings, Rose St, New Town	220 6040	♿ ✓ ☺ 🚭 ❌	D3 46

Mediterranean

Alphabet	92 St Johns Road, Corstophine	316 4466	♿ WC ✓ ☺ 🚭	K11 136
Malmaison Brasserie	1 Tower Place, Leith	468 5000	♿ WC ✓ ☺	
Vine Leaf, The	22a Nicolson Street, Newington	662 9191	♿ WC ✓ ☺ 🚭	E5 24

Mexican

Basement, The	10a-12a Broughton Street, Broughton	557 0097	✓	D2 66
Blue Parrot Cantina	49 St Stephen Street, Stockbridge	0800 698 1405	✓	C2 86
Coconut Grove	3 Lochrin Terrace, Tollcross	0800 698 1409	♿ WC ✓ ☺	B6 92
Gringo Bills	110 Hanover Street, New Town	220 1208	✓ ☺	C3 44
Haw House, The	44 Candlemaker Row, Old Town	220 4420	✓	D5 24
Miro's Cantina	184 Rose Street, New Town	0800 698 1433	✓	C3 62

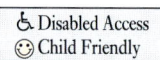

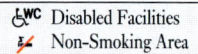

KEY:
♿ Disabled Access WC Disabled Facilities ✓ Vegetarian-Friendly
☺ Child Friendly 🚭 Non-Smoking Area ❌ Separate Non-Smoking Room

CATEGORY INDEX

Mexican continued
Mothers Restaurant	107-109 St Leonards St, Southside	0800 698 1461 ♿	✓ 🚭	E6 101
Pancho Villas	240 Canongate, Royal Mile	557 4416 ♿ wc	✓ ☺	E4 28
Viva Mexico	41 Cockburn Street, Old Town	226 5145	✓ ☺	D4 18

Modern British
Malmaison Brasserie	1 Tower Place, Leith	468 5000 ♿ wc	✓ ☺	G8 111
Rhodes & Co	3-15 Rose Street, New Town	0800 698 1445 ♿ wc	✓ ☺	D3 40
Rotisserie	Holiday Inn, Corstophine Road	0870 400 9026 ♿ wc	✓ ☺ 🚭	A5 135

Modern Scottish
A Room in the West End	69 William Street South, East Lane	226 1036	✓	B4 68
Black Bo's	57/61 Blackfriars St, off Royal Mile	0800 298 2994	✓	E4 110
Bridge, The at The Carlton Hotel	19 North Bridge, Old Town	472 3022 ♿ wc	✓ 🚭 🚭	D3 20
Caerketton Restaurant	Mauricewood Road, Nr Penicuik	0800 698 1406 ♿ wc	✓ ☺	K11 143

Modern Scottish continued
Carriage House, The	45 Morningside Road, Morningside	466 7666 ♿ wc	✓ ☺	B7 92
Channings Restaurant	South Learmouth Gardens, West End	315 2225	✓ 🚭	A2 78
Dial	44-46 George IV Bridge, Old Town	225 7179	✓ ☺ 🚭	D5 28
Fenwick's Restaurant	15 Salisbury Place, Newington	667 4265 ♿	✓ ☺	E7 106
Forth Element Restaurant	Newhaven Place, Newhaven Harbour	467 8736 ♿ wc	✓ ☺ 🚭	F8 116
Inn Over The Green	24 Milton Road East, Outskirts	0800 698 1428 ♿ wc	✓ ☺	K11 138
King's Wark, The	36 The Shore, Leith	554 9260	✓ 🚭	G8 111
New Bell Restaurant, The	233 Causewayside, Southside	668 2868 ♿	✓ ☺ 🚭	E7 102
Stockbridge Restaurant, The	54 St Stephen Street, Stockbridge	0800 698 1451	✓	B2 80

Mongolian
Khublai Khans	43 Assembly Street, Leith	555 0005 ♿ wc	✓ ☺ 🚭	G8 118

Nepalese
Khukuri, The	8 West Maitland Street, West End	228 2085 ♿	✓ ☺	A5 80

Non-Smoking
Annabelle's	27 Sciennes Road, Southside	667 0700 ♿ wc	✓ ☺ 🚭 🚭	
Channings Restaurant	South Learmouth Gardens, West End	315 2225	✓ 🚭	A2 78
Inn Over The Green	24 Milton Road East, Outskirts	657 0200 ♿ wc	✓ ☺ 🚭	K11 138
Loopy Lorna's	24 Dean Haugh Street, Stockbridge	332 4476	✓ ☺ 🚭	B2 86
Patisserie Florentin Ltd	5 North West Circus Place, Stockbridge	220 0225	☺ 🚭	C2 129
Potters Fine Dining Restaurant	Salisbury View Hotel, 64 Dalkeith Road	662 9010	✓ 🚭 🚭	E7 106

North Indian Frontier Cuisine
Namaste North Indian Frontier	41-42 West Preston Street, Newington	466 7061	✓ ☺	E7 106

Oriental
Sampans	Holiday Inn, Corstophine Road	0870 400 9026 ♿ wc	✓ ☺ 🚭	A5 135

Outside Catering
Absolut Catering	10 Stewart Gardens, Outskirts	476 5018		171
E H C M Ltd	64 Jane Street, Leith	553 5733		171

Outside Catering continued

edinburghcatering.com	53-55 Broughton Street, Broughton	0800 698 1412		168
Haddows Caterers	15 Rosneath Street, Marchmont	530 1858	☺ ✗ ✗	168
Patisserie Florentin Ltd	5 North West Circus Place, Stockbridge	220 0225	✓ ☺ ✗ ✗	C2 129

Patisserie

Patisserie Florentin Ltd	5 North West Circus Place, Stockbridge	220 0225	♿ ✓ ☺ ✗ ✗	C2 129

Pavement Café

Vittoria Restaurant & Italian Coffee Bar	113 Brunswick Street, Leith Walk	556 6171	✓ ☺	E1 69

Peking

Joanna's Cuisine	42 Dalmeny Street, off Leith Walk	554 5833	✓	E1 111

Scottish

A Room In The Town	18 Howe Street, New Town	225 8204	♿ LWC ✓ ✗ ✗	C2 40
Fine Dining at Open Arms Hotel	The Green, Dirleton	01620 850 241	✓ ☺	L10 144
Grain Store Restaurant	30 Victoria Street, Old Town	225 7635	♿ LWC ✓ ✗	D4 14
No 27 Charlotte Square	27 Charlotte Square, New Town	243 9339	✓ ☺ ✗ ✗	B3 68
No.3 Royal Terrace	3 Royal Terrace, New Town	0800 698 1438	✓ ✗	E2 35
Stac Polly	29-33 Dublin Street, New Town	0800 298 3436	✓ ☺ ✗	D2 56
Stac Polly	8-10 Grindlay Street, Lothian Road	0800 298 3438	✓ ☺	C5 88
Tower	Museum of Scotland, Chambers St	0800 698 1485	✓ ☺ ✗	D5 15
Wee Windaes	144 High Street, Royal Mile	0800 698 1455	✓ ☺	D4 18
Witchery, The	352 Castlehill, Royal Mile	0800 698 1491	✓	D4 27

Scottish/European

Bouzy Rouge	1 Alva Street, West End	225 9594	✓ ☺	B4 77
Carvers Restaurant at George Hotel	19-21 George Street, New Town	240 7181	♿ ✓ ☺ ✗	D2 54
Inn Over The Green	24 Milton Road East, Outskirts	657 0200	♿ LWC ✓ ☺ ✗	K11 138

stac polly
THE SCOTTISH RESTAURANTS

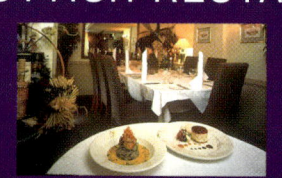

"Brilliant, braw, scintillating, choose your own adjective" **Bill Clapperton - Evening News**

29-33 Dublin St, Edinburgh **FREEPHONE 0800 298 3425**
8-10 Grindlay St, Edinburgh **FREEPHONE 0800 298 3426**

The Witchery by the Castle

Edinburgh's most spectacular and atmospheric restaurants and luxurious suites located in an historic building at the gates of Edinburgh Castle.

Open 7 days for Lunch 12-4pm (last entry)
Dinner 5.30-11.30pm (last entry)
Theatre Suppers £9.95 two courses 5.30-6.30pm and 10.30-11.30pm

Castlehill • The Royal Mile • Edinburgh
www.thewitchery.com mail@thewitchery.com
Reservations recommended 0800 698 1493

TOWER RESTAURANT

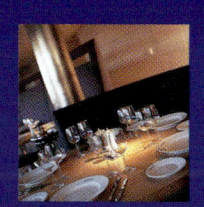

RESERVATIONS 0800 698 1485
mail@tower-restaurant.com www.tower-restaurant.com

TOWER RESTAURANT
Museum of Scotland Chambers Street Edinburgh EH1 1JF

CATEGORY INDEX

Scottish/European continued

La Commedia (Pearl of the Orient)	20 Leopold Place, London Road	556 6748	✓ ☺ ⚡ ✗	E2	62
Montpeliers	159 Bruntsfield Place, Bruntsfield	0800 698 1434		B7	90
Point Restaurant	34 Bread Street, West End	221 5555	♿ WC ✓ ☺	C5	26

Scottish/French

Peters Cellars	11-13 William Street, West End	226 3161	✓ ☺	B4	82
The Grill Room, Sheraton Grand Hotel	1 Festival Square, Lothian Road	229 9131	♿ WC ✓ ☺ ⚡	B5	98

Scottish/International

Carriage House, The	45 Morningside Road, Morningside	466 7666	♿ WC ✓ ☺	B7	92
Hadrian's, The Balmoral Hotel	1 Princes Street, New Town	0800 698 1440	♿ WC ✓ ☺ ⚡	D3	36
Howie's	208 Bruntsfield Place, Bruntsfield	0800 698 1421	♿ WC ✓ ☺ ⚡	B7	92
Howie's	63 Dalry Road, West End	0800 698 1422	♿ WC ✓ ☺ ⚡	A6	77
Howie's	4/6 Glanville Place, Stockbridge	0800 698 1423	♿ WC ✓ ☺ ✗	B2	76
Howie's	29 Waterloo Place, New Town	0800 698 1424	♿ ✓ ☺ ✗	D3	60
Number One, The Balmoral Hotel	1 Princes Street, New Town	0800 698 1439	♿ WC ✓ ☺ ⚡	D3	36

Seafood

Skerries	4 West Coates, West End	337 6169	✓ ☺ ✗	A5	73

Seafood/Game

Stockbridge Restaurant, The	54 St Stephen Street, Stockbridge	0800 698 1451	✓	B2	80

South African

Ndebele	57 Home Street, Tollcross	0800 698 1436	♿ ✓ ☺ ⚡ ✗	C6	134

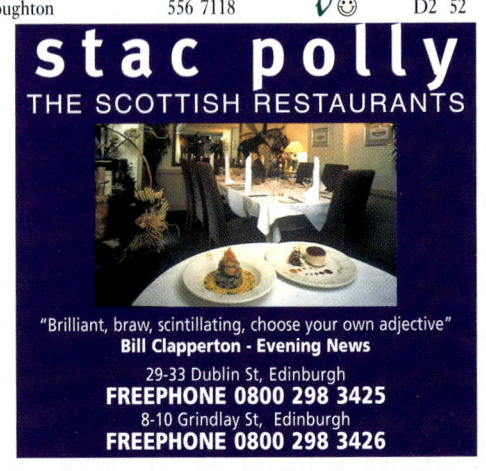

Spanish

Barioja	15 Jeffrey Street, Old Town	0800 698 1499	♿ ✓ ☺	E4	16
Tapas Tree, The	1 Forth Street, Broughton	556 7118	✓ ☺	D2	52

---

original, best & totally fresh!

Negociants is edinburgh's original cafe bar, serving coffees, food and drink until 3 in the morning. It's as fresh as it ever was!

Negociants

also **Medina** — Moroccan style nightclub open 7 nights from 10pm

lothian street edinburgh. 0131 225 6513

---

stac polly
THE SCOTTISH RESTAURANTS

"Brilliant, braw, scintillating, choose your own adjective"
Bill Clapperton - Evening News

29-33 Dublin St, Edinburgh
FREEPHONE 0800 298 3425
8-10 Grindlay St, Edinburgh
FREEPHONE 0800 298 3426

CATEGORY INDEX

Spanish/Scottish
Iggs Restaurante	15 Jeffrey Street, Old Town	0800 698 1501		E4	16

Takeaway
Central	15-16 Teviot Place, Old Town	226 6898		149
Dragon Way Takeaway	28 Warrender Park Road, Marchmont	0800 298 3470		

Tandoori
Balli's	89 Hanover Street, New Town	226 3451		C3	51

Thai
Ayutthaya	14b Nicholson Street, Old Town	0800 698 1402		E5	11
Erawan Express	176 Rose Street, New Town	220 0059		C3	53
Erawan Oriental	14 South St Andrew Street, New Town	556 4242		D3	53
Samui Thai	95 Gilmore Place, Tollcross	0800 698 1447		B6	98
Siam Erawan	48 Howe Street, New Town	226 3675		C2	86
Songkran	24a Stafford Street, West End	0800 698 1449		B4	70
Sukhothai	23 Brougham Place, Tollcross	229 1537		C6	88
Tawan Thai	15 Dalry Road, Haymarket	313 2797		A6	76
Thai Orchid	44 Grindlay Street, Lothian Road	0800 698 1452		B5	90

Traditional British
Sealscraig, The	23 Edinburgh Road, South Queensferry	331 1098		J10	144

Turkish
Nargile Mezeriye Restaurant	73 Hanover Street, New Town	225 5755		D3	40

Vegetarian
Bann UK	5 Hunter Square, Old Town	0800 197 3515		D4	14
La Commedia (Pearl of the Orient)	20 Leopold Place, London Road	556 6748		E2	62
Susie's Diner	51-53 West Nicolson Street, Southside	667 8729		E6	108

Vegetarian/Vegan
Baked Potato Shop	56 Cockburn Street, Old Town	225 7572		D4	68

Inspired Dining...

Maison BIeue

lunch special – 3 courses £4.90
pre-threatre – 3 courses £9.90

Open 12 noon - 12 midnight
Tel: 226 1900
Map Ref: D4

36-38 Victoria Street

ALPHABETICAL INDEX

RESTAURANT	TEL	MAP	PG	RESTAURANT	TEL	MAP	PG
394 Bistro	447 9287			Browns Restaurant	225 4442	C3	42
A Room In The Town	225 8204	C2	40	Bruntsfield Links Hotel, The	229 3046	C7	134
A Room in the West End	226 1036	B4	68	Buffalo Grill, The	667 7427		
Abbotsford Restaurant	225 5276			Buntoms Thai	229 6971		
Absolut Catering	0800 698 1401			Cactus Jacks	228 6006		
Al Frescos	556 7771			Caerketton Restaurant	0800 698 1406	K11	143
Alfredo's Ristorante	226 6990			Cafe 1812	556 4766		
Almond Restaurant	335 3777			Cafe Disperato	4493092		
Alonzi Donato	554 1686			Cafe Europa	667 6116	E6	
Alp-Horn Restaurant	225 4787			Cafe Hub	473 2067	D4	20
Alphabet	316 4466	K11	136	Cafe India	449 3092		
Amber Inn Chinese Restaurant	558 3028			Cafe Marlayne	0800 698 1462	C3	51
Annpurna Restaurant	662 1807			Cafe Provencal	220 6105	B4	70
Apartment, The	228 6456			Cafe' Rouge	225 4515		
Atrium, The	228 8882			Cafe Royal Oyster Bar	556 1884		
Au Bar	228 2648	B4	74	Caledonia	557 5600		
Ayutthaya	0800 698 1402	E5	164	Caley Ale House, The	337 1006	A5	80
Babylon Cafe	622 7142	E5	132	Caley Bistro	622 7170		
Babylon Takeaway	229 7793		165	Canons' Gait	556 4481	E4	122
Backstage Bistro	229 1978			Caprice Restaurant	665 2991		
Baked Potato Shop	225 7572	D4	68	Caribbean Connection	228 1345		
Balli's	226 3451	C3	51	Caruso's	660 6440		
Balti Kings Restaurant	662 9212			Carvers Restaurant at			
Balti Raj, The	0800 698 1403		158	George Hotel Intercontinental	240 7181	D2	54
Balti Raj, The	466 7281			Casa De La Fiesta, La	229 8386		
Bam Bou	556 0200			Castle Inn	476 1590		
Bamboo Garden	225 2382			CEC Catering	0800 698 1407		171
Bank Hotel	556 9940	D4		Cellars Bistro, The	538 8111		
Bann UK	0800 197 3515	D4	14	Central	226 6898		149
Bar Italia	0800 698 1410			Central Marque	466 6660		
Bar Java	467 7527			Channings Restaurant	315 2225	A2	78
Bar Napoli	225 2600			Chatterbox	667 9406		
Bar Roma	226 2977	B3	42	Chenzo's Restaurant	01506 855 163		
Barioja	0800 698 1499	E4	16	Chez Jules	225 8544		
Basement, The	557 0097	D2	66	Chi San Chinese Restaurant	555 5771		
Bay of Bengal	225 2361	D4	28	Chi Wai	669 8544		
Belfry, The	221 0291			Chilli Connection	0800 298 3467		160
Bell's Diner	225 8116	B2	74	China Kitchen Restaurant	557 3876		
Bella Pasta	225 2044	D4	38	Chinese Home Cooking	668 4946		
Bella Pasta	225 4808	D3	18	Chiquito Restaurant & Bar	657 4444		
Bellini Fine-Dining	476 2602	D2	46	Chisolms, Caledonian Hilton Hotel	200 9941	B4	69
Beluga	0800 698 1404	D5	22	Christopher North House Hotel	225 2720	B2	
Bennetti's	225 6252			Ciao	558 1138		
Bewley's	220 1969			Ciao Roma	557 3777		
Biblios	226 7177			City Limits	538 7368		
Bierex	667 2335	E7	130	City Restaurant, The	667 2819	E5	30
Bistro Tapas Bar, The	225 2973			Clarinda's	557 1888		
Black Bo's	0800 298 2994	E4	110	Cochise	466 7666		
Blonde	668 2917			Cockatoo Family Fare, The	660 1211		
Blossom Garden, The	663 7796			Coconut Grove	0800 698 1409	B6	92
Blue Moon Cafe	557 0911			Conservatory Restaurant, The	557 3222		
Blue Parrot Cantina	0800 698 1405	C2	86	Cooks	662 0340		
Bombay Bicycle	229 3839			Country Hotel & Restaurant	663 3495		
Bonham, Restaurant at the	623 9319	A3	78	Country Kitchen	225 4469		
Bookstop Cafe	226 6929	D5	130	Courtyard Country Inn, The	660 3200		
Bouzy Rouge	225 9594	B4	77	Craigs Restaurant	556 0111		
Braidburn Inn	667 3867			Cramond Brig Hotel	339 4350		
Brattisani	667 5808			Cramond Gallery Bistro	312 6555		
Brewsters	555 1570			Cramond Inn, The	336 2035		
Bridge, The at The Carlton Hotel	472 3022	D3	20	Creelers	0800 542 4384		
Britannia Spice	555 2255	F8	116	Crowne Plaza Edinburgh	557 9797		

ALPHABETICAL INDEX

Curry Club	539 8110			Gathering Bistro & Bar, The	333 1275	K11	135
Curry Pot	228 9997			Gigis'	226 5061		
Dalmeney House	331 1888			Giuliano's	0800 698 1415		
Daniel's Bistro	0800 698 1459	G8	114	Giuliano's on the Shore	0800 698 1416		
Dante's Restaurant	441 7427			Gleneagles Hotel, The	01764 694 435		
Dario's	229 9625			Goblin Ha Hotel	01620 810 244	L11	144
Daruma-Ya	554 7660			Golden Bengal	225 6633	D4	11
Davaar House	01383 721 886			Golden Dragon	225 7327		
De:alto	228 8153			Golf Hotel	01620 892202	L10	146
De Niros	0800 698 1481	E6		Goodyear, The	667 9988		
Delifrance Boulangerie	220 0474			Gordon's Trattoria	225 7992	D4	16
Denzlers Restaurant	554 3268			Grain Store Restaurant	225 7635	D4	14
Deveaus at Open Arms Hotel	01620 850 241	L10	144	Granary, The	220 0550		
Dial	225 7179	D5	28	Grange, The	01620 893 344		
Dix-Neuf	220 6119			Great Wall Chinese Restaurant	229 7747	B5	95
Dolphin Inn	665 3354	K11	140	Green Craigs	01875 870301		
Dome, The	624 8624	D3	48	Gringo Bills	220 1208	C3	44
Doric Tavern & McGuffies Bar	225 1084	D4	126	Gringo Joe's	228 1010		
Dragon Way	0800 298 3413	E7	102	Guildford Arms	556 4312	D3	129
Dragon Way	01875 813 551			Gurkha, The	447 8114		
Dragon Way	668 1328			Guru Balti Restaurant	221 9779		
Dragon Way Takeaway	0800 298 3470			GY	0800 458 0067		154
Dsk	478 7246			Haddows Caterers	530 1858		168
Dubh Prais Restaurant	0800 542 4351			Hadrian's, The Balmoral Hotel	0800 698 1440	D3	36
Duck's at Le Marché Noir	0800 698 1411	C1	65	Haldanes	0800 542 4383		
Dunedin Restaurant, Stakis Grosvenor Hotel	527 1406			Hampton Hotel, The	337 1130		
				Hanoi Vietnamese Restaurant	228 8868		
Dungeon Restaurant at Dalhousie Castle	01875 820 153			Hard Rock Cafe	260 3000	D3	44
				Harp Toby Hotel	334 8235		
Dynasty Chinese Restaurant	653 3200			Harry Ramsden's	551 5566		
E H C M Ltd	553 5733		171	Haw House, The	220 4420	D5	24
edinburghcatering.com	0800 698 1412			Haymarket Chinese Restaurant	228 8288		
Efes	229 7833			Heavenly Restaurant, The	447 8096		
EH1	220 5277			Henderson's	225 2131		
Elephant House, The	220 5355	D5	128	Hendersons Bistro	225 2605		
Elephants & Bagels	668 4404	E5	126	Henry J. Beans	459 1999	B4	70
Engine Shed, The	662 0040			Hill Street Bistro	226 3458		
Erawan Express	220 0059	C3	53	Hilton Edinburgh Airport	519 4400	J11	138
Erawan Oriental	556 4242	D3	53	Hilton Edinburgh Grosvenor	226 6001	A5	74
Est Est Est	0800 698 1413	B3	38	Himalaya	229 8216		
Etrebelle	332 7688			Hong Kong Delight	229 1690		
Evergreen Chinese Restaurant	538 7012			Hopetoun House	331 2451		
Fabio's	334 2300			Howie's	0800 698 1417	B2	76
Fairmile	445 2056			Howie's	0800 698 1418	D3	60
Famous Cavalier	663 4492			Howie's	0800 698 1420	A6	77
Famous Peacock Inn The	552 8707			Howie's	0800 698 1419	B7	92
Far Pavillions, The	332 3362			Human Be-In, The	662 8860	E6	130
Fenwick's Restaurant	667 4265	E7	106	Hunters Tryst Restaurant	445 1797		
Ferri's	556 5592			Iggs Restaurante	0800 698 1501	E4	16
Filmhouse Café Bar	229 5932	B5	133	Iguana	0800 698 1425	D5	24
Fine Dining at Open Arms Hotel	01620 850 241			Il Castello	229 2730	C5	28
Fingals Cave	225 9575			Il Giardino D'Italia	229 3325		
Fishers	554 5666			Il Restaurante Corallo	662 7008		
Fishers in the City	225 5109			Il Teatro	229 8386		
(fitz) Henry	0800 698 1460	G9	114	In House Cuisine	4672 345		
Food Plantation, The	557 9583			India Cottage, The	0800 698 1426	J11	140
Forth Element Restaurant (Next Generation)	467 8736	F8	116	Indian Cavalry Club, The	228 3282	A5	74
				Indigo Yard	0800 298 3416	B3	72
Fortune Cookie	229 7853			Inn Over The Green	0800 698 1428	K11	138
Frankie & Benny's	669 0839			International Chinese Restaurant	337 5165		
French Corner Bistro, The	226 1890			Isabel's Café	662 4014		
Garfunkels	225 4579			Istanbul	622 7734		
Garibaldis	220 3007						

183

ALPHABETICAL INDEX

Italian Place, The	447 9724			
J M French Bistro	225 9397			
Jacksons	0800 542 4352			
Jacques	229 6080	C6	96	
Jasmine Chinese Restaurant	0800 698 1429	B5	100	
Joanna's Cuisine	554 5833	E1	111	
Johnstournburn House	449 3847			
Joy Chinese Restaurant	440 4207			
Joypur Indian Restaurant	555 3683			
Kaffe Politik	446 9873	C7	134	
Kalpna	0800 698 1457	E6	108	
Karens Cantonese Restaurant	661 8981			
Kariba Coffee	220 1818	D4	125	
Kasim's	662 4812			
Kavios	467 7746	G8	118	
Kenningtons (at Jenners)	225 2442			
Khublai Khans	555 0005	G8	118	
Khukuri, The	228 2085	A5	80	
Khushi Tandoori	556 8092			
Khushis	556 8996			
King's Spice	0800 698 1504	G9	114	
King's Wark, The	554 9260	G8	111	
Kweilin	0800 698 1430	C2	58	
L'Amore d'Italia	228 5069	B6	96	
La Bagatelle	0800 698 1431	C6	96	
La Banda	467 7874			
La Campana	668 2868			
La Commedia (Pearl of the Orient)	556 6748	E2	62	
La Gavotte	557 8451	E2	44	
La Kamargne	554 9999			
La Lanterna	226 3090	D3	60	
La P'tite Folie	225 7983	C3	44	
La Piazza	0800 698 1432	B4	84	
La Rocca Italian Restaurant	557 4435			
La Rusticana	225 2832			
Lady Nairne Hotel	661 3396			
Lafayette	225 8678	B3	36	
Lancers Brasserie	332 3444			
Lanna Thai Restaurant	653 2788			
Laurieston Farm Restaurant	312 7071			
Lazio's	229 7788	B5	96	
Le Bistro	477 7010			
Le Café Saint-Honore	0800 542 4386			
Le Chamberlin at George Hotel Intercontinental	240 7181	D3	54	
Le Sept	225 5428			
Lee On	229 7732			
Lee's Restaurant	667 3223			
Lianachan	556 6922			
Littlejohn's	226 6300			
Logie Bairds Bar	556 9043			
Loon Fung	556 1781			
Loon Fung Seafood Restaurant	229 5757			
Loopy Lorna's	332 4476	B2	86	
Lorenzo's	226 2426	D4	26	
Loveate Bistro	467 6820			
Lower Aisle Restaurant, The	225 5147			
Luigi's Ristorante	01383 726 666	J10	146	
Mackenzies Restaurant	441 2587			
Made in France	221 1184	C6	90	
Made in Italy	622 7328		150	
Magnum, The	0800 542 4372			
Maharajah's	220 2273	D5	12	

Maison Bleue	226 1900	D4	21	
Mal's Diner	467 7397			
Malmaison Brasserie	468 5000	G8	111	
Mamma Roma	558 1628			
Mamma's American Pizza Co	225 6464			
Mamma's American Pizza & Panzerotti	558 7177			
Mariachi	538 0022			
Marine Hotel	01620 892 406			
Marmara Tavern	662 8093			
Marmaris	622 7555			
Marque, The	466 6660			
Marrakech Hotel & Restaurant	556 7293			
Martins Restaurant	0800 542 4363			
Masala Pot Takeaway & Restaurant	620 7080			
Maxi's	343 3007			
Maxie's	667 0845			
McNulty's Coffee Shop	556 2290			
Mediterraneo	557 6900			
Merchants	0800 542 4371			
Metro (Apex)	474 3466			
Metropole	668 4999	E7	130	
Millenium Spice	01620 895 418	L10		
Mills Mount Restaurant	225 9746			
Ming's Chinese Restaurant	332 4593			
Miro's Cantina	0800 698 1433	C3	62	
Modern India	556 4547	E2	38	
Montpeliers	0800 698 1434	B7	90	
Mother India	662 9020			
Mothers Restaurant	0800 698 1461	E6	101	
Mountains of India	556 9862	C1	58	
Mozart (Christopher North House Hotel)	225 2720			
MP's Bistro	478 4000	E3	35	
Mussel Inn	225 5979	C3	48	
Namaste North Indian Frontier Restaurant	0800 698 1435	E7	106	
Nargile Mezeriye Restaurant	225 5755	D3	40	
National Trust for Scotland	243 9300			
Native State	662 9788	E5	122	
Ndebele	0800 698 1436	C6	134	
Negociants	225 6313	D5	121	
New Bangalore	0800 698 1408	C6	98	
New Bell Restaurant, The	668 2868	E7	102	
New Jasmin House	226 1883			
New LB	554 5292			
New Loon Wah Chinese Restaurant	661 3995			
New Star of Bengal	346 0204			
Nexus Café Bar	478 7069	D2	60	
Nile Valley Restaurant	667 8200	E6	101	
No 1 Brasserie	226 7177			
No 27 Charlotte Square	243 9339			
No.3 Royal Terrace	0800 698 1438	E2	35	
Norton House Hotel	333 1275			
Number One, The Balmoral Hotel	0800 698 1439	D3	36	
Off The Wall Restaurant	558 1497	E4	11	
Old Aberlady Inn, The	01875 870 503	L10	144	
Old Boat House, The	331 5429			
Old Bordeaux The	664 1734			
Oloroso	447 8722			
Orchid Chinese Restaurant	229 1181			
Orchid Garden	554 5292			

184

Manchester Food Guide — ALPHABETICAL INDEX

Name	Phone	Grid	Page
Orchid Lodge	226 2505		
Oriental Dining Centre	221 1288		
Ortegas	557 5754		
Overtures	557-8339		
Palm Court	556 2414		
Palumbo Restaurant	229 5025		
Pancho Villas	557 4416	E4	28
Park Bar	229 3834		
Parrots	229 3252		
Pasquale's	228 3115	B6	92
Passepartout	332 4476		
Pataka Restaurant	668 1167	E7	105
Patio Restaurant	226 3653	C3	64
Patisserie Florentin Ltd	220 0225	C2	129
Pavilion, The	445 5584		
Peach Garden	334 5901		
Peacock Inn	552 8707		
Peckham's Underground	228 2888		
Peevers	225 4787/225 1546		
Peking Inn Chinese Restaurant	229 6789		
Pepe's Taverna	337 9774		
Peters Cellars	226 3161	B4	82
Piatto Verde	228 2588		
Pierre Victoire	225 1037		
Pigs Bistro	667 6676		
Pindi Restaurant	226 4848		
Ping On	332 3621	B2	56
Pizza Alvito	558 2680		
Pizza Express (North Bridge)	557 6411		
Pizza Express (Deanhaugh St)	332 7229		
Pizza Factory, The	662 4727		153
Pizza Hut (Hanover St)	226 3652		
Pizza Hut (North Bridge)	226 3038		
Pizza Primo	229 2002		
Plaisir du Chocolat	556 9524	E4	121
Podricious	0800 698 1442	C3	58
Point Restaurant	221 5555	C5	26
Poldrate's Restaurant	01620 826 882		
Polo Fusion	622 7722		
Pompadour, Caledonian Hilton Hotel	200 9941	B4	69
Potters Fine Dining Restaurant	662 9010	E7	106
Premier Mandarin Cuisine	556 2321		
Prestonfield House Hotel	0800 542 4382		
Prince Balti House	657 1155	K11	136
Quayside, The	665 1066		
Queen's Spice	331 4300		
Quills	557 4484		
Raeburn House Hotel	332 8000		
Raffaelli Restaurant	225 6060		
Rainbow Arch	0800 698 1443	B5	88
Raj, The	553 3980		
Rajdhani Indian Restaurant	553 1518		
Ratho Park	333 1242		
Redholme House Hotel	447 5111		
Reform, The	558 9992		
Restaurant Martin Wishart	553 3557		
Restaurant on The Mile	667 1597		
Rhodes & Co	0800 698 1445	D3	40
Rialto Restaurant	229 8386		
Rick's	226 1370	C3	56
Ristorante Gennaro	226 3706		
Ristorante Lazio	229 7788		
Ristorante Sant Andrea	669 2850		
Ristorante Tinelli	652 1932		
Ritz Bar & Grill, The	317 8800	K11	136
Rock, The	555 2225		
Rotisserie	0870 400 9026	A5	135
Royal Scot Hotel	334 9191		
Rutland Hotel Gallery Restaurant	229 3402		
Ryan's Bar	226 6669	B4	84
Salata Verdi Salad Restaurant	553 3762		
Salsa Hut	554 4344		
Sambuca	667 3307	E7	104
Sampans	0870 400 9026	A5	135
Samui Thai	0800 698 1447	B6	98
San Marco	332 1569	B2	72
Santa Lucia Ristorante	01383 624 462	J10	148
Santini	229 9131		
Sawadee Siam	313 2797		
Scalini's (Lonico Ltd)	0800 542 4369		
Scots Pantry	557 5130		
Scotsman Hotel	556 5565		
Sealscraig, The	331 1098	J10	144
Shalimar Indian Restaurant	220 0603	A5	86
Shamiana	228 2265		
Shanaz	226 2862		
Shanghai Pearl	652 1743		
Shenanigans	556 2358		
Shezan Tandoori	557 5098	E2	65
Ship on the Shore	555 0409		
Shish Mahal	665 3121	K11	140
Siam Erawan	226 3675	C2	86
Silvio's	553 3557		
Skerries	0800 698 1448	A5	73
Skippers Bistro	0800 542 4385	G8	115
Smoke Stack	556 6032	D2	61
Songkran	0800 698 1449	B4	70
Songkran II	225 4804		
Sophie's	229 1690		
Southern Cross Cafe	622 0622		
Spice Cottage	229 1000		
Spices of Life	0800 698 1450		
St John's Restaurant	334 2857	K11	138
Stable Bar	664 0773		
Stac Polly	0800 298 3408	D2	56
Stac Polly	0800 298 3409	C5	88
Stand Comedy Club, The	558 7373	D2	68
Starbank Inn, The	552 4141	F8	116
Stills Canteen	622 6202		
Stockbridge Buffalo Grill, The	332 3864/667 7427		
Stockbridge Restaurant, The	0800 698 1451	B2	80
Sukhothai	229 1537	C6	88
Sun Inn, The	663 2456		
Suruchi	0800 298 3418	E5	22
Susie's Diner	667 8729	E6	108
Szechuan House	229 4655		
Tabu Restaurant	474 3446		
Tai Hu House	551 3244		
Tamara	556 0773		
Tampopo Japanese Noodle Bar	220 5254		
Tandoori Night	229 1818		
Tandooriland	667 1035		
Tantallon Inn	01620 892 238		
Tapas Ole	556 2754		

185

ALPHABETICAL INDEX

Tapas Ole	225 7069		
Tapas Tree, The	556 7118	D2	52
Taurasi Ristorante	01383 623 798	J10	146
Tawan Thai	313 2797	A6	76
Templar Lodge Hotel	01620 842 999		
Tex Mex	225 1796		
TGI Fridays	0800 197 3527	C3	68
TGI Fridays	226 6543		
Thai Orchid	0800 698 1452	B5	90
The Grill Room, Sheraton Grand Hotel	229 9131	B5	98
The Terrace, Sheraton Grand Hotel	221 6422	B5	98
Theatre Royale Bar	557 2142	E2	128
Three Sisters	662 6801	D5	
Ti Amo	0800 698 1482	E5	12
Tiffin Restaurant	476 7055		
Tiles	558 1507	D3	128
Tillmouth Park	01890 882 255		
Timberbush	476 8080	G8	
Tippoo Sahib	226 2862		
Tonic	225 6431		
Tony's	447 8781		
Topaz	667 8845		
Topiary Restaurant at The Grange Hotel	667 5681		
Tower	0800 698 1485	D5	15

Trafalgar Suite Restaurant	556 7597		
Tron, The	226 0931		
Twenty 4 Seven Catering & Events	0800 698 1453		
Unicorn Inn	220 4799		
Verandah Restaurant	337 5828		
Vine Leaf, The	662 9191	E5	24
Vito's Restaurant	225 5052		
Vittoria Restaurant & Italian Coffee Bar	0800 698 1454	E1	69
Viva Mexico	226 5145	D4	18
Waiting Room, The	452 9707	B7	133
Wat's Chinese Restaurant	668 1818		
Waterfront Wine Bar & Bistro	554 7427		
Waterline, The	554 6294		
Waterloo Kebab House	556 2832 or 558 9140		
Wee Windaes	0800 698 1455	D4	18
Whigams Wine Cellars	0800 542 4373		
Whinrig	449 3848		
Wigwam	225 6127		
Witchery, The	0800 698 1491		
Wok Wok	220 4340		
Woodside Bistro	333 5226		
Yangtze	229 6971		
Yee Kiang	554 5833		
YO! Sushi	220 6040	D3	46
Yumi	226 3579/337 2173		

Published by
Marc Wilkinson
SNAP*fax*® Partnership
3 Boroughloch Square
Edinburgh
EH8 9NJ
TEL: 0131 662 1122
FAX: 0131 662 1188

National Account Manager
Kenny Murphy

Area Sales Manager
Warren Paul

Advertising Executives
Amanda Brown
Kevin Devlin
John Goodman
Rosie Jeffrey

Production
Rolf Rae Hansen
Caroline Rae
Graeme Blaikie

Design and Artwork
Rachel Black, Paulene Scott
The Almond Consultancy, Edinburgh

Front Cover Painting
Ian Thompson

Contributors
Justin Anderson (JA), Ailsa Bates (AB), Mairi Ball (MAB), Iain Barbour (IB), Margaret Beveridge (MB), Graeme Blaikie (GB), David, Cairns (DC), Jonathon Coates (JC), Pam Cowburn (PC), Caroline Darke (CD), Paul Donald (PD), Mark Drummond (MD), Andrew Dunlop (AD), Jody Fitcher (JF), John Flint (JJF), Judy Flint (JJF), Georgina Glass (GG), Nuala Gormley (NG), Keith Hardy (KH), David Hay (DH), Neil Hamblen (NH), Rolf Rae Hansen (RRH), Keith Hardy (KH), Vicky Innes (VI), Marianne Jack (MJ), Dawn Kofie (DK), Charles Krasun (CK), Amy Louie (AL), Annie McCormack (AMcC), Emma McGowan (EM), John McNally (JM), Paula McNally (PM), Eddie Millar (EdM), Brian Monteith (BM), Sam Morris (SJM), Andrew Morton (AM), Marie Murphy (MM), Breda O'Reilly (BO'R), Chris Peck (CP), Claire Ritchie (CR), Caroline Rae (CSR), Danny Ratnaike (DDR), Kirsty Regan (KR), Dominic Stephenson (DS), Helen Stringfellow (HS), Debbie Sunley (DS), Peter Sunley (PS), Lyndsey Thompson (LJT), Carole Tweedie (CT), Jessica Werb (JW).

ISBN 0 9528878 7 8
Ninth Edition

The publisher cannot accept responsibility for errors contained within this publication.

Copyright © 2001 SNAP*fax*®

Please be aware that by using freephone numbers advertised in this Guide you will be disclosing your own telephone number. We may then use this number to contact you, either by calling or sending a text message. Please withhold your number when phoning, or contact us at the address below if you do not wish to be contacted.

360° panoramic **moving** pictures on the **internet**

With an etour you can take your customers on 360° virtual tour of your conference venue, hotel, restaurant or visitor attraction without them leaving their seat.

Users of the etours 360° still imaging solution include:

- Residential and commercial property agents
- Hotels and Guest houses
- Conference venues
- Tourist attractions
- Exhibition venues
- Sports, entertainment and news organisations

etours
360 virtual tours

see the big picture

For more information call free on **08000 832 360**
or visit our web site at **www.360etours.net**

Maison BLEUE

a unique dining experience…

36-38 Victoria Street
Tel/Fax: 0131 226 1900
MAP REF: D4

RHODES & CO

Gary Rhodes restaurant offers excellent food in a modern and comfortable surroundings at a very reasonable price. A unique dining experience.

All day eating available from 11.30am - 9.45pm
Fixed price menu from 6.00pm - 9.45pm

Rhodes and Co
3-15 Rose Street
Edinburgh EH2 2YJ
Tel: 0800 698 1445
Fax: 0131 220 9199

MAPS

Nº 27 CHARLOTTE SQUARE

The National Trust for Scotland

The Restaurant

Home of fine Scottish Cuisine

Open
Tuesday - Saturday
6 - 11pm
Last Reservations
at 9.30pm

For reservations
please call
0131 243 9339

'...dignified and simple ...'

MAPS

stac polly
THE SCOTTISH RESTAURANTS

"Brilliant, braw, scintillating, choose your own adjective"

Bill Clapperton - Evening News

29-33 Dublin St, Edinburgh
FREEPHONE 0800 298 3431

8-10 Grindlay St, Edinburgh
FREEPHONE 0800 298 3432

TOWER RESTAURANT

OPEN 7 DAYS
Monday to Saturday 10am - 11pm Sunday 12pm - 11pm

TOWER RESTAURANT
Museum of Scotland
Chambers Street
Edinburgh EH1 1JF
RESERVATIONS
0800 698 1488

mail@tower-restaurant.com
www.tower-restaurant.com

the KING'S Spice

The Newest Restaurant in Town

For the very best in Indian & Bangladeshi Cuisine whether to sit-in or take-away.

OPEN 7 DAYS • FULLY LICENSED
TAKE-AWAY MENUS & DELIVERY AVAILABLE

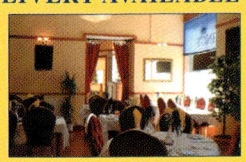

BUFFET LUNCH: Mon-Fri 12noon-2pm
BUFFET NIGHT: SUN-THURS 5.30pm-10.30pm
A LA CARTE MENU AVAILABLE

50-54 HENDERSON STREET, LEITH
FREEPHONE: 0800 698 1504
FAX: 0131 555 3104

A TRUE DINING EXPERIENCE

ti amo

Finest Quality Cuisine Created in-house

Winner of
TRINACRIA D'ORO
(Sicilian Golden Spoon Award)

Fish · Pasta · Chicken
Steak · Risottos · Pizza etc

Special Occasions
(weddings, birthdays)

Healthy Choice Menu &
Catch of the Day

Designated Non-Smoking
Area Available

Open 7 Days
12pm till late

16 Nicolson Street
(opp Festival Theatre)
TEL 0800 698 1482
FAX 0131 622 7878

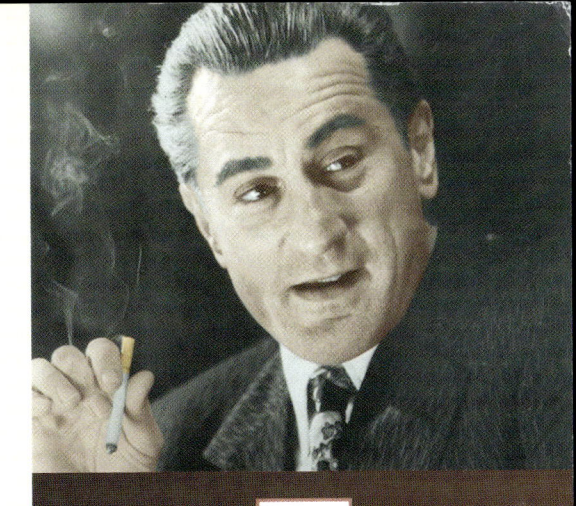

De Niro's Ristorante

"THANK YOU FOR A MEMORABLE EXPERIENCE"
LORD RICHARD ATTENBOROUGH

"QUALITY BASIC INGREDIENTS... COMFORT IN A WELCOMING ATMOSPHERE"
THE LIST

"THE BEST SPAGHETTI CARBONARA I'VE EVER TASTED."
RORY FORD, EVENING NEWS

Open 7 days 12-11.30pm
140 Nicolson Street
Freephone: 0800 698 1481
Fax: 0131 622 7878

"I believe in God and Cable TV"